Stakeholder Engagement and Sustainability Reporting

T0298896

In a context of growing social and environmental concerns, the role of large enterprises and corporations in encouraging sustainability has drawn increasing attention in recent years. Both academic debates and public-opinion research have called into question the extended responsibilities of firms in our increasingly inter-connected world. By studying issues associated with the greatest challenges mankind is currently facing – from climate change to social exclusion – the scientific community is aware of the need to account for the actions and agendas of companies, especially large ones. They are becoming important global political actors with great power, but also unprecedented responsibilities. With this in mind, the authors believe that it is more important than ever that large enterprises, on the one hand, take into account the opinion of their stakeholder while defining their strategies and, on the other hand, disclose material and relevant information on their ability to contribute to sustainability while delivering value for all of their stakeholders. A consensus is being reached on the responsibility of large enterprises to report in a triple bottom perspective – not only on their financial performances, but also on their social and environmental outcomes. Consequently, it is important to understand what elements organizations need to report on in order to provide stakeholders with relevant and comprehensive sustainability reports. Against this background, this book presents a significant and original contribution, both empirically and theoretically, to the social and environmental accounting literature by studying the various features of stakeholder engagement in sustainability reporting.

Marco Bellucci is a postdoctoral research fellow in accounting at the University of Florence. He holds a PhD with distinction in business administration and management from the University of Pisa. His research interests include corporate social responsibility, sustainability reporting, social enterprises and third sector organizations. He is social economy unit coordinator at ARCO Action Research for CO-development and project manager of the Yunus Social Business Centre of the University of Florence under the patronage of Nobel laureate Muhammad Yunus. Additionally, he was a visiting scholar at the Schulich School of Business at York University in Toronto and is the author of many articles in various respected scholarly journals.

Giacomo Manetti is associate professor of accounting at the Department of Economics and Management of the University of Florence. He holds a PhD in planning and control from the University of Florence. He teaches financial accounting and business administration at the School of Economics and Management. His research interests include stakeholder theory, corporate social responsibility, sustainability reporting and assurance, the third sector and accounting history. Additionally, he is the author of many scholarly articles and four books and was a visiting scholar at the Schulich School of Business at York University in Toronto in 2012.

Finance, Governance and Sustainability: Challenges to Theory and Practice Series
Series Editor: Professor Güler Aras
Yildiz Technical University, Turkey;
Georgetown University, Washington DC, USA

Focusing on the studies of academicians, researchers, entrepreneurs, policy makers and government officers, this international series aims to contribute to the progress in matters of finance, good governance and sustainability. These multidisciplinary books combine strong conceptual analysis with a wide range of empirical data and a wealth of case materials. They will be of interest to those working in a multitude of fields, across finance, governance, corporate behaviour, regulations, ethics and sustainability.

Strategy, Structure and Corporate Governance
Nabyla Daidj

Corporate Behavior and Sustainability
Doing Well by Being Good
Edited by Güler Aras and Coral Ingley

Corporate Social Responsibility and Sustainable Development
Social Capital and Corporate Development in Developing Economies
Risa Bhinekawati

Cosmopolitan Business Ethics
Towards a Global Ethos of Management
Jacob Dahl Rendtorff

Sustainability Accounting and Integrated Reporting
Edited by Charl de Villiers and Warren Maroun

Women on Corporate Boards
An International Perspective
Edited by Maria Aluchna and Güler Aras

Stakeholder Engagement and Sustainability Reporting
Marco Bellucci and Giacomo Manetti

For more information about this series, please visit www.routledge.com/Finance-Governance-and-Sustainability/book-series/FINGOVSUST

Stakeholder Engagement and Sustainability Reporting

Marco Bellucci and Giacomo Manetti

with a foreword by Linda Thorne

Routledge
Taylor & Francis Group

LONDON AND NEW YORK

First published 2019
by Routledge
2 Park Square, Milton Park, Abingdon, Oxon OX14 4RN

and by Routledge
52 Vanderbilt Avenue, New York, NY 10017, USA

First issued in paperback 2020

Routledge is an imprint of the Taylor & Francis Group, an informa business

British Library Cataloguing-in-Publication Data
A catalogue record for this book is available from the British Library

Library of Congress Cataloging-in-Publication Data
Names: Bellucci, Marco, author. | Manetti, Giacomo, author.
Title: Stakeholder engagement and sustainability reporting / Marco Bellucci
    and Giacomo Manetti.
Description: Abingdon, Oxon ; New York, NY : Routledge, 2018. | Series:
    Finance, governance and sustainability: challenges to theory and practice
    series ; 10
Identifiers: LCCN 2018009736| ISBN 9780815373155 (hardback) |
    ISBN 9781351243957 (ebook) | ISBN 9781351243926 (mobipocket)
Subjects: LCSH: Sustainable development reporting. | Corporations—
    Investor relations. | Sustainable development.
Classification: LCC HD60.3 .B45 2018 | DDC 338.9/27—dc23
LC record available at https://lccn.loc.gov/2018009736

ISBN 13: 978-0-367-58824-3 (pbk)
ISBN 13: 978-0-8153-7315-5 (hbk)

Typeset in Times New Roman
by Swales & Willis Ltd, Exeter, Devon, UK

To our wives

Contents

Figures

Tables

Foreword

Linda Thorne

In the context of growing social and environmental concerns, the role of large enterprises and corporations in encouraging sustainability has drawn increasing attention in recent years. Both academic debates and public opinion research have called into question firms' extended responsibilities in our increasingly inter-connected world. By studying issues associated with the greatest challenges mankind currently faces – from climate change to social exclusion – the scientific community is aware of the need to account for companies' actions and agendas (Crane & Matten, 2016).

This volume examines and emphasizes the need for stakeholder engagement in promoting corporate social responsibility (CSR). By so doing, it stands in direct contrast to Milton Friedman's perspective on the responsibility of business as focusing solely on owners' and shareholders' economic interests (Friedman, 2007; 1970). Many agree that Friedman's perspective is becoming progressively untenable as corporations are increasingly willing, for various reasons, to address the needs and expectations of their stakeholders (not just shareholders) and to create shared value (not just shareholder value). For example, statements pertaining to expanded corporate commitment – even though some may be rhetorical in nature – can be found in companies' sustainability reports or integrated annual reports, particularly in high-impact sectors and sectors with high legitimacy concerns. Organizations operating in these fields must deal with social and environmental issues every day and are very sensitive to the interests of several stakeholder groups. More specifically, the analysis presented in this volume focuses on these sectors and includes the chemical, energy, food and beverage, forest and paper products, mining, textile and apparel, tobacco and waste management sectors.

Friedman offers an excellent starting definition of CSR. According to Friedman, CSR is when a company – or managers acting on its behalf – has a "social conscience and take[s] seriously its responsibilities for providing employment, eliminating discrimination, avoiding pollution" (1970) and voluntarily addresses objectives beyond shareholders' economic interests. In other words, CSR implies that companies adopt expanded responsibilities beyond the narrow economic interests of shareholders, consider the interests of a wide collection of firm stakeholders (McGuire, 1963; Carroll, 1999), and undertake courses of action that are "desirable in terms of the values and objectives of society" (Bowen, 1953).

Given the evolving expectations of both consumers and investors, corporations are increasingly communicating to an expanded stakeholder audience regarding how corporate sustainability strategies are integrated into their business models. Over the past 40 years, companies have begun to pay greater attention to environmental and social issues (Cho, 2009; De Villiers, Rinaldi, & Unerman, 2014; Buhr, Gray, & Milne, 2014; Guthrie & Parker, 1989). At the same time, there has been substantial growth in research that tackles social and environmental accounting topics (Deegan, 2002). This growing interest has raised new questions regarding the underlying objectives of corporations and the best ways to account for (and report on) CSR and the extent to which the objectives of various stakeholder communities have been addressed (Gray, 2016; Adams & McNicholas, 2007). The development of the reporting of social and environmental information has resulted in various narratives that articulate – with varying degrees of thoroughness and misdirection – organizations' relationships with their stakeholders and with the environment (Gray, 2010; Brown & Dillard, 2014; Kolk, 2004.

Guided by the Global Reporting Initiative (GRI), stakeholder engagement has increasingly played a key role in dictating the information to be included in sustainability reports (Brown & Dillard, 2014; Manetti & Bellucci, 2016; Manetti, 2011). Stakeholder engagement is the process by which companies interactively engage with their stakeholders to understand their key corporate objectives and priorities. Stakeholder engagement can act as a powerful tool for dialogic communication and accounting (Bebbington, Brown, Frame, & Thomson, 2007; Brown & Dillard, 2014) and a channel for interactive mutual learning while also promoting transformative action and social change (Bebbington et al., 2007; Dillard & Brown, 2012). By definition, stakeholder engagement is a re-iterative process that fosters an open and evolving relationship between a corporation and its stakeholders and thus ensures that stakeholders' evolving expectations can be addressed (Manetti & Bellucci, 2016).

By studying the various features of stakeholder engagement in sustainability reporting, this volume makes a significant and original contribution – both empirically and theoretically – to the social and environmental accounting literature. CSR research has evolved from a specialty area of interest and research to one that is pervasive and crosses national boundaries and corporate cultures.

To advance our understanding of the extent to which corporations value, engage and address the needs of various corporate stakeholders, this volume presents research that bridges the divide between traditional sociological research and archival studies by providing insight into the properties of information on which sustainability activities are reported, and in so doing, provides insight on stakeholder engagement's importance for and impact on social and environmental accounting. This volume aims to provide insight for both experienced and emerging researchers on the complexities of the information on which CSR research is based. As a result, I believe that this volume is an invaluable resource for graduate students and established scholars regarding the current state of CSR research and corporate accountability.

References

Adams, C. A., & McNicholas, P. (2007). Making a difference: Sustainability reporting, accountability and organisational change. *Accounting, Auditing & Accountability Journal, 20*(3), 382–402.

Bebbington, J., Brown, J., Frame, B., & Thomson, I. (2007). Theorizing engagement: The potential of a critical dialogic approach. *Accounting, Auditing & Accountability Journal, 20*(3), 356–381.

Bowen, H. R. (1953). *Social responsibilities of the businessman* (No. 3). New York: Harper.

Brown, J., & Dillard, J. (2014). Integrated reporting: On the need for broadening out and opening up. *Accounting, Auditing & Accountability Journal, 27*(7), 1120–1156. http://doi.org/doi:10.1108/AAAJ-04-2013-1313

Buhr, N., Gray, R., & Milne, M. J. (2014). Histories, rationales, voluntary standards and future prospects for sustainability reporting. In J. Bebbington, J. Unerman, & B. O'Dwyer (Eds), *Sustainability accounting and accountability*. London: Routledge.

Carroll, A. B. (1999). Corporate social responsibility: Evolution of a definitional construct. *Business and Society, 38*(3), 268–295.

Cho, C. H. (2009). Legitimation strategies used in response to environmental disaster: A French case study of Total SA's Erika and AZF incidents. *European Accounting Review, 18*(1), 33–62.

Crane, A., & Matten, D. (2016). Engagement required: The changing role of the corporation in society. In D. Barton, D. Horvath, & M. Kipping (Eds), *Re-imagining capitalism: Building a responsible, long-term model*. Oxford: Oxford University Press.

Deegan, C. (2002). Introduction: The legitimising effect of social and environmental disclosures-a theoretical foundation. *Accounting, Auditing & Accountability Journal, 15*(3), 282–311.

De Villiers, C., Rinaldi, L., & Unerman, J. (2014). Integrated reporting: Insights, gaps and an agenda for future research. *Accounting, Auditing & Accountability Journal, 27*(7), 1042–1067. http://doi.org/doi:10.1108/AAAJ-06-2014-1736

Dillard, J., & Brown, J. (2012). Agonistic pluralism and imagining CSEAR into the future. *Social and Environmental Accountability Journal, 32*(1), 3–16.

Friedman, M. (2007) The social responsibility of business is to increase its profits. In W. C. Zimmerli, M. Holzinger, and K. Richter (Eds), *Corporate ethics and corporate governance*. Berlin: Springer.

Friedman, M. (1970). The social responsibility of business is to increase its profits. *The New York Times Magazine*, September 13, 1970. The New York Times Company.

Gray, R. (2010). Is accounting for sustainability actually accounting for sustainability . . . and how would we know? An exploration of narratives of organisations and the planet. *Accounting Organizations and Society, 35*(1), 47–62. http://doi.org/10.1016/j.aos.2009.04.006

Gray, R. (2016). Reading for displeasure: Why bother with social accounting at all? *Social and Environmental Accountability Journal, 36*(2), 153–161. http://doi.org/10.1080/0969160X.2016.1197625

Guthrie, J., & Parker, L. D. (1989). Corporate social reporting: A rebuttal of legitimacy theory. *Accounting and Business Research, 19*(76), 343–352.

Kolk, A. (2004). A decade of sustainability reporting: Developments and significance. *International Journal of Environment and Sustainable Development, 3*(1), 51-64. http://doi.org/10.1504/IJESD.2004.004688

Lee, M. D. P. (2008). A review of the theories of corporate social responsibility: Its evolutionary path and the road ahead. *International Journal of Management Reviews*, *10*(1), 53–73.

Manetti, G. (2011). The quality of stakeholder engagement in sustainability reporting: Empirical evidence and critical points. *Corporate Social Responsibility and Environmental Management*, *18*(2), 110–122.

Manetti, G., & Bellucci, M. (2016). The use of social media for engaging stakeholders in sustainability reporting. *Accounting, Auditing & Accountability Journal*, *29*(6), 985–1011. http://doi.org/10.1108/AAAJ-08-2014-1797

McGuire, J. W. (1963). *Business and society*. New York: McGraw-Hill.

Acknowledgements

We are sincerely and deeply grateful to Linda Thorne, Luca Bagnoli, Kristina Abbotts, Andrew Crane and all others who supported this project and provided academic guidance and human inspiration. We also wish to thank Sofia Biagini, Dania Cantatori, Gabriele Citrolo, Joseph Mazziotti and Vanessa Pezzetta. Finally, we are grateful to our families for their lasting encouragement and love.

Although this monograph is the result of a team effort, Marco Bellucci can be considered the author of sections 2.1, 3.1, 4.2, 4.3, 4.4, 5, 6 and Giacomo Manetti the author of section 2.2, 2.3, 3.2, 4.1. Section 1 has been written by both authors.

1   Introduction

Currently, many of the largest economies in the world are corporations, not nations. Many multinationals' revenues surpass the budgets of entire countries. For example, Apple's turnover exceeds Austria's revenues by a few billion dollars, while the revenues of British Petroleum easily compete with the federal budget of Mexico[1] (CIA, 2016; Fortune, 2016). Although we acknowledge that dollar-value company revenues are not equivalent to governments' dollar-value budgets, this illustrative comparison nevertheless reveals the vast power held by corporations and raises important questions regarding large firms' accountability and responsibility to civil society.

Particularly in the context of growing environmental concerns, the role of large enterprises in promoting sustainability is increasingly highlighted. Both academic conversations and public opinion debates increasingly question firms' extended responsibilities in the frame of contemporary and inter-connected societies. In studying issues associated with the greatest challenges mankind currently faces – from climate change to social exclusion – the current scientific community is fully aware of the need to account for companies' actions and agendas, especially those of large companies (Aras & Crowther, 2008; Crane & Matten, 2016). Large firms are becoming global political actors – but with great power comes greater responsibility.

As shown later in this volume, many authors agree that the historically prevailing thesis that a firm's first and only responsibility is to maximize value for shareholders (cf. Friedman, 1970) is becoming progressively untenable (cf. Freeman, 1984). Enterprises themselves are increasingly willing – for different reasons – to show their commitment to the needs and expectations of their stakeholders (not just those of their shareholders), their aspiration to create shared value (not only value for shareholders) and to make every element of their business sustainable. Although they vary case by case from genuine to be completely rhetoric, statements on this commitment are commonly found in the sustainability reports and integrated annual reports of companies operating in various sectors, even and especially in the most impactful ones, such mining and oil and gas (Bini, Bellucci, & Giunta, 2018).

Given consumers' and investors' evolving expectations, corporations currently face the need to communicate to internal and external stakeholders how their business model is integrated with aspects of sustainability. In the last 40 years, companies have exhibited increasing interest in environmental and social issues (Aras & Crowther, 2016; Bagnoli, 2004); at the same time, the research attention devoted to social and environmental accounting topics has grown substantially (Bini et al., 2018; Deegan, 2002). This growing interest has raised new questions on the real objectives of large corporations and the best ways to account for and report on the degree to which these objectives have been achieved. The development of social and environmental accounting and reporting in recent decades has resulted in a wide range of actual and potential accounts of extended organizational interactions with society and with the natural environment: such accounts can be understood as narratives of events that articulate, with varying degrees of thoroughness and misdirection, the relationships between the organization and its stakeholders and the environment (Gray, 2010).

With that in mind, we believe it is now more important than ever that large enterprises take into account their stakeholders' opinions when defining their strategies on the one hand and, on the other, disclose material and relevant information regarding their ability to contribute to sustainability while delivering value to all their stakeholders. An increasing consensus is being reached on large enterprises' responsibility to report not only on their financial performance but also on their social and environmental outcomes. Consequently, in practical terms, it is important to understand the elements on which organizations need to report to provide stakeholders with relevant and comprehensive sustainability reports.

In the past two decades, stakeholder dialogue and engagement have played an increasingly important role in defining the contents of integrated and sustainability reporting (Fasan & Mio, 2017; Manetti, 2011) in accordance with the principle of materiality and relevance of information disclosed (Global Reporting Initiative, 2013; Unerman & Bennett, 2004). According to the materiality principle, material aspects are those that reflect the organization's significant economic, environmental and social impacts or that substantively influence stakeholders' assessments and decisions (Global Reporting Initiative, 2013). Stakeholder engagement can represent a powerful tool for dialogic communication and accounting (Bebbington, Brown, Frame, & Thomson, 2007; Brown & Dillard, 2014) and a channel for interactive mutual learning that is capable of promoting transformative action and social change (Bebbington et al., 2007; Bellucci & Manetti, 2017; Passetti, Bianchi, Battaglia, & Frey, 2017). Moreover, stakeholder engagement is a milestone policy in social and environmental accounting because it allows an organization to interact with its stakeholders in a two-way dialogue in which the engager and the engaged mutually learn from this cooperation and potentially revise their expectations, strategies and behaviors (Manetti & Bellucci, 2016; Manetti, Bellucci, & Bagnoli, 2016; Owen, Swift, & Hunt, 2001).

Against this background, this volume aims to contribute to the social and environmental accounting literature by studying the role and features of stakeholder engagement in sustainability reporting.

This contribution is structured as follows. The next chapter introduces and discusses corporations' extended responsibilities in contemporary societies and considers the opposition between shareholder and stakeholder theories. Alongside the evolution of enterprises' objectives lies the evolution of reporting and the need to account for an integrated and broader set of information. Consequently, the concept of sustainability and the role of enterprises and accounting in sustainability are framed in light of social and environmental accounting.

The third chapter provides a literature review on sustainability reporting, materiality assessment and stakeholder engagement. Many local and global factors currently advocate for social and environmental reporting: the increasing relevance of beneficial relations with stakeholders, the growing concern about business ethics and CSR and the mounting importance of ethical investment have all increased the need for new accounting methods that organizations and their stakeholders can use to mutually address these issues. After analyzing the main motivations underlying sustainability reporting, we discuss the topic of materiality and the salience of information in social and environmental reports through the lens of the materiality principle and the main sustainability reporting guidelines. We then discuss how the involvement of every relevant group of stakeholders can represent the most straightforward way to produce comprehensive, relevant and material sustainability reports.

The fourth chapter provides a theoretical framework based on stakeholder theory and the involvement of stakeholders in decision making and sustainability reporting. We introduce a review of the different definitions of stakeholders and the diverse approaches to stakeholder theory. Consequently, the process of stakeholder engagement is theoretically divided into three phases: 1) stakeholder identification and analysis; 2) interaction with stakeholders; and 3) evaluation and reporting. Each phase is analyzed by considering the contributions of the most relevant authors and our own elaboration. Then, we discuss the theory underlying the possible achievement of materiality among the information in sustainability reports through stakeholder engagement. The last section of the fourth chapter is dedicated to a review of stakeholder engagement tools in practice and to a focus on social media as a tool that supports dialogic accounting.

Many theoretical tools introduced in the fourth chapter are then used to support our empirical analysis. The fifth chapter adopts a deep empirical focus on how sustainability reports address the topic of stakeholder engagement, the distinctive features of this involvement process and the role of stakeholder engagement in assessing materiality and defining the contents of such a disclosure. To pursue this objective, we opted for a mixed methodology built on content analysis – a research technique based on the objective, systematic and quantitative description of the manifest content of communications (Berelson, 1952). We analyze 211 sustainability reports that were published in 2016 in compliance with the Global Reporting Initiative (GRI) G4 guidelines from organizations operating in eight sectors with high social and environmental impact (Chemicals, Energy, Food and Beverage Products, Forest and Paper Products, Mining, Textiles and Apparel, Tobacco and Waste Management). We focus on these sectors because of the legitimate concerns they raise: organizations operating in these sectors must wrestle various societal, organizational and environmental issues linked to sustainability and legitimacy and are very sensitive to the interests of several stakeholder groups. The results of this content analysis are discussed in detail in the last section of the fifth chapter. Through this empirical analysis, we aim to contribute to the stakeholder theory literature and sustainability reporting literature original insights on the properties of information regarding stakeholder engagement policies and practices stated in sustainability reports.

Finally, we draw conclusions that summarize our contribution, offer supplementary comments on our main results and practical implications, and provide several ideas for further research on stakeholder engagement in social and environmental accounting.

Note

1 Considering the 2010 spillage of the BP-operated Deepwater Horizon oil platform in the Gulf of Mexico, this association is not completely casual.

References

Aras, G., & Crowther, D. (2008). The social obligation of corporations. *Journal of Knowledge Globalization, 1*(1). www.journal.kglobal.org/index.php/jkg/article/view/22

Aras, G., & Crowther, D. (2016). *The durable corporation: Strategies for sustainable development*. London: Taylor & Francis.

Bagnoli, L. (2004). *Quale responsabilità sociale per l'impresa?* (Vol. *21*). Milano: Franco Angeli.

Bebbington, J., Brown, J., Frame, B., & Thomson, I. (2007). Theorizing engagement: The potential of a critical dialogic approach. *Accounting, Auditing & Accountability Journal, 20*(3), 356–381.

Bellucci, M., & Manetti, G. (2017). Facebook as a tool for supporting dialogic accounting? Evidence from large philanthropic foundations in the United States. *Accounting, Auditing & Accountability Journal, 30*(4), 874–905. doi:10.1108/AAAJ-07-2015-2122

Berelson, B. (1952). *Content analysis in communication research*. New York: Free Press.

Bini, L., Bellucci, M., & Giunta, F. (2018). Integrating sustainability in business model disclosure: Evidence from the UK mining industry. *Journal of Cleaner Production, 171*(Supplement C), 1161–1170. doi:https://doi.org/10.1016/j.jclepro.2017.09.282

Brown, J., & Dillard, J. (2014). Integrated reporting: On the need for broadening out and opening up. *Accounting, Auditing & Accountability Journal, 27*(7), 1120–1156. doi:doi:10.1108/AAAJ-04-2013-1313

CIA. (2016). The World Factbook. Retrieved September 2016, www.cia.gov/library/pub
lications/the-world-factbook/fields/2056.html

Crane, A., & Matten, D. (2016). Engagement required: The changing role of the corporation in society. In D. Barton, D. Horvath, & M. Kipping (Eds), *Re-imagining capitalism: Building a responsible, long-term model*. Oxford: Oxford University Press.

Deegan, C. (2002). Introduction: The legitimising effect of social and environmental disclosures-a theoretical foundation. *Accounting, Auditing & Accountability Journal, 15*(3), 282–311.

Fasan, M., & Mio, C. (2017). Fostering stakeholder engagement: The role of materiality disclosure in Integrated Reporting. *Business Strategy and the Environment, 26*(3), 288–305.

Fortune. (2016). Global 500. Retrieved September 2016, http://beta.fortune.com/global500

Freeman, R. E. (1984). *Strategic management: A stakeholder approach*. Boston: Pitman.

Friedman, M. (1970). The social responsibility of business is to increase its profits. *New York Times Magazine*, September 13, 1970, 122–126.

Global Reporting Initiative. (2013). *Reporting principles and standard disclosure*. Amsterdam: Global Reporting Initiative.

Gray, R. (2010). Is accounting for sustainability actually accounting for sustainability . . . and how would we know? An exploration of narratives of organisations and the planet. *Accounting Organizations and Society*, *35*(1), 47–62. doi:10.1016/j.aos.2009.04.006

Manetti, G. (2011). The quality of stakeholder engagement in sustainability reporting: Empirical evidence and critical points. *Corporate Social Responsibility and Environmental Management*, *18*(2), 110–122.

Manetti, G., & Bellucci, M. (2016). The use of social media for engaging stakeholders in sustainability reporting. *Accounting, Auditing & Accountability Journal*, *29*(6), 985–1011. doi:10.1108/AAAJ-08-2014-1797

Manetti, G., Bellucci, M., & Bagnoli, L. (2016). Stakeholder engagement and public information through social media: A study of Canadian and American public transportation agencies. *The American Review of Public Administration*, *47*(8), 991–1009. doi:10.1177/0275074016649260

Owen, D. L., Swift, T., & Hunt, K. (2001). Questioning the role of stakeholder engagement in social and ethical accounting, auditing and reporting. *Paper presented at the Accounting Forum*. http://lists.exeter.ac.uk/items/BDDBDFDB-0CBB-F6C5-00CC-60A158A4435A.html

Passetti, E., Bianchi, L., Battaglia, M., & Frey, M. (2017). When democratic principles are not enough: Tensions and temporalities of dialogic stakeholder engagement. *Journal of Business Ethics*, online.

Unerman, J., & Bennett, M. (2004). Increased stakeholder dialogue and the internet: Towards greater corporate accountability or reinforcing capitalist hegemony? *Accounting, Organizations and Society*, *29*(7), 685–707.

2 Business and sustainability

2.1 Enterprises' extended role in society

2.1.1 The purpose of business

What purpose do enterprises serve in the context of contemporary societies? This question is trivial only on first glance, as enterprises can play various roles in society. Moreover, many other questions arise from this question, such as whether enterprises can have more than one objective, how to measure their performance relative to their objective (or objectives) and how to effectively report on the degree to which their objective(s) has been achieved.

Enterprises[1] represent an ingenious coordination mechanism for natural, human and financial capital, which, when skillfully combined, create value in a way that humans cannot achieve on their own (Crane & Matten, 2016). However, large enterprises' success as economic institutions has given them a role in society that far exceeds their initial economic purpose (Bagnoli, 2004; Ciepley, 2013; Scherer, Palazzo, & Baumann, 2006).

We believe that enterprises, especially large corporations and companies, currently have new roles and responsibilities that are as much social and environmental as they are economic. We agree with the argument of Crane and Matten (2016) that the idea that large enterprises are economic actors with a solely economic function in society is becoming increasingly untenable. Enterprises are often among the world's dominant institutions, with the largest ones eclipsing most national governments in terms of revenues, employment, logistical capabilities and global presence (Ciepley, 2013). The power, scope and influence of modern corporations are such that these organizations are currently key actors in social change. When we consider the greatest challenges mankind currently faces – from poverty (Biggeri, Ballet, & Comim, 2011) to climate change (Backman, Verbeke, & Schulz, 2017) – it is now inconceivable to ignore the actions and agendas of companies, especially large ones (Aras & Crowther, 2008b; Crane & Matten, 2016).

However, in most industrialized nations, economists, management scholars, policy makers, corporate executives and special interest groups are currently engaged in a debate over corporate governance (Aras & Crowther, 2008b;

Jensen, 2001). At the heart of this debate is a remarkable division of opinion about the fundamental purpose of enterprises in society. While much of the discord is due to the complexity of the issues and to the strength of the conflicting interests that are likely to be affected by the outcome of the debate, political, social, evolutionary and emotional forces that are not usually considered to operate in the domain of business and economics also fuel the controversy (Jensen, 2001). As argued by Jensen (2001), at the economy-wide or social level, the major question is as follows: if we could dictate the criterion or objective function to be maximized by firms (and thus the performance criterion by which corporate executives choose among alternative policy options), what would it be? Alternatively, to put the issue even more simply: how do we want the firms in our economy to measure their own performance? How do we want them to determine what is better versus what is worse?

2.1.2 Shareholder theory versus stakeholder theory

The discussion on corporate purpose has centered largely on the debate between those advocating a shareholder view of the firm and those promoting a more stakeholder-oriented perspective (Crane & Matten, 2016)

Those subscribing to the shareholder view argue that enterprises exist to maximize value for shareholders and that this value maximization is the only true way to effectively evaluate executives in manager-driven firms (Jensen, 2001; Sundaram & Inkpen, 2004). Most economists would argue simply that managers must use the maximization of the firm's long-term market value as a criterion for evaluating performance and deciding between alternative courses of action. This value maximization proposition is rooted in 200 years of research in economics and finance (Jensen, 2001): in the field of finance, for example, the logic of shareholder value maximization is considered so obvious that textbooks simply assert it rather than argue for it. Deviation from this objective is described as an agency problem resulting from the separation of ownership and control and the failure to meet it is assumed to be corrected by corporate boards, shareholder voice, shareholder exit and the market for corporate control (Sundaram & Inkpen, 2004). Entire generations of managers have been groomed to believe in the idea that an enterprise's central purpose is to maximize shareholder value; therefore, any attempt to rethink enterprises' role and responsibilities will clearly need to engage with such assumptions (Crane & Matten, 2016).

Friedman (1970) argues that firms should do no more than abide by the letter of the law and that the additional costs associated with social spending represent only a competitive disadvantage for firms. Managers' pursuits of their desired social missions degrade firms' ability to maximize shareholder wealth. Sundaram and Inkpen (2004) argue five reasons why shareholder value maximization should be the preferred corporate goal: (1) the goal of maximizing shareholder value is pro-stakeholder; (2) maximizing shareholder value creates the appropriate incentives for managers to assume entrepreneurial risks; (3) having more than one objective function will make governing difficult, if not impossible; (4) it is easier to make shareholders out of stakeholders than vice versa; and (5) in the event of a breach of contract or trust, stakeholders – in contrast to shareholders – have protection (or can seek remedies) through contracts and the legal system. The shareholder view assumes that the enterprise is an instrument for wealth creation and that this function is its sole social responsibility (Garriga & Melé, 2013).

However, Sundaram and Inkpen (2004) argue that by no means should firms ignore other stakeholders and that there are no boundary conditions for the way in which shareholder value creation logic must be applied in practice. Supporters of this view believe that adopting shareholder value as the objective function will lead organizations to make decisions that enhance outcomes for multiple stake-holders; additionally, they reject the view that managers will somehow become negligent in their moral (and legal) duty to stakeholders if they actively and vigor-ously pursue a fiduciary responsibility to shareholders, and they remain skeptical of the argument that a stakeholder approach to governance leads to either a com-petitive advantage or better behavior.

Despite his terse dismissal of social performances as "hypocritical window-dressing", "fraud", and worse, Friedman (1970) nonetheless acknowledges that a firm's investment in social responsibility could make it easier for the firm to attract desirable employees, reduce the wage bill or lessen losses from pilferage and sabotage or have other worthwhile effects (Barnett & Salomon, 2012). In not-ing that social responsibility can generate valuable goodwill for firms, he provides a basis for the counter-argument by stakeholder theorists that corporate social per-formance and corporate financial performance are positively related (Barnett & Salomon, 2012). Many theoretical and empirical debates have focused on the rela-tionship between corporate social performance and firm financial performance (Aras, Aybars, & Kutlu, 2010; Crowther & Aras, 2007).

Those arguing for the stakeholder view suggest that a corporation's purpose is "creating value for stakeholders", including but not necessarily prioritizing share-holders (Crane & Matten, 2016; Freeman, 1984; Freeman, Harrison, & Wicks, 2007; Freeman, Wicks, & Parmar, 2004). Stakeholder theory – the main chal-lenger to the shareholder view – argues that managers should make decisions that consider the interests of all of a firm's stakeholders (Ciepley, 2013; Jensen, 2001). We will examine stakeholder theory in depth in Section 4.1 of this volume. In a sense, both views agree that the original goal when creating the corporate form was to achieve a more efficient means of creating value in society; however, these views differ in their view of what exactly that value is – whether simply share-holder value, economic value more broadly, or societal value – and who that value is created for: shareholders or stakeholders more broadly (Crane & Matten, 2016). Stakeholder theory – the origins of which are commonly credited to Freeman (1984) – argues that as a firm's management of its relationships with the myriad groups that have an interest, or "stake", in the firm improves, the more successful the firm will be over time (Barnett & Salomon, 2012). Stakeholders include all individuals or groups that can substantially affect or be affected by a firm's welfare – a category that includes not only financial claimholders but also employees, customers, communities and government officials (Jensen, 2001; Moratis & Brandt, 2017). Widely different conceptualizations of what a stakeholder is have emerged, as different definitions are generated to serve different purposes, each focusing on attributes that are relevant to the context (Miles, 2017). Whilst this profusion of stakeholder definitions is indicative of the richness of stakeholder theory and its widespread appeal, which have resulted in multi-contextual applications, theorists recognize that it is also highly problematic (Miles, 2017). We will return to the point of stakeholder classification in Section 4.2.

From the alternative to shareholder primacy emerges the concept of corporate social responsibility (CSR) – a responsibility not just to shareholders but also to other stakeholders and society (Ciepley, 2013). Justifications for CSR vary, ranging from long-term self-interest to the ethical principle that one should act in consideration of the consequences of one's actions for all, avoiding harm and perhaps even providing help (Garriga & Melé, 2013; Lopatta, Jaeschke, & Chen, 2017).

Opponents of shareholder theory argue that in highlighting the centrality of shareholder value maximization, Friedman (1970) was mistaken for at least two main reasons. The first is equality, as it is right to create, measure and report value for every stakeholder, and the second is efficiency, as social and stakeholder-oriented activities such as CSR can increase a firm's ability to attract customers (Barnett & Salomon, 2012). In other words, CSR is not only a matter of ethics but also a matter of economical performance: in many businesses, the worsening of relationships with stakeholders will compromise or end activities through strikes, boycotts or community protests. Moreover, as argued by Ciepley (2013) and Stout (2012), the maximization of short-term share prices would not be economically efficient in terms of allocating resources to produce sustained growth. Given these premises, the broad success of the stakeholder theory introduced by Freeman (1984) is not surprising.

2.1.3 New responsibilities for a traditional purpose

During the 1960s and 1970s, the relationship between business and society was re-examined, and new theories on corporation's responsibilities to society emerged (Dierkes & Antal, 1986; Roberts, 1992; Zappa, 1957). In that period, several authors (Davis, 1973; Roberts, 1992; Steiner, 1972; Terzani, 1989) argued that although business is fundamentally an economic institution, larger firms exert significant influence in society and have the responsibility to use some economic resources in an altruistic manner to help meet social goals (Roberts, 1992).

Much of the business and management literature indicates that businesses have a responsibility toward the public good. We can find a compromise between the prevalent opposing views: while corporations were founded to produce economic value for their creators, in the 21st century, they have the potential to do more and to produce value for not only shareholders but also stakeholders. While enterprises undoubtedly aim to produce value for shareholders (because without it, there is no financial viability and a lack of investments), not all authors agree that corporations must maximize this value in respect to the value for other stakeholders. Friedman's point is unquestionably straightforward; however, from a normative perspective more than from a positivistic perspective, many scholars believe that an enterprise's responsibility is to create value for all its stakeholders. It is necessary to take into account both corporations' initial economical purpose and their increasing social and environmental roles and responsibilities. Enterprises, especially large ones, currently have so much economic, social, environmental and political potential that much of the literature has argued that even if producing value for all stakeholders was not corporations' initial purpose, it is definitely their actual role and responsibility. Moreover, this potential is increasing, especially nowadays, when large corporations' role in society is enlarging and the regulatory power of national states is retrenching simultaneously.

Crane and Matten (2016) outline three main drivers of a more pronounced social and political role for larger enterprises: political, economic and technological drivers. From a political standpoint, liberalization has created a space in which national governments have gradually ceded more influence and governing space to private actors, most notably, companies and civil society groups, since the 1980s. Recent discussions on corporate citizenship (Crane & Matten, 2004; Matten & Crane, 2005; Matten, Crane, & Chapple, 2003; Néron & Norman, 2008; Warhurst, 2001; Whelan, Monn, & Grant, 2013) highlight the new political role of corporations in society by arguing that corporations increasingly act as quasi-governmental actors and take on what had originally been governmental tasks (Aßländer & Curbach, 2017).

Moreover, from an economic standpoint, the rise of international trade regimes, the emergence of global markets for capital, commodities and labor, and the global spread of supply chains and production networks have created huge economic opportunities for companies and corporations. Finally, large enterprises have assumed a much more exposed role in society because of technological progress. In recent decades we have seen unprecedented innovation in telecommunication and transport technology globally.

One increasingly influential way of thinking about enterprises' extended purpose is to conceive of certain types of organizations as social purpose companies that aim to combine social goals with financial sustainability (Bagnoli, 2004; Haigh, Walker, Bacq, & Kickul, 2015). As such, social purpose companies specifically identify their purpose as the advancement of social or environmental goals – much as a non-profit would – but typically seek to achieve these goals through commercial or market-based tools, as a company would (Crane & Matten, 2016). On an international level, these companies, which share the objective of solving a social or environmental issue instead of only pursuing profit, can present different features and take different legal forms, such as social enterprises (Defourny & Nyssens, 2008, 2010; Galera & Borzaga, 2009; Mook, Chan, & Kershaw, 2015), benefit corporations (André, 2012; Hiller, 2013), social cooperatives (Bellucci, Bagnoli, Biggeri, & Rinaldi, 2012; Borzaga, Depedri, & Tortia, 2009; Galera & Borzaga, 2009; Thomas, 2004) and social businesses (Crane, Matten, & Spence, 2008; Yunus, 2007; Yunus, Moingeon, & Lehmann-Ortega, 2010). A discussion of these forms is beyond the scope of this work.

Nonetheless, whether we consider the extended responsibilities of every corporation or call into question new entrepreneurial forms as social purpose enterprises, we find that companies are increasingly called to report on their economical, social and environmental performance to all their stakeholders, particularly given that effective public policy to address global issues such as climate change should be built on a data-driven analysis of firm-level strategies (Backman et al., 2017). Companies, even those that operate in critical sectors such as mining and agroforestry, are increasingly aware of this responsibility, even though their commitment to this responsibility varies case by case and sector by sector. Confirming this point, the annual reports of big companies that contain sustainability reports often feature expressions such as the following:

> We will deliver an attractive and differentiated value proposition to our shareholders, business partners and other stakeholders by having the right assets and technical expertise, the right people working with our partners, and a commitment to responsible mining that will support us in delivering the products that make our world work. We are focused on delivering our targeted returns to shareholders while creating value for all our partners and stakeholders.
>
> (AngloAmerican, 2013)

A move toward a redefined corporate purpose must involve rethinking how corporate performance is conceived, assessed and reported. In fact, one of the most prominent questions arising from the one postulated at the beginning of this section is whether – from the point of view of enterprises' expanded social or even political role – the measures used by companies, professionals or researchers are actually the most salient. Although there have been significant advances in determining the materiality of issues to be reported, many of the metrics used still focus primarily on inputs – or, at best, outputs – rather than actual outcomes for or impacts on relevant stakeholders (Crane & Matten, 2016). As Salazar, Husted, and Biehl (2012) contend, firm-level measures of corporate social performance tend to focus on inputs, such as the value of corporate contributions or the number of volunteer hours donated, rather than the impacts of the firm's CSR activities on the intended beneficiaries (e.g., lives saved, improvements in health, incomes raised, increased happiness, etc.) (Aras & Crowther, 2008b; Manetti, Bellucci, Como, & Bagnoli, 2015).

If the answer to our introductory question is that enterprises have an economical purpose and social and environmental roles and responsibilities, it also necessary to rethink the original function of accounting and reporting in light of a broader and multi-dimensional set of objectives (Crowther, 1996, 2012; De Villiers, Rinaldi, & Unerman, 2014). The following sections will respectively analyze the general function of corporate reporting and the adaptations that are necessary in order to take into account and report on environmental and social performance.

2.2 The path to integrated reporting

2.2.1 The evolution of corporate reporting

At the individual organization level, the most basic governance issue is illustrated in the following argument:

> Every organization has to ask and answer the question: What are we trying to accomplish? Or, to put the same question in more concrete terms: how do we keep score? When all is said and done, how do we measure better versus worse?
>
> (Jensen, 2001)

A conventional perspective on the topic notes that corporate reporting provides a way for the organization or its representatives to communicate the company's past actions, the results of those actions and the company's intended future actions (Crowther, 2012); this process is undertaken partly to satisfy legal requirements and partly to allow any interested party to undertake an evaluation of the effectiveness of the company's past actions and the expected outcomes of its future activity (Crowther, 1996; Jensen, 2001).

This communication may be directed toward the business's owners, investors or prospective future investors or any permutation or combination of stakeholders who are associated with the business in any way (Aras & Crowther, 2008a; Crowther, 2012). Indeed, this communication may even be directed toward society at large on the basis that all members of society are either current or potential stakeholders in the business (Crowther, 1996). In fact, the purpose of corporate reporting has changed from one primarily of stewardship and accountability to shareholders to a more outward-looking and forward-looking perspective (Crowther, 2012). One of the driving forces for this change in orientation has been the discourse on environmentalism and, more recently, sustainability (see Section 2.3); nevertheless, other forces are also involved:

> Modern accounting was born on the basis that there was a need to record the actions of the individual and its effects as a basis for the planning of future action. This need was brought about by the need for a separation of the public and private actions of an individual and the need to record, and account for, the public actions because of the involvement of others in these public actions. Thus the medieval methods of bookkeeping, with the indistinguishability of public from private actions, was inappropriate to this modern world in which capitalist enterprise was beginning to arise. Capitalism required the ability to precisely measure activities, and this was the founding basis of management accounting.
>
> (Crowther, 2012)

Indeed, the literature has argued (Sombart, 1915) that capitalism would not have been possible without the techniques of double-entry bookkeeping and its subsequent metamorphosis into management accounting (Crowther, 2012). This accounting provided a mechanism to illuminate the activities of all involved in the capitalist enterprise and to record both the effects of past actions and the expected results of future actions (Crowther, 2012). The modern world therefore witnessed the genesis of the modern firm as a mechanism that enables individuals to coordinate within an enterprise and to combine capital and expertise from different individuals. It also saw the concomitant genesis of modern accounting in providing a representation of a firm's actions as distinct from the individuals comprising that firm (Crowther, 2012).

The "archaeology" of corporate reporting until the 1970s was simply the archaeology of the financial accounting aspects of reporting, as little else was considered to be significant (Crowther, 2012):

> This recognition of the use made of the corporate report has of course affected the way in which the report is produced as well as the contents and format of the report itself. Thus the earliest reports consisted merely of the financial reporting information of balance sheet, profit and loss account and increasing amounts of analysis of such information and notes to provide greater detail. The incorporation of the chairman's report provided an acknowledgement that financial information alone was insufficient to explain the actions of the company in the past and its prospects for the future. This was then extended, in recognition of the increasing size and complexity of organisations and the increasing divorce of investment from involvement in management of the organisation, to provide details about the activities and plans of the organisation. At the same time, over the last 25 years the report itself has changed from a plain statement to an increasingly glossy product containing maps, charts and pictures in a multi-coloured production designed to have mass appeal.
>
> (Crowther, 2012)

Generally speaking, the corporate governance debate has focused merely on internal mechanisms and on disclosure and transparency, with a primary focus on the suppliers of finance (Daily, Dalton, & Cannella, 2003; Kolk, 2008; Shleifer & Vishny, 1997). In this regard, a broader notion of corporate governance that relates to the entire range of stakeholder demands – including, but not limiting to, shareholder demands – seems to be emerging (Kolk, 2008).

The last 30 years have seen considerable development in the academic literature on accounting and accountability systems for the combined management and reporting of financial and non-financial performance (De Villiers et al., 2014). Academics and practitioners have analyzed the interaction between management's strategic propositions, organizational control systems and performance measurement and reporting systems (García-Sánchez & Noguera-Gámez, 2017; Parker, 2012). With their increased level of responsibility and accountability to their stakeholders, corporations have felt that there is a need to develop a code for corporate governance to guide them toward appropriate stakeholder relations (Aras & Crowther, 2008a).

As argued by De Villiers et al. (2014), among several proposals advanced by scholars within the accounting, management and governance domains (Giovannoni & Pia Maraghini, 2013; Nixon & Burns, 2012), four frameworks have emerged: the Balanced Scorecard,[2] the triple bottom line (see Section 2.3 of this volume), sustainability reporting (see Section 3.1) and integrated reporting (we will focus on this framework later in the text). While drawing on multiple strands, the early development of integrated reporting policies and practices appears to have been informed and driven largely by considerations linked to social and environmental reporting (De Villiers et al., 2014):

> Until the latter part of the twentieth century much social and environmental reporting took place via the medium of corporate annual reports. Although these reports were predominantly financial in orientation, some organisations used parts of their annual reports to disclose selected information about their social and environmental impacts and their policies towards managing the interactions between the organisation, the society in which it operated, and the natural environment.
>
> (Unerman, 2000, cited in De Villiers et al., 2014)

Research indicates that these social and environmental disclosures within annual reports were initially motivated by organizational or managerial desires to meet the perceived information requirements of the stakeholders who held the most economic power relative to the reporting organization (Brown & Dillard, 2014; Deegan, 2002; Neu, Warsame, & Pedwell, 1998):

> As social and environmental reporting became more widely practiced, and as the amount of social and environmental information reported by many organisations expanded, increasingly organisations began to separate out social and environmental disclosures, using media other than the annual report to disclose much of this information . . . For many of these organisations, the annual report became primarily focused on communicating information of core relevance to their financial stakeholders . . . Information considered to be primarily of relevance to other stakeholders was published (often in increasing volume and complexity) in stand-alone social and environmental reports and/or other interactive media (such as sustainability web sites).
>
> (De Villiers & Van Staden, 2011)

The growth in stand-alone social and environmental reporting practices was accompanied by the development of initiatives to create voluntary reporting standards to guide organizations in initiating and implementing these reporting practices. The Institute of Social and Ethical Accountability (commonly known as AccountAbility – see Section 3.2 of this volume) and the Global Reporting Initiative (GRI) (see Section 3.1) were among the membership organizations that developed the most enduring and widely adopted reporting and assurance standards for social and environmental reporting (Brown & Dillard, 2014; Gray,

Milne, & Buhr, 2014). It is reasonable to argue that the amount of information disclosed on the relationship between governance and sustainability will increase not only as firms gain a clearer understanding of that relationship but also as they understand the benefits of greater disclosure in this respect (Aras & Crowther, 2008a). As for financial reporting standards, one of the aims of such standardization in social and environmental reporting was to enhance the credibility and comparability of reports compiled in compliance with the standards (De Villiers et al., 2014).

2.2.2 Integrated reporting

In the current business environment, company disclosure must focus on non-financial information and on its connections with financial performance (Fasan & Mio, 2017). As illustrated further in the text, social and environmental reporting has a long history (Gray et al., 2014; Guthrie & Parker, 1989):

> Initially this reporting took place predominantly through disclosures within corporate annual (financial) reports. Over the past two decades, however, social and environmental disclosures have increasingly been made in separate stand-alone reports in addition to a variety of other media such as web sites (Cho, 2009). These stand-alone social and environmental reports have become more complex (and long) as a greater range of issues has been disclosed to meet the supposed information needs of a range of stakeholders.
>
> (De Villiers et al., 2014)

Possibly in response to the increased complexity and length of stand-alone reports, there have been recent moves to recombine some social and environmental disclosures with financial disclosures in single reports. In contrast to earlier social and environmental disclosures made within annual reports, where social and environmental information was not integrated with the financial information, these recent moves have sought to integrate social, environmental, financial and governance information (Dey, Burns, Hopwood, Unerman, & Fries, 2010; García-Sánchez & Noguera-Gámez, 2017; Hopwood, Unerman, & Fries, 2010). The resulting practices have come to be known as integrated reporting (De Villiers et al., 2014), which is poised as an evolution of mainstream reporting (Adams & Simnett, 2011).

Integrated reporting – a new standard for corporate communication – helps in completing financial and other corporate reports and results in concise communication about how an organization's strategy, governance, performance and prospects lead to value creation over the short, medium and long terms (International Integrated Reporting Committee, 2011). Integrated reporting aims to illustrate the relation between the company's business model[3] and all forms of capital (financial capital, manufactured capital, human capital, social capital, intellectual capital and natural capital) (Bini, Dainelli, & Giunta, 2016): "Integrated Reporting makes clearer the linkages between the organization's strategy, governance and financial performance and the social, environmental and economic context within which it operates" (International Integrated Reporting Committee, 2011). In fact, one of the main distinguishing features of integrated reporting is its aim of providing a concise report that can indicate an organization's most material social, environmental and economic actions, outcomes, risks and opportunities in a manner that reflects the integrated nature of these factors for the organization (De Villiers et al., 2014).

The International Integrated Reporting Council (IIRC) has gained a considerable amount of attention since its formation in 2010 (Busco, Frigo, Quattrone, & Riccaboni, 2014; Eccles & Krzus, 2010). The IIRC is: "a global coalition of regulators, investors, companies, standard setters, the accounting profession and NGOs. Together, this coalition shares the view that communication about value creation should be the next step in the evolution of corporate reporting" (IIRC, 2013b). The IIRC proposes that organizations generate only a single report that draws together financial and non-financial information (Busco et al., 2014; De Villiers et al., 2014; Eccles & Krzus, 2010, 2014). The IIRC's mission is to shift the norm of accounting for financial information in isolation from non-financial information toward integrated thinking, which is embedded within mainstream management and accounting practices and should enable integrated reporting to become the corporate reporting norm (De Villiers et al., 2014; IIRC, 2013a, 2013b).

A definition of integrated reporting is provided in *The International <IR> Framework* (2013b), which represents the main document of the IIRC guidelines: "A concise communication about how an organization's strategy, governance, performance and prospects, in the context of its external environment, lead to the creation of value in the short, medium and long term" (IIRC, 2013b). Moreover, integrated reporting is defined as a process "founded on integrated thinking that results in a periodic integrated report by an organization about value creation over time and related communications regarding aspects of value creation" (IIRC, 2013b).

Integrated reporting is a "hybrid practice that spans between the different worlds of financial reporting and sustainability reporting" and aims to providing a true and fair view of firm value and thereby account for sustainability (Fasan & Mio, 2017). For the IIRC, the main purpose of integrated reporting is to provide a broader and more connected account of organizational performance than that provided by traditional financial and/or sustainability-specific reporting (De Villiers et al., 2014).

Following the guidelines provided by the IIRC (2013b), the aim of an integrated report is to provide insight about the resources and relationships used and affected by an organization, collectively referred to as "the capitals" in the <IR> Framework. An integrated report also aims to explain how the organization interacts with the external environment and these capitals to create value over the short, medium and long terms.

IIRC guidelines define capitals as "stocks of value that are increased, decreased or transformed through the activities and outputs of the organization" (IIRC, 2013b):

They are categorized in this Framework as financial, manufactured, intellectual, human, social and relationship, and natural capital, although organizations preparing an integrated report are not required to adopt this categorization or to structure their report along the lines of the capitals. The ability of an organization to create value for itself enables financial returns to the providers of financial capital. This is interrelated with the value the organization creates for stakeholders and society at large through a wide range of activities, interactions and relationships. When these are material to the organization's ability to create value for itself, they are included in the integrated report.

(IIRC, 2013b)

The following principles, contained in the <IR> Framework and hereby presented in Table 2.1, should guide the preparation of an integrated report.

How is an integrated report structured in practice? As presented in Table 2.2, an integrated report should include eight core elements that are "fundamentally linked to each other and are not mutually exclusive" (IIRC, 2013b).

Table 2.1 Guiding principles for an integrated report

Principle	Description (as provided in the <IR> Framework)
Strategic focus and future orientation	"An integrated report should provide insight into the organization's strategy, and how it relates to the organization's ability to create value in the short, medium and long term, and to its use of and effects on the capitals"
Connectivity of information	"An integrated report should show a holistic picture of the combination, interrelatedness and dependencies between the factors that affect the organization's ability to create value over time"
Stakeholder relationships	"An integrated report should provide insight into the nature and quality of the organization's relationships with its key stakeholders, including how and to what extent the organization understands, takes into account and responds to their legitimate needs and interests"
Materiality	"An integrated report should disclose information about matters that substantively affect the organization's ability to create value over the short, medium and long term"
Conciseness	"An integrated report should be concise"
Reliability and completeness	"An integrated report should include all material matters, both positive and negative, in a balanced way and without material error"
Consistency and comparability	"The information in an integrated report should be presented: (a) on a basis that is consistent over time; and (b) in a way that enables comparison with other organizations to the extent it is material to the organization's own ability to create value over time"

Source: IIRC (2013b).

Table 2.2 Content elements of an integrated report

Principle	Description (as provided in the <IR> Framework)
Organizational overview and external environment	"What does the organization do and what are the circumstances under which it operates?"
Governance	"How does the organization's governance structure support its ability to create value in the short, medium and long term?"
Business model	"What is the organization's business model?"
Risks and opportunities	"What are the specific risks and opportunities that affect the organization's ability to create value over the short, medium and long term, and how is the organization dealing with them?"
Strategy and resource allocation	"Where does the organization want to go and how does it intend to get there?"
Performance	"To what extent has the organization achieved its strategic objectives for the period and what are its outcomes in terms of effects on the capitals?"
Outlook	"What challenges and uncertainties is the organization likely to encounter in pursuing its strategy, and what are the potential implications for its business model and future performance?"
Basis of presentation	"How does the organization determine what matters to include in the integrated report and how are such matters quantified or evaluated?"

Source: IIRC (2013b).

Accounting and business professionals are increasingly expected to report on social and environmental impacts, and they are showing increasing willingness to do so, despite previously paying little attention to these factors (Brown & Dillard, 2014). BASF, ENI, Vodafone, and Unilever are some of many organizations that have adopted the integrated reporting approach and the guidelines provided by the IIRC.[4]

However, opinions are divided among academics, businesspeople, public policy makers and civil society groups on whether integrated reporting truly enhances sustainability (De Villiers et al., 2014). Some view integrated reporting as a potential tool for mainstreaming sustainability within companies and capital markets, while others see it as an excessively narrow approach to enhancing sustainability, especially from the point of view of non-financial stakeholders (Brown & Dillard, 2014). As argued by Brown and Dillard (2014):

> for some, integrated reporting is a potent tool to mainstream sustainability in companies and capital markets, while for others it perpetuates the myth that a singular, standardized narrative will somehow satisfy accounting's public interest responsibilities. For yet others, the International Integrated Reporting

Council's (IIRC's) proposals are "a masterpiece of obfuscation and avoidance of any recognition of the prior 40 years of research and experimentation" that, if they take over from the Global Reporting Initiative (GRI), threaten to push us "even further away from any plausible possibility that sustainability might be seriously embraced by any element of business and politics".

(Milne & Gray, 2012)

Although integrated reporting has the potential to represent a win-win solution that, on one hand, meets substantive organizational accountability measures and, on the other hand, is cost-effective for organizations, many academic scholars have criticized the scope and substance of the integrated reporting agenda (Abdifatah & Mutalib, 2016). Their main concern is the possibility that integrated reporting's focus on sustainability could be too diluted among the other dimensions. For example, Milne (2013) and Brown and Dillard (2014) criticize the IIRC proposals' emphasis on value to investors and unceasing advocacy of the business case approach. Empirical findings indicate that integrated reporting practice, albeit still in an early stage, suffers many of the problems of previous organizational reporting techniques (Setia, Abhayawansa, Joshi, & Huynh, 2015; Solomon & Maroun, 2012; Wild & van Staden, 2013); for instance, although studies confirm a significant increase in the amount of non-financial disclosures following the adoption of integrated reporting (Setia et al., 2015; Solomon & Maroun, 2012), integrated reports are sometimes permeated with rhetorical disclosures and are biased toward reporting only positive outcomes (Solomon & Maroun, 2012). In addition, empirical studies reveal that companies continue to follow the traditional and non-integrated technique of "silo reporting" and provide limited disclosures on the organizational value creation/destruction process in the context of multiple capitals (Abdifatah & Mutalib, 2016; Wild & van Staden, 2013), which is what really matters for sustainability.

As we will study in Section 3.1, there are important differences between the concepts of IIRC integrated reporting, sustainability reporting, and social and environmental reporting. In order to make sense of this debate and to support our decision to focus on sustainability reporting as the best tool to report on sustainability and integrate the triple bottom line perspective, at this point in our volume, we must take a step back and focus on the concept of sustainability itself and on the role and history of sustainability reporting.

2.3 The concept of sustainability

2.3.1 Defining sustainability

As there has been a vast increase in interest in and concern for corporate governance, there has also been a similar growth in interest in sustainability (Aras & Crowther, 2008a). Something is considered sustainable if it can be maintained at a certain level or rate over the long term. In other words, sustainability is the ability to self-sustain and is a concept that should be considered when analyzing any phenomenon characterized by input and output. From deciding the winning pace in a marathon, balancing one's lifestyle in respect to one's income flow, developing the business plan for an enterprise in the forest industry, to the global utilization of non-renewable energy resources, the sustainability concept indicates the need to balance inputs and outputs, given the social, economic and environmental system in which we are operating. Every human and non-human activity features inputs and outputs that can be considered the outputs and inputs of other activities, respectively. In a closed system, in fact, the outputs of all parts of the system are linked to the inputs of other parts, and vice versa:

> All living organisms, including man himself, are open systems. They have to receive inputs in the shape of air, food, water, and give off outputs in the form of effluvia and excrement. Deprivation of input of air, even for a few minutes, is fatal. Deprivation of the ability to obtain any input or to dispose of any output is fatal in a relatively short time. All human societies have likewise been open systems. They receive inputs from the earth, the atmosphere, and the waters, and they give outputs into these reservoirs; they also produce inputs internally in the shape of babies and outputs in the shape of corpses. Given a capacity to draw upon inputs and to get rid of outputs, an open system of this kind can persist indefinitely.
>
> (Boulding, 1966)

Originating in the ecology field, sustainability can be defined as "the ability of the whole or parts of a biotic community to extend its form into the future" (Ariansen, 1999). Consequently, from an environmental standpoint, sustainability is a state that requires that humans and organizations carry out their activities in a way that protects the functions of the earth's ecosystem as a whole (Evans, 2012).

The Brundtland Commission's definition of sustainable development as "development which meets the needs of the present without compromising the ability of future generations to meet their own needs" (World Commission for Environment and Development, 1987) brought the concept of sustainability to a broader social consciousness in 1987 (Laine, 2010). The "Brundtland Report" was the culmination of a much longer process of examining interactions between humans and the environment (Bebbington, 2001; Lele, 1991).

The United Nations-established Brundtland Commission, formally known as the World Commission on Environment and Development (WCED), deliberately gave sustainable development a vague meaning because it helped the concept to gain broader acceptance (Laine, 2010; Reid, 2013). However, as a result, sustainability means different things to different people in different contexts, as pointed out by Bebbington (2001) and Aras and Crowther (2008a). Nevertheless, sustainable development enjoys widespread acceptance as an appropriate goal for humankind even though there is no common understanding of what this elusive goal actually is and how it can be achieved (Biggeri & Ferrannini, 2014; Laine, 2010; Meadowcroft, 2000; Reid, 2013; Robinson, 2004).

Generational equity, in its dual meaning of inter-generational equity and intra-generational equity, represents a central element of the culture of sustainability. First, inter-generational equity is present generations' moral duty to guarantee the same growth opportunities to future generations without compromising their ability to dispose of appropriate and sufficient natural assets (Padilla, 2002; Solow, 1974). Second, intra-generational equity is concerned with equity between people of the same generation. This concept is distinct from inter-generational equity, which deals with equity between present and future generations. On the international level, intra-generational equity may refer to the principle of environmental, social and economic equity between rich and poor countries, developed and developing countries, the north and south of the world, and so on; on the national level, it may refer to equity between people and groups, men and women, social classes or religious groups, the young and the elderly, people with power and people without power, and so on.

In the context of business and society, we can distinguish "strong" and "weak" forms of sustainability. The former prioritizes natural resources and requires a radical transformation of the economic system, whereas the latter opts to solve environmental problems within the bounds of the present system and moderate reforms (Luke, 2013; Redclift, 2005). These views differ regarding the extent of change required to obtain sustainability. Followers of strong sustainability claim that fundamental, structural change is required, while followers of weak sustainability believe that sustainability is achievable with incremental adjustments to the current system. The former perspective leads to abandoning or deeply redefining infinite economic growth as a dominant goal of our socio-economic system and raises new questions about how we measure development and wellbeing in our society:

> The "weak" sustainability position does not question the present mode of economic development and views sustainable development as being compatible with some modified version of "business as usual". In contrast, the "strong" sustainability position throws this assumption into doubt and seeks to redefine the ends which human populations . . . should seek.
>
> (Bebbington, 2001)

The notion of "weak" sustainability suggests that achieving sustainable development is considered to be contingent upon further economic growth, since without it, society and social actors will not possess the resources required for innovating and developing further measures for environmental protection (Adams, 1995; Daly, 1996; Dobson, 2000; Ekins, 1993; Laine, 2010). In contrast to "strong sustainability", which directs humans to first preserve their supplies of natural capital (Scruton, 2012), in weak sustainability, nature and natural resources are considered to be of solely instrumental value for increasing human welfare (Redclift, 2005; Shrivastava, 1995). This debate between "weak" and "strong" sustainability is also reflected in terminology. "Sustainable development" usually means ameliorating but not challenging continued economic growth, while "sustainability" focuses attention on humans' need to continue to live within environmental constraints (Robinson, 2004).

In Table 2.3, we summarize the key differences between the strong and weak sustainability perspectives.

2.3.2 The role of enterprises in sustainability

Responding to the call from new ecology movements in the 1960s and 1970s, some firms accepted greater responsibility for their operations on "Spaceship Earth" (Boulding, 1966; Fuller, 1968; Ward, 1966) by working with communities and other stakeholders (Freeman, 1984) in ways that implicitly addressed the so-called "triple bottom line" of "people, planet, profit" (Elkington, 1997; Luke, 2013; Manetti, 2006). The pursuit of sustainability involves an examination of both environment and development issues and the interplay between these concepts (Bebbington, 2001). Redclift (2002) characterizes environmental issues as concerns with the "limits which nature presents to human beings", while development issues are concerned with the "potential for human material development locked up in nature". Combining these two concepts is clearly problematic.

CSR and the triple bottom line (Elkington, 1997) include economic, environmental and social dimensions as the three pillars of sustainability (Ariansen, 1999; Evans, 2012; Laine, 2010; Luke, 2013; Redclift, 2005). In fact, sustainability is becoming increasingly relevant for firms' long-term success: it is advocated that businesses that fail to rethink their business model with a focus on sustainability will fail to create competitive advantage in the long term (Aras & Crowther, 2016; Laine, 2010; Nidumolu, Prahalad, & Rangaswami, 2009).

Much of the literature indicates that the business sector has a crucial role to play in global society's journey toward sustainability (Aras & Crowther, 2008a).

Table 2.3 Strong and weak forms of sustainability

Aspects	Weak sustainability	Strong sustainability
Substitution of natural capital	Manufactured capital of equal value can substitute for natural capital.	The existing stock of natural capital must be maintained and possibly enhanced because the functions it performs cannot be duplicated by manufactured capital.
Extent of change	Sustainability is achievable with incremental adjustments to the current system.	Fundamental, structural change is likely to be required.
Role of economic development	Economic development is actually essential for the pursuit of sustainability.	Economic growth may need to be redefined or abandoned as a dominant goal.

While we provided an initial discussion of this topic in Section 2.1, the role of corporations in the journey toward sustainability is still debated:

> Global society has a right to expect business to do that at which it is most accomplished, i.e. to pursue traditional modes of efficiency, to seek market-lead innovation and to respond rapidly and successfully to changes in the "playing field" - changes in markets, prices, incentives, tastes and so on. It is not clear whether business can be expected to provide, on its own initiative, the innovative ways of thinking, the drastic re-design of life-styles, the costly structural re-adjustments and the major redistribution of wealth which are patently essential for a sustainable future.
>
> (Bebbington & Gray, 1996)

A rapidly increasing number of companies are publishing different kinds of sustainability and CSR reports and requesting consultancies on sustainability issues (Barth & Wolff, 2009; Deegan, Rankin, & Tobin, 2002; KPMG, 2015; Laine, 2010). Through these disclosures, business actors disseminate their views on environmental and social issues and on sustainable development in general. Since these organizations represent very powerful social actors, these disclosures also "construct reality" (Phillips & Hardy, 2002) and affect how society at large perceives sustainability (Hines, 1988). The significance of corporate non-financial environmental disclosures – and particularly of carbon reporting – appears to be growing due to increased concerns about the impacts of global climate change (Aras & Crowther, 2016; Bebbington & Larrinaga-Gonzalez, 2008; Kolk, Levy, & Pinkse, 2008). Thus, there is a clear need to better understand both the corporate motivations to engage in such reporting and the rhetoric that organizations use in these reports while pursuing particular ends (Cho, 2009; Laine, 2010).

One of the most central questions to emerge from this section of our volume is the following: what are the features of a sustainable business? Bebbington and Gray (1996) argue that:

> at minimum, a sustainable business is one which leaves the environment no worse off at the end of each accounting period than it was at the beginning of that accounting period. For full sustainability, the sustainable business would also re-dress some of the excesses of current un-sustainability and consider the intra-generational inequalities. It is perfectly clear that few, if any, businesses, especially in the developed economies, come anywhere near to anything that looks remotely like sustainability.

Gray and Milne (2002) conceptualize a sustainable enterprise as one that leaves the natural environment and social justice no worse off at the end of the accounting period than they were at the beginning of that period and claim that approximating this state (especially the social justice requirement) is difficult and raises contestable issues.

We believe that a sustainable enterprise is one that is able to sustain the creation of social and economic capital without radically compromising the environment's natural capital. However, many companies and organizations have adopted a business view of sustainability, which is akin to "weak sustainability". In fact, the business view often concentrates on win-win situations, and case examples describe organizations that have succeeded in diminishing environmental impacts while simultaneously increasing profitability (Elkington, 1999; Fritsch, Schmidheiny, & Seifritz, 2012).

If sustainability is not considered explicitly, every claim risks becoming rhetorical. As suggested by Gray (2010), "sustainability" can become synonymous with other concepts such as "social responsibility" or "environmental management" and, most especially, can offer no threat to traditional corporate attitudes and activities (Bonacchi, 2007; Buhr & Reiter, 2006; Gladwin, Krause, & Kennelly, 1995; Livesey & Kearins, 2002; Milne, Kearins, & Walton, 2006). Thus, a suite of increasingly pervasive narratives of sustainability comprising relatively benign, win-win cocktails of economic achievement, managerial excellence, environmental probity and social responsibility have emerged (Gray, 2010). Within these narratives lies an additional signifier for "sustainability" – that of the "sustainability of the business": while this notion is rarely addressed explicitly in the claims reviewed here, it more comfortably adapts to the preconceptions of "business as usual" (Gray, 2010). In essence, it seems that no business can succeed without the approval of its stakeholders as a socially and environmentally responsible entity, and consequently, there is an unexamined presupposition that the business is indeed responsible (Gray, 2010).

To assess if the sustainability narrative is genuine or if the sustainability rhetoric requires a close, case-by-case approach, we must once again summon the relevance of stakeholders because stakeholders have a critical role in corporations' legitimization[5] process, and we must understand what factors are more material in light of sustainability reporting. Moreover, we claim that engaging stakeholders and impacted communities[6] is an essential tool for enterprises' effective decision making regarding sustainability issues:

> A particular aspect of the human dimensions of sustainability that deserves special mention is the need to develop methods of deliberation and decision making that actively engage the relevant interests and communities in thinking through and deciding upon the kind of future they want to try and create.
> (Robinson, 2004)

Important parts of the academic literature on these topics argue from both a normative and an instrumental perspective[7] that enterprises should accept the responsibility to consider the opinion of stakeholders, including the communities representing the environment in which they are operating. Since there is a wide diversity of viewpoints regarding what sustainability is and what it entails, it is important to develop tools and processes that allow diversity to be expressed in a constructive way without creating paralysis. We will return to this point in Section 4.4 of this volume.

2.3.3 How to measure sustainability?

After outlining the main concepts (and misconceptions) of sustainability, one may wonder how to measure sustainability and how to account for it, especially regarding enterprises. There have been many attempts to identify a range of key factors that might be taken as indicators of moves toward or away from sustainability (Atkinson, 2000; Bonacchi & Rinaldi, 2006; Gray, 2010; Gray & Bebbington, 2001; Gray, Owens, & Adams, 1996; Ranganathan, 1998). These attempts can be roughly divided in two main areas according to whether they are based on financial or non-financial representations.

The various attempts to offer financial accounts of organizations' sustainability appear to be motivated by the simple assumption that only through financial representation is it possible to speak to businesses in a language that they will recognize and accept. The main approach to constructing a financial account of an organization's un-sustainability is identifying the "sustainable costs" of organizations' activity (Bebbington & Gray, 2001; Ekins, Simon, Deutsch, Folke, & De Groot, 2003; Gray, 1992, 2010; Lohmann, 2009; Taplin, Bent, & Aeron-Thomas, 2006). As argued by Gray (2010):

> this approach employs the concept of the maintenance of capital as an analogue for environmental sustainability and identifies: man-made, renewable/ substitutable and critical natural capital at the level of the organisation. The "sustainable organization" would be one which maintained these three capitals over an "accounting" period. The "sustainable cost" is the amount that the organisation would have had to spend if it had been sustainable.

There are also several studies that approach the assessment of sustainability through non-financial quantification. Some of these experiments embrace the utilization of different concepts such as the conservation of bio-diversity (Jones, 1996, 2003; Pallot, 1997), the monitoring of inputs and outputs for assessing progress toward sustainability targets in specific cases studies (Lamberton, 2000) or the development of performance indicators of more sustainable practices (Ranganathan, 1998).

Moreover, one of the dominant discourses around sustainability that has grown rapidly in recent years is that surrounding the notion of an "ecological footprint" (EF) (Wackernagel & Rees, 1998). The ecological footprint concept is linked directly to the planet's carrying capacity and seeks to measure the amount of land usage that an activity requires for its support (Gray, 2010). The first academic publication on the ecological footprint was authored by Rees (1992), but the ecological footprint concept and calculation method was first developed in the PhD dissertation of Mathis Wackernagel under Rees's supervision at the University of British Columbia in Vancouver, Canada, from 1990 to 1994.[8] Then, the seminal book on the ecological footprint became *Our Ecological Footprint: Reducing Human Impact on the Earth* (Wackernagel & Rees, 1998). The typical image used to describe this indicator is that three planets would be required to support the world's population if India and China obtained the level of consumption enjoyed by the USA (Dresner, 2008; Meadows, Randers, & Meadows, 2004). In other words, the ecological footprint is a measure of humans' impact on ecosystems and is typically estimated in terms of the land or amount of natural capital consumed each year to supply resources to a human population or to an organization (Wackernagel & Rees, 1998). The basic idea is that every individual, process, activity and region has an impact on the earth, via resource use, the generation of waste and the use of services provided by nature (Blomqvist et al., 2013). These impacts can be converted to biologically productive areas for which one can account:

> The EF is presented as a simple operational indicator to aid in monitoring progress towards (un)sustainability, i.e. maintenance (loss) of natural capital. It accounts for the flows of energy and matter to and from a specific economy or activity, converted into corresponding land and water area needed to support these flows. Six land categories are included in the procedure, namely consumed/degraded land (built environment), gardens, crop land, pasture land and grasslands, productive forest, and energy land . . . The power of the method is the fact that all human exploitation of resources and environment is reduced to a single dimension, namely land and water area needed for its support.
>
> (Blomqvist et al., 2013)

Ecological footprints can be calculated for people, activities, organizations and regions. In short, how are ecological footprints calculated in practice?

> First, consumption is determined in a particular spatial domain for each relevant category. This includes food, housing, transportation, consumer goods and services. Next, the land area appropriated by each consumption category is estimated for different land categories. This includes land appropriated by fossil energy use, built environment, gardens, crop land, pasture/grassland and managed forest. This is based on both resource and waste flows, and leads to a consumption/land-use matrix. Summing all the area figures in this matrix gives an estimate of the EF of the region considered.
>
> (Blomqvist et al., 2013)

Although there are considerable inevitable difficulties in the measurement and application of the notion (Blomqvist et al., 2013; Fiala, 2008), the ecological footprint remains a very powerful and widely employed device to determine (un)sustainability at the organizational level (Gray, 2010).

Much of the literature indicates that in recent decades, there has been a growing awareness of incorporating sustainability into business management (Wang, Halim, Adhitya, & Srinivasan, 2010). Moreover, there is growing global consensus that organizations are responsible for respecting human rights, including non-discrimination, gender equality, freedom of association, collective bargaining, child labor, forced or compulsory labor, and indigenous rights (Global

Reporting Initiative, 2013). Decision makers commonly address the economic aspect of sustainability, and in the last decade, increasing attention has been paid to the environmental aspect. The social dimension of sustainability, however, is in an earlier stage of development, including themes and indicators, such as poverty (e.g., the percent of the population living below the poverty line), gender equality (e.g., the ratio of the average female wage to the average male wage), mortality (e.g., the mortality rate of children under five years old and the life expectancy at birth), sanitation, drinking water, healthcare access and education level, which are to be considered along the supply chain as a whole (Wang et al., 2010). Indeed, gender equality issues are another important topic within the culture of sustainability. In fact, enterprises increasingly have the responsibility to report on their actions regarding these topics (Pulejo, 2012). From the triple bottom line perspective, GRI and many other reporting guidelines now request that data, activities, outcomes and impacts be divided by gender in order to give to readers the opportunity to assess the effectiveness of the gender equality policies adopted.

As shown in this section, social and environmental sustainability issues are increasingly intertwined with business strategies in every sector and especially for larger companies. Thus, we must address how to effectively report on the sustainability-focused business activities that enterprises carry out. As noted by Gray (2010):

> it has been said more than once that if one was looking to solve the problems of the world one would be unlikely to choose accounting as one's starting point; however if we are to consider narratives of sustainability at the organisational level, then it is accounts – in the broadest sense of the term – that we need to embrace.

The next chapter will provide more insights on the processes underlying social, environmental and sustainability reporting.

Notes

1 In this volume, we will use the word "enterprise" to indicate an organization involved in the provision of goods or services to users or consumers; where not otherwise stated, we also refer to this general concept when using the words "corporation", "firm" and "business". We recognize that these notions refer to different things in different legal frameworks, and we leave the analysis of the different roles of stakeholder engagement within these specific legal forms for further research.
2 In this volume, we will not analyze the Balanced Scorecard as an internal strategic management system; instead, we will focus on reporting tools aimed at disclosing economic, social and environmental information to the public.
3 A company's business model is considered a tool that allows managers to better understand, capture, analyze, and manage their businesses (Amit & Zott, 2001; Magretta, 2002). It is also increasingly used as a representation device that can offer valuable information to external users (Beattie & Smith, 2013; Magretta, 2002; Morris, 2013; Nielsen, 2010; Perkmann & Spicer, 2010). The business model is seen as a platform

that provides a comprehensive and integrated description of a company's value creation process, which is how resources, processes, and partnerships are combined to achieve long-term profitability (Nielsen, 2010). When a company's commitment to sustainability affects its strategy and its operation methods, the disclosure of sustainability information through the business model platform might signal the authenticity of its sustainability rhetoric to its stakeholders.

4 On March 1, 2010, the Johannesburg Stock Exchange (JSE) adopted the King III (King Report on Corporate Governance) principles as part of its listing requirements, recommending integrated reporting and requires listed companies to issue integrated reports.

5 Organizations aim to operate within the boundaries and norms of society in order to ensure that their activities are seen as legitimate. According to Lindblom (1994), legitimacy is the condition or status that exists when an entity's value system is congruent with the value system of the larger social system of which the entity is a part. When a disparity, whether real or perceived, exists between the two value systems, there is a threat to the entity's legitimacy. In other words, legitimacy can be viewed as a generalized perception or assumption that an entity's actions are desirable, proper or appropriate within a socially constructed system of norms, values, beliefs and definitions (Suchman, 1995). This definition implies that legitimacy is a desirable social good, that it is more than a matter of optics, and that it may be defined and negotiated at various levels of society (Mitchell, Agle, & Wood, 1997).

6 The word "community" is often over-used. In this volume, we define a community as a social group of any size whose members live in a specific space, share a system of government, and often have a common cultural and historical heritage.

7 Section 4.1.2 of this volume will provide an analysis of the diverse approaches – positive, instrumental and normative – to stakeholder theory.

8 Wackernagel and Rees were first to use the concept of "appropriated carrying capacity": then, to make the idea of this measurement tool more accessible, Rees, inspired by a computer technician who praised his new computer's "small footprint on the desk", coined the term "ecological footprint" (Safire, 2008).

References

Abdifatah, A. H., & Mutalib, A. (2016). The trend of integrated reporting practice in South Africa: ceremonial or substantive? *Sustainability Accounting, Management and Policy Journal, 7*(2), 190–224.

Adams, S., & Simnett, R. (2011). Integrated reporting: An opportunity for Australia's not-for-profit sector. *Australian Accounting Review, 21*(3), 292–301.

Adams, W. (1995). *Green development: Environment and sustainability in a developing world*. London: Routledge.

Amit, R., & Zott, C. (2001). Value creation in e-business. *Strategic Management Journal, 22*(6–7), 493–520.

André, R. (2012). Assessing the accountability of the benefit corporation: Will this new gray sector organization enhance corporate social responsibility? *Journal of Business Ethics, 110*(1), 133–150.

AngloAmerican. (2013). *Annual report 2013*. Retrieved from www.angloamerican.com/investors/annual-reporting

Aras, G., & Crowther, D. (2008a). Governance and sustainability: An investigation into the relationship between corporate governance and corporate sustainability. *Management Decision, 46*(3), 433–448.

Aras, G., & Crowther, D. (2008b). The social obligation of corporations. *Journal of Knowledge Globalization, 1*(1). www.journal.kglobal.org/index.php/jkg/article/view/22

Aras, G., & Crowther, D. (2016). *The durable corporation: Strategies for sustainable development*. London: Taylor & Francis.

Aras, G., Aybars, A., & Kutlu, O. (2010). Managing corporate performance: Investigating the relationship between corporate social responsibility and financial performance in emerging markets. *International Journal of Productivity and Performance Management, 59*(3), 229–254.

Ariansen, P. (1999). Sustainability, morality and future generations. In W. M. Lafferty & O. Langhelle (Eds), *Towards sustainable development: On the goals of development – and the conditions of sustainability* (pp. 84–96). London: Palgrave Macmillan UK.

Aßländer, M. S., & Curbach, J. (2017). Corporate or governmental duties? Corporate citizenship from a governmental perspective. *Business & society, 56*(4), 617–645.

Atkinson, G. (2000). Measuring corporate sustainability. *Journal of Environmental Planning and Management, 43*(2), 235–252. doi:10.1080/09640560010694

Backman, C. A., Verbeke, A., & Schulz, R. A. (2017). The drivers of corporate climate change strategies and public policy: A new resource-based view perspective. *Business & society, 56*(4), 545–575.

Bagnoli, L. (2004). *Quale responsabilità sociale per l'impresa?* (Vol. *21*). Milano: Franco Angeli.

Barnett, M. L., & Salomon, R. M. (2012). Does it pay to be really good? Addressing the shape of the relationship between social and financial performance. *Strategic Management Journal, 33*(11), 1304–1320.

Barth, R., & Wolff, F. (2009). *Corporate social responsibility in Europe: Rhetoric and realities*. Cheltenham: Edward Elgar Publishing.

Beattie, V., & Smith, S. J. (2013). Value creation and business models: Refocusing the intellectual capital debate. *The British Accounting Review, 45*(4), 243–254.

Bebbington, J. (2001). Sustainable development: A review of the international development, business and accounting literature. *Univ of Aberdeen Acct, Finance & Mgmt Working Paper, 00–17*. doi:http://dx.doi.org/10.2139/ssrn.257434

Bebbington, J., & Gray, R. (1996). Sustainable development and accounting: Incentives and disincentives for the adoption of sustainability by transnational corporations. In H. Blokdijk (Ed.), *Environmental and sustainable development* (pp. 107–151). Amsterdam: Limperg Instituut.

Bebbington, J., & Gray, R. (2001). An account of sustainability: Failure, success and a reconceptualization. *Critical Perspectives on Accounting, 12*(5), 557–587.

Bebbington, J., & Larrinaga-Gonzalez, C. (2008). Carbon trading: Accounting and reporting issues. *European Accounting Review, 17*(4), 697–717.

Bellucci, M., Bagnoli, L., Biggeri, M., & Rinaldi, V. (2012). Performance measurement in solidarity economy organizations: The case of fair trade shops in Italy. *Annals of Public and Cooperative Economics, 83*(1), 25–59. doi:10.1111/j.1467-8292.2011.00453.x

Biggeri, M., & Ferrannini, A. (2014). *Sustainable human development: A new territorial and people-centred perspective*. Basingstoke: Palgrave Macmillan.

Biggeri, M., Ballet, J., & Comim, F. (2011). *Children and the capability approach*. Basingstoke: Palgrave Macmillan.

Bini, L., Dainelli, F., & Giunta, F. (2016). Business model disclosure in the Strategic Report: Entangling intellectual capital in value creation process. *Journal of intellectual capital, 17*(1), 83–102. doi:10.1108/JIC-09-2015-0076

Blomqvist, L., Brook, B. W., Ellis, E. C., Kareiva, P. M., Nordhaus, T., & Shellenberger, M. (2013). Does the shoe fit? Real versus imagined ecological footprints. *PLoS Biol, 11*(11), e1001700.

Bonacchi, M. (2007). Sustainable development performance and sustainability: Are stake-holders the missing link? Paper presented at the Seminar at Darden School of Business, USA.

Bonacchi, M., & Rinaldi, L. (2006). A performance measurement system for sustainability. In M. Epstein & J. Manzoni (Eds), *Studies in managerial and financial accounting* (Vol. 16, pp. 49–77). Oxford: Elsevier.

Borzaga, C., Depedri, S., & Tortia, E. (2009). The role of cooperative and social enterprises: A multifaceted approach for an economic pluralism. *European Search Institute on Cooperative and Social Enterprises*. https://papers.ssrn.com/sol3/papers.cfm?abstract_id=1622143

Boulding, K. E. (1966). The economics of the coming spaceship earth. In H. Jarrett (Ed.), *Environmental quality issues in a growing economy* (pp. 3–14). Baltimore: Johns Hopkins University Press.

Brown, J., & Dillard, J. (2014). Integrated reporting: On the need for broadening out and opening up. *Accounting, Auditing & Accountability Journal, 27*(7), 1120–1156. doi:10.1108/AAAJ-04-2013-1313

Buhr, N., & Reiter, S. (2006). Ideology, the environment and one worldview: A discourse analysis of Noranda's environmental and sustainable development reports. *Advances in Environmental Accounting and Management, 3*, 1–48.

Busco, C., Frigo, M. L., Quattrone, P., & Riccaboni, A. (2014). *Integrated reporting*. Dordrecht: Springer.

Cho, C. H. (2009). Legitimation strategies used in response to environmental disaster: A French case study of Total SA's Erika and AZF incidents. *European Accounting Review, 18*(1), 33–62.

Ciepley, D. (2013). Beyond public and private: Toward a political theory of the corporation. *American Political Science Review, 107*(01), 139–158.

Crane, A., & Matten, D. (2004). *Business ethics: A European perspective: managing corporate citizenship and sustainability in the age of globalization*. Oxford: University Press Oxford.

Crane, A., & Matten, D. (2016). Engagement required: The changing role of the corporation in society. In D. Barton, D. Horvath, & M. Kipping (Eds), *Re-imagining capitalism: Building a responsible, long-term model*. Oxford: Oxford University Press.

Crane, A., Matten, D., & Spence, L. J. (2008). *Corporate social responsibility: Readings and cases in a global context*. London: Routledge.

Crowther, D. (1996). Corporate performance operates in three dimensions. *Managerial Auditing Journal, 11*(8), 4–13.

Crowther, D. (2012). A social critique of corporate reporting. In D. Crowther, *Semiotics and web-based integrated reporting*. Edition 2 reprint, London: Routledge.

Crowther, D., & Aras, G. (2007). Is the global economy sustainable? In S. Barber (Ed.), *The geopolitics of the city* (pp. 165–194). London: Forum Press.

Daily, C. M., Dalton, D. R., & Cannella, A. A. (2003). Corporate governance: Decades of dialogue and data. *Academy of Management Review, 28*(3), 371–382.

Daly, H. E. (1996). *Beyond growth: The economics of sustainable development*. Boston: Beacon Press.

Davis, K. (1973). The case for and against business assumption of social responsibilities. *Academy of Management Journal, 16*(2), 312–322.

De Villiers, C., & Van Staden, C. J. (2011). Where firms choose to disclose voluntary environmental information. *Journal of Accounting and Public Policy, 30*(6), 504–525.

De Villiers, C., Rinaldi, L., & Unerman, J. (2014). Integrated reporting: Insights, gaps and an agenda for future research. *Accounting, Auditing & Accountability Journal, 27*(7), 1042–1067. doi:10.1108/AAAJ-06-2014-1736

Deegan, C. (2002). Introduction: The legitimising effect of social and environmental disclosures-a theoretical foundation. *Accounting, Auditing & Accountability Journal, 15*(3), 282–311.

Deegan, C., Rankin, M., & Tobin, J. (2002). An examination of the corporate social and environmental disclosures of BHP from 1983–1997: A test of legitimacy theory. *Accounting, Auditing & Accountability Journal, 15*(3), 312–343.

Defourny, J., & Nyssens, M. (2008). Social enterprise in Europe: Recent trends and developments. *Social Enterprise Journal, 4*(3), 202–228.

Defourny, J., & Nyssens, M. (2010). Conceptions of social enterprise and social entrepreneurship in Europe and the United States: Convergences and divergences. *Journal of social entrepreneurship, 1*(1), 32–53.

Dey, C., Burns, J., Hopwood, A., Unerman, J., & Fries, J. (2010). Integrated reporting at Novo Nordisk. In A. Hopwood, J. Unerman, & J. Fries (Eds) *Accounting for sustainability: Practical insights* (pp. 215–232). London: Earthscan.

Dierkes, M., & Antal, A. B. (1986). Whither corporate social reporting: Is it time to legislate? *California Management Review, 28*(3), 106–121.

Dobson, A. (2000). *Green political thought*. Hove: Psychology Press.

Dresner, S. (2008). *The principles of sustainability*. London: Earthscan.

Eccles, R. G., & Krzus, M. P. (2010). *One report: Integrated reporting for a sustainable strategy*. Hoboken: John Wiley & Sons.

Eccles, R. G., & Krzus, M. P. (2014). *The integrated reporting movement: Meaning, momentum, motives, and materiality*. Hoboken: John Wiley & Sons.

Ekins, P. (1993). Making development sustainable. In W. Sachs (Ed.), *Global ecology: A new arena of political conflict* (pp. 91). London: Zed Books.

Ekins, P., Simon, S., Deutsch, L., Folke, C., & De Groot, R. (2003). A framework for the practical application of the concepts of critical natural capital and strong sustainability. *Ecological Economics, 44*(2), 165–185.

Elkington, J. (1997). *Cannibals with forks. The triple bottom line of 21st century*. Oxford: Capstone publishing.

Elkington, J. (1999). The link between accountability and sustainability: Theory put into practice. Paper presented at the Conference on the Practice of Social Reporting for Business, ISEA, January 19, Commonwealth Conference Centre, London.

Evans, T. L. (2012). *Occupy education: Living and learning sustainability* (Vol. 22). New York: Peter Lang.

Fasan, M., & Mio, C. (2017). Fostering stakeholder engagement: The role of materiality disclosure in Integrated Reporting. *Business Strategy and the Environment, 26*(3), 288–305.

Fiala, N. (2008). Measuring sustainability: Why the ecological footprint is bad economics and bad environmental science. *Ecological economics, 67*(4), 519–525.

Freeman, R. E. (1984). *Strategic management: A stakeholder approach*. Boston: Pitman.

Freeman, R. E., Harrison, J. S., & Wicks, A. C. (2007). *Managing for stakeholders: Survival, reputation, and success*. New Haven: Yale University Press.

Freeman, R. E., Wicks, A. C., & Parmar, B. (2004). Stakeholder theory and "the corporate objective revisited". *Organization Science, 15*(3), 364–369.

Friedman, M. (1970). The social responsibility of business is to increase its profits. *New York Times Magazine*, September 13, 1970, 122–126.

Fritsch, B., Schmidheiny, S., & Seifritz, W. (2012). *Towards an ecologically sustainable growth society: Physical foundations, economic transitions, and political constraints.* Dordrecht: Springer Science & Business Media.

Fuller, R. B. (1968). *Operating manual for spaceship earth.* New York: Dutton.

Galera, G., & Borzaga, C. (2009). Social enterprise: An international overview of its conceptual evolution and legal implementation. *Social Enterprise Journal, 5*(3), 210–228.

García-Sánchez, I. M., & Noguera-Gámez, L. (2017). Integrated reporting and stakeholder engagement: The effect on information asymmetry. *Corporate social responsibility and environmental management.* https://onlinelibrary.wiley.com/doi/abs/10.1002/csr.1415

Garriga, E., & Melé, D. (2013). Corporate social responsibility theories: Mapping the territory. In Michalos, Alex C., Poff CM, & Deborah C (Eds)*Citation classics from the Journal of Business Ethics* (pp. 69–96). Dordrecht: Springer.

Giovannoni, E., & Pia Maraghini, M. (2013). The challenges of integrated performance measurement systems: Integrating mechanisms for integrated measures. *Accounting, Auditing & Accountability Journal, 26*(6), 978–1008.

Gladwin, T. N., Krause, T. S., & Kennelly, J. J. (1995). Beyond eco-efficiency: Towards socially sustainable business. *Sustainable Development, 3*(1), 35–43.

Global Reporting Initiative. (2013). *Reporting principles and standard disclosure.* Amsterdam: Global Reporting Initiative.

Gray, R. (1992). Accounting and environmentalism: An exploration of the challenge of gently accounting for accountability, transparency and sustainability. *Accounting, Organizations and Society, 17*(5), 399–425.

Gray, R. (2010). Is accounting for sustainability actually accounting for sustainability. . . and how would we know? An exploration of narratives of organisations and the planet. *Accounting Organizations and Society, 35*(1), 47–62. doi:10.1016/j.aos.2009.04.006

Gray, R., & Bebbington, J. (2001). *Accounting for the environment.* Thousand Oaks: Sage.

Gray, R., & Milne, M. (2002). Sustainability reporting: Who's kidding whom? *Chartered Accountants Journal of New Zealand, 81*(6), 66–70.

Gray, R. H., Milne, M., & Buhr, N. (2014). Histories, rationales, voluntary standards and future prospects or sustainability reporting: CSR, GRI, IIRC and Beyond. In J. Bebbington, J. Unerman, & B. O'Dwyer (Eds), *Sustainability accounting and accountability* (pp. 51–71). London: Routledge.

Gray, R., Owen, D., & Adams, C. (1996). *Accounting & accountability: Changes and challenges in corporate social and environmental reporting.* Upper Saddle River: Prentice Hall.

Guthrie, J., & Parker, L. D. (1989). Corporate social reporting: A rebuttal of legitimacy theory. *Accounting and Business Research, 19*(76), 343–352.

Haigh, N., Walker, J., Bacq, S., & Kickul, J. (2015). Hybrid organizations: Origins, strategies, impacts, and implications. *California Management Review, 57*(3), 5–12.

Hiller, J. S. (2013). The benefit corporation and corporate social responsibility. *Journal of Business Ethics, 118*(2), 287–301.

Hines, R. D. (1988). Financial accounting: in communicating reality, we construct reality. *Accounting, Organizations and Society, 13*(3), 251–261.

Hopwood, A. G., Unerman, J., & Fries, J. (2010). *Accounting for sustainability: Practical insights.* London: Earthscan.

International Integrated Reporting Committee. (2011). *Towards integrated reporting: Communicating value in the 21st century.* London: International Integrated Reporting Committee.

IIRC. (2013a). Business model–background paper for <IR>. Retrieved from http://integratedreporting.org//wp-content/uploads/2013/03/Business_Model.pdf

IIRC. (2013b). *The international <IR> framework*. London: IIRC.

Jensen, M. C. (2001). Value maximization, stakeholder theory, and the corporate objective function. *Journal of applied corporate finance, 14*(3), 8–21.

Jones, M. J. (1996). Accounting for biodiversity: A pilot study. *The British Accounting Review, 28*(4), 281–303.

Jones, M. J. (2003). Accounting for biodiversity: Operationalising environmental accounting. *Accounting, Auditing & Accountability Journal, 16*(5), 762–789.

Kolk, A. (2008). Sustainability, accountability and corporate governance: Exploring multinationals' reporting practices. *Business Strategy and the Environment, 17*(1), 1–15.

Kolk, A., Levy, D., & Pinkse, J. (2008). Corporate responses in an emerging climate regime: The institutionalization and commensuration of carbon disclosure. *European Accounting Review, 17*(4), 719–745.

KPMG. (2015). *Currents of change: The KPMG Survey of Corporate Responsibility Reporting 2015*. Netherlands: KPMG.

Laine, M. (2010). Towards sustaining the status quo: Business talk of sustainability in Finnish corporate disclosures 1987–2005. *European Accounting Review, 19*(2), 247–274. doi:10.1080/09638180903136258

Lamberton, G. (2000). Accounting for sustainable development: Case study of city farm. *Critical Perspectives on Accounting, 11*(5), 583–605.

Lele, S. M. (1991). Sustainable development: A critical review. *World Development, 19*(6), 607–621.

Lindblom, C. K. (1994). The implications of organizational legitimacy for corporate social performance and disclosure. Paper presented at the Critical Perspectives on Accounting Conference, New York.

Livesey, S. M., & Kearins, K. (2002). Transparent and caring corporations? A study of sustainability reports by the Body Shop and Royal Dutch/Shell. *Organization & Environment, 15*(3), 233–258.

Lohmann, L. (2009). Toward a different debate in environmental accounting: The cases of carbon and cost–benefit. *Accounting, Organizations and Society, 34*(3), 499–534.

Lopatta, K., Jaeschke, R., & Chen, C. (2017). Stakeholder engagement and corporate social responsibility (CSR) performance: International evidence. *Corporate Social Responsibility and Environmental Management, 24*(3), 199–209.

Luke, T. W. (2013). Corporate social responsibility: An uneasy merger of sustainability and development. *Sustainable Development, 21*(2), 83–91. doi:10.1002/sd.1558

Magretta, J. (2002). Why business models matter. *Harvard Business Review, 80*(5), 86–92.

Manetti, G. (2006). *Il triple bottom line reporting: Dal coinvolgimento degli stakeholder alle verifiche esterne* (Vol. 30). Milano: Franco Angeli.

Manetti, G., Bellucci, M., Como, E., & Bagnoli, L. (2015). Investing in volunteering: Measuring social returns of volunteer recruitment, training and management. *VOLUNTAS: International Journal of Voluntary and Nonprofit Organizations, 26*(5), 2104–2129. doi:10.1007/s11266-014-9497-3

Matten, D., & Crane, A. (2005). Corporate citizenship: Toward an extended theoretical conceptualization. *Academy of Management Review, 30*(1), 166–179.

Matten, D., Crane, A., & Chapple, W. (2003). Behind the mask: Revealing the true face of corporate citizenship. *Journal of Business Ethics, 45*(1), 109–120. doi:10.1023/a:1024128730308

Meadowcroft, J. (2000). Sustainable development: A new (ish) idea for a new century? *Political Studies, 48*(2), 370–387.

Meadows, D., Randers, J., & Meadows, D. (2004). *Limits to growth: The 30-year update*. White River Junction: Chelsea Green Publishing.

Miles, S. (2017). Stakeholder theory classification: A theoretical and empirical evaluation of definitions. *Journal of Business Ethics*, *142*(3), 437–459.

Milne, M. J. (2013). Phantasmagoria, sustain-a-babbling and the communication of corporate social and environmental accountability. In L. Davison, & R. Craig (Eds), *The Routledge companion to accounting communication* (pp. 135–153). London: Routledge.

Milne, M. J., & Gray, R. (2012). W(h)ither ecology? The triple bottom line, the Global Reporting Initiative, and corporate sustainability reporting. *Journal of Business Ethics*, *118*(1), 13–29. doi:10.1007/s10551-012-1543-8

Milne, M. J., Kearins, K., & Walton, S. (2006). Creating adventures in wonderland: The journey metaphor and environmental sustainability. *Organization*, *13*(6), 801–839.

Mitchell, R. K., Agle, B. R., & Wood, D. J. (1997). Toward a theory of stakeholder identification and salience: Defining the principle of who and what really counts. *Academy of Management Review*, *22*(4), 853–886. doi:10.2307/259247

Mook, L., Chan, A., & Kershaw, D. (2015). Measuring social enterprise value creation. *Nonprofit Management and Leadership*, *26*(2), 189–207.

Moratis, L., & Brandt, S. (2017). Corporate stakeholder responsiveness? Exploring the state and quality of GRI-based stakeholder engagement disclosures of European firms. *Corporate Social Responsibility and Environmental Management*, *24*(4), 312–325..

Morris, L. (2013). Business model warfare: The strategy of business breakthroughs. *Journal of Business Models*, *1*(1), 13–37.

Néron, P.-Y., & Norman, W. (2008). Citizenship, Inc. Do we really want businesses to be good corporate citizens? *Business Ethics Quarterly*, *18*(01), 1–26.

Neu, D., Warsame, H., & Pedwell, K. (1998). Managing public impressions: environmental disclosures in annual reports. *Accounting, Organizations and Society*, *23*(3), 265–282.

Nidumolu, R., Prahalad, C. K., & Rangaswami, M. R. (2009). Why sustainability is now the key driver of innovation. *Harvard Business Review*, *87*(9), 56–64.

Nielsen, C. (2010). Conceptualizing, analyzing and communicating the business model. *Department of Business Studies, Aalborg University, WP*, *2*, 1–24.

Nixon, B., & Burns, J. (2012). The paradox of strategic management accounting. *Management Accounting Research*, *23*(4), 229–244.

Padilla, E. (2002). Intergenerational equity and sustainability. *Ecological Economics*, *41*(1), 69–83.

Pallot, J. (1997). Infrastructure accounting for local authorities: Technical management and political context. *Financial Accountability & Management*, *13*(3), 225–242.

Parker, L. D. (2012). Qualitative management accounting research: Assessing deliverables and relevance. *Critical Perspectives on Accounting*, *23*(1), 54–70.

Perkmann, M., & Spicer, A. (2010). What are business models? Developing a theory of performative representations. *Research in the Sociology of Organizations*, *29*, 265–275.

Phillips, N., & Hardy, C. (2002). *Discourse analysis: Investigating processes of social construction* (Vol. 50). Thousand Oaks: Sage Publications.

Pulejo, L. (2012). *La gender equality nell'economia dell'azienda. Strategie e strumenti di mainstreaming di genere per lo sviluppo sostenibile* (Vol. 1). Milano: Franco Angeli.

Ranganathan, J. (1998). Sustainability rulers: Measuring corporate environmental and social performance. World Resources Institute, Sustainable Enterprise Initiative. Retrieved from www.wri.org/publication/sustainability-rulersmeasuring-corporate-environmental-social-performance

Redclift, M. (2002). *Sustainable development: Exploring the contradictions*. London: Routledge.

Redclift, M. (2005). Sustainable development (1987–2005): An oxymoron comes of age. *Sustainable Development*, *13*(4), 212–227.

Rees, W. E. (1992). Ecological footprints and appropriated carrying capacity: What urban economics leaves out. *Environment and urbanization*, *4*(2), 121–130.

Reid, D. (2013). *Sustainable development: An introductory guide*. London: Routledge.

Roberts, R. W. (1992). Determinants of corporate social responsibility disclosure: An application of stakeholder theory. *Accounting, Organizations and Society*, *17*(6), 595–612.

Robinson, J. (2004). Squaring the circle? Some thoughts on the idea of sustainable development. *Ecological Economics*, *48*(4), 369–384.

Safire, W. (2008). Footprint. *The New York Times*. www.nytimes.com/2008/02/17/magazine/17wwln-safire-t.html

Salazar, J., Husted, B. W., & Biehl, M. (2012). Thoughts on the evaluation of corporate social performance through projects. *Journal of Business Ethics*, *105*(2), 175–186.

Scherer, A. G., Palazzo, G., & Baumann, D. (2006). Global rules and private actors: Toward a new role of the transnational corporation in global governance. *Business Ethics Quarterly*, *16*(04), 505–532.

Scruton, R. (2012). *How to think seriously about the planet: The case for an environmental conservatism*. Oxford: Oxford University Press.

Setia, N., Abhayawansa, S., Joshi, M., & Huynh, A. V. (2015). Integrated reporting in South Africa: Some initial evidence. *Sustainability Accounting, Management and Policy Journal*, *6*(3), 397–424. doi:10.1108/SAMPJ-03-2014-0018

Shleifer, A., & Vishny, R. W. (1997). A survey of corporate governance. *The Journal of Finance*, *52*(2), 737–783.

Shrivastava, P. (1995). The role of corporations in achieving ecological sustainability. *Academy of Management Review*, *20*(4), 936–960. doi:10.2307/258961

Solomon, J., & Maroun, W. (2012). *Integrated reporting: The influence of King III on social, ethical and environmental reporting*. London: The Association of Chartered Certified Accountants.

Solow, R. M. (1974). Intergenerational equity and exhaustible resources. *The Review of Economic Studies*, *41*, 29–45.

Sombart, W. (1915). *The quintessence of capitalism: A study of the history and psychology of the modern business man*. New York: EP Dutton.

Steiner, G. A. (1972). Social policies for business. *California Management Review*, *15*(2), 17–24.

Stout, L. A. (2012). *The shareholder value myth: How putting shareholders first harms investors, corporations, and the public*. Oakland: Berrett-Koehler Publishers.

Suchman, M. C. (1995). Managing legitimacy: Strategic and institutional approaches. *Academy of Management Review*, *20*(3), 571–610.

Sundaram, A. K., & Inkpen, A. C. (2004). The corporate objective revisited. *Organization Science*, *15*(3), 350–363.

Taplin, J. R., Bent, D., & Aeron-Thomas, D. (2006). Developing a sustainability accounting framework to inform strategic business decisions: A case study from the chemicals industry. *Business Strategy and the Environment*, *15*(5), 347–360.

Terzani, S. (1989). *Introduzione al bilancio di esercizio*. (Quinta edizione. ed.). Padova: Cedam.

Thomas, A. (2004). The rise of social cooperatives in Italy. *VOLUNTAS: International Journal of Voluntary and Nonprofit Organizations*, *15*(3), 243–263.

Wackernagel, M., & Rees, W. (1998). *Our ecological footprint: Reducing human impact on the earth*. Gabriola: New Society Publishers.

Wang, P. C., Halim, I., Adhitya, A., & Srinivasan, R. (2010). Evaluating triple bottom line sustainability of global supply chains using dynamic simulation. Paper presented at the 2010 AIChE Annual Meeting, Salt Lake City.

Ward, B. (1966). *Spaceship earth*. New York: Columbia University Press.

Warhurst, A. (2001). Corporate citizenship and corporate social investment. *Journal of Corporate Citizenship*, *1*(1), 57–73.

Whelan, G., Moon, J., & Grant, B. (2013). Corporations and citizenship arenas in the age of social media. *Journal of Business Ethics*, *118*(4), 777–790.

Wild, S., & van Staden, C. (2013). Integrated reporting: Initial analysis of early reporters–an institutional theory approach. Paper presented at the 7th Asia Pacific Interdisciplinary Accounting Research Conference, Kobe.

World Commission for Environment and Development. (1987). *Our common future.* Oxford: Oxford University Press.

Yunus, M. (2007). *Creating a world without poverty: Social business and the future of capitalism.* New York: PublicAffairs.

Yunus, M., Moingeon, B., & Lehmann-Ortega, L. (2010). Building social business models: Lessons from the Grameen experience. *Long Range Planning*, *43*(2), 308–325.

Zappa, G. (1957). *Le produzioni nell'economia delle imprese.* Milano: Giuffrè editore.

3 Materiality in sustainability reporting

3.1 Social and environmental sustainability reporting

3.1.1 Framing sustainability reporting

Within the accounting literature, sustainability and sustainable development have been considered in the context of social and environmental sustainability reporting (hereafter "sustainability reporting" or SR[1]) because accounting for sustainable development and SR share some concerns and consider the same range of issues, namely, the social and environmental impacts of corporate activity (Bebbington, 2001). Therefore, what is the function of sustainability reporting?

> Sustainability reporting helps organizations to set goals, measure performance, and manage change in order to make their operations more sustainable. A sustainability report conveys disclosures on an organization's impacts – be they positive or negative – on the environment, society and the economy. In doing so, sustainability reporting makes abstract issues tangible and concrete, thereby assisting in understanding and managing the effects of sustainability developments on the organization's activities and strategy.
>
> (Global Reporting Initiative, 2013c)

SR examines the areas in which accounting affects its functional environment and seeks to develop accounting tools to assess these effects. As seen in the previous chapter, the sustainability concept has gained wider acceptance, and there has been a worldwide trend toward the greater use of sustainability reports. In recent decades, companies have paid growing interest to environmental and social issues, and there has been substantial growth in the research attention devoted to social and environmental accounting topics (Bagnoli, 2004; Barth & Wolff, 2009; Deegan, Rankin, & Tobin, 2002; Elkington, 1999; Epstein, 2007; Kolk, 2008; Laine, 2010; Manetti & Toccafondi, 2011; Thorne, Mahoney, & Manetti, 2014).

The emergence of large-scale business organizations in Europe and the United States in the last third of the 19th century gave rise to concerns about corporate social responsibility (CSR) (Epstein, 2007). The development of social and environmental accounting and reporting in the last 40 years has resulted in a wide range of actual and potential accounts of organizational interactions with society and the natural environment: these accounts can be understood as narratives of events that articulate – with varying degrees of thoroughness and misdirection – the organization's relationships with its "stakeholders and its immediate substantive environment" (Gray, 2010).

While in the early 1990s, the focus on environmental reporting was accompanied by growing interest in social reporting beginning in approximately the mid-1990s, the principal focus in recent years has been either triple bottom line reporting or sustainability reporting (Gray & Milne, 2002). It is important to note that despite appearances, these two latter concepts are not synonyms. Although in practice, there is a great deal of confusion regarding the use of terms such as "sustainability reporting" and "social and environmental reporting" and even "social, environmental and sustainability reporting", on a theoretical level, much of the literature argues that it is important to highlight the specific features of each concept.

First, as stated in Section 2.3.2, the concept of the triple bottom line refers to the notion that organizations contemplating issues related to sustainable development need to depart from working toward a single financial bottom line and to focus additionally on social and environmental performance or social and environmental bottom lines (Gray, 2010; Gray & Milne, 2002). The merit of the triple bottom line is that it promotes the idea that for full accountability, an organization must produce, alongside its financial statements, a full set of both social and environmental disclosures (Gray, 2010; Gray & Milne, 2002):

> That is, with the growth in environmental reporting and social reporting, the company's annual report would contain, in addition to such matters as the chair's review, director's report and financial review, detailed social and environmental statements. For a truly meaningful "triple bottom line" these social and environmental statements would be as important, detailed, rigorous and reliable as the financial statements. But this is where the problems arose - the social and environmental information included by the few that approached any kind of triple bottom line reporting tended to be assertive, partial and to cherry-pick the "good news". As accountability statements they were, and still are, at very best, partial.
>
> (Gray & Milne, 2002)

Second, SR requires a stronger commitment than social and environmental reporting do. A sustainability report should contain a complete and transparent statement about the extent to which the organization contributed to – or, more likely, diminished – the sustainability of the planet (Gray, 2010; Gray & Milne, 2002). In other words, as reported by Gray and Milne (2002), a sustainability report requires a detailed and complex analysis of the organization's interactions with ecological systems, resources, habitats and societies.

3.1.2 The motivations underlying sustainability reporting

Currently, various domestic and international factors advocate reporting. The increasing concerns about stakeholders, the growing concern about business ethics (Ciappei & Ninci, 2006) and CSR and the increasing importance of ethical investment have all increased the need for new accounting methods by which organizations and their stakeholders can address these topics (Gray, 2010; Laine, 2010; Lopatta, Jaeschke, & Chen, 2017). Accordingly, an increasing number of companies are publishing various kinds of sustainability and CSR reports (KPMG, 2015). The number of corporations' published reports that include sustainability information is growing around the world. According to data from CorporateRegister.com, a repository of over 77,000 reports by 13,400 different organizations in 159 countries, the global output of sustainability reports increased from 26 in 1992 to 5,819 in 2011 (Eccles, Krzus, Rogers, & Serafeim, 2012) and reached 8,477 in 2015. Nearly 95 percent of the largest 250 companies worldwide issue sustainability reports, of which 46 percent are independently assured (Edgley, Jones, & Atkins, 2015).

KPMG has regularly published a survey on sustainability reporting at regular intervals since 1993: the growth in the number of countries and companies covered in these reports (KPMG, 2015) is just one indication of how sustainability reporting has evolved into a mainstream business practice in recent decades. In 2015, KPMG issued the ninth edition of the report, which reflects the current state of non-financial reporting worldwide. Below is a summary of the key trends highlighted by KPMG (2015):

- Almost three-quarters of N100 companies now report on CR (corporate responsibility). The current rate of CR reporting among the G250 is over 90 percent;
- More companies now report on CR in the Asia Pacific region than in any other region;
- Four emerging economies have the highest CR reporting rates in the world: India, Indonesia, Malaysia and South Africa;
- Companies in the retail sector have the furthest to go, lagging behind all other sectors;
- Including CR data in annual financial reports is now a firmly established global trend: almost three in five companies currently do so, in contrast to only one in five in 2011;
- The number of companies stating that they produce integrated reports remains low: approximately one in ten;
- Third-party independent assurance of CR information is now firmly established as standard practice among the world's largest companies (G250). Almost two-thirds invest in assurance;
- Major accountancy organizations continue to dominate the market for third-party assurance among G250 and N100 companies;
- The Global Reporting Initiative (GRI) remains the most popular voluntary reporting guideline worldwide, but use of GRI declined among the world's largest companies.

Additionally, KPMG (2015) continues to study the overall quality of sustainability reporting around the globe. In 2013, KPMG analyzed the quality of reporting among the world's largest companies using a proprietary assessment and scoring methodology based on seven criteria: "stakeholder engagement", "materiality", "risk, opportunity and strategy", "targets and indicators", "transparency and balance", "suppliers and value chain" and "corporate responsibility and governance". Assessing the quality of reporting is important because "poor quality reports tend to be associated with poor performance in the mind of the reader. Few companies practice 'total greenwash' these days but readers certainly give more credence to a higher quality report" (KPMG, 2013). According to KPMG (2013), companies in the electronics and computers sector led the G250 in terms of reporting quality, while the lowest scoring sectors were oil and gas, trade and retail, metals, engineering and manufacturing, and construction and building materials. European companies demonstrate significantly greater reporting quality than other regions; Italy, Spain and the UK have the highest average scores, reflecting the relative maturity of reporting in these markets compared with those of countries such as China, where widespread reporting is a relatively new phenomenon. KPMG repeated this analysis in 2015 and identified that CR reporting quality improved slightly in the Asia Pacific region but declined slightly elsewhere; however, companies are improving their ability to report the environmental and social trends and risks that affect their businesses (KPMG, 2015).

Moreover, in recent years, the topic of sustainability has also gained prominence within the agenda of national and international policy makers. In the European Union (EU), Directive 2014/95/EU on the disclosure of non-financial and diversity information, which entered into force on December 6, 2014, and amended Directive 2013/34/EU, requires large companies to disclose in their management reports information on policies, risks and outcomes regarding environmental matters, social and employee aspects, respect for human rights, anticorruption and bribery issues, and diversity in their boards of directors. The EU originally introduced an official requirement for non-financial disclosure in 2003 (Directive 51/2003) further to a 2001 recommendation.

In response to corporate collapses such as Enron and WorldCom, the United States introduced new corporate governance disclosure requirements under the Sarbanes-Oxley Act in 2002; additionally, listed US companies must also report on their environmental performance under Securities and Exchange Commission regulations (Items 101 and 103 of Regulation S-K).

Hence, in recent years, there has been an increased call for transparency among companies – especially large ones – from two main angles: accountability requirements in the context of corporate governance, which expand to staff-related and ethical aspects, and sustainability reporting, which has broadened from environment concerns to include social and financial issues as well (Kolk, 2008). Policy makers and academics have argued that the demand for external communication regarding new types of value drivers is increasing as companies progressively base their competitive strengths – and thus their companies' value – on know-how, patents, skilled employees and other intangibles (Nielsen, 2010).

One may conclude that in many cases, large enterprises create sustainability reports in whole or in part to comply with the increasing number of regulations on reporting social and environmental elements. We believe that compliance with the law is not the only or the main reason why enterprises – especially large ones – issue sustainability reports, as confirmed by the practice of business to also publish information on unregulated topics. Although many governments and institutions have stimulated this kind of disclosure directly or indirectly, corporate sustainability reporting has been and remains a mostly voluntary activity oriented at providing an account of the societal and environmental implications of doing business to internal and external stakeholders (Kolk, 2008). It is relevant to note that companies can have a range of reasons for publishing (or not publishing) a sustainability report other than national or international regulations.

Following Kolk (2004), we hereby discuss a set of motivations beyond simple compliance with the law. The following lists contain various motivations that were mentioned in a study by SustainAbility and UNEP (1998) featuring inter-views with reporters and non-reporters. Basing on the results of that study, the main reasons for reporting include:

> enhanced ability to track progress against specific targets; facilitating the implementation of the environmental strategy; greater awareness of broad environmental issues throughout the organisation; ability to clearly convey the corporate message internally and externally; improved all-round credibil-ity from greater transparency; ability to communicate efforts and standards; licence to operate and campaign; reputational benefits, cost savings identifi-cation, increased efficiency, enhanced business; development opportunities and enhanced staff morale.

Additionally, the reasons for not reporting included:

> doubts about the advantages it would bring to the organisation, competitors are neither publishing reports, customers (and the general public) are not inter-ested in it, it will not increase sales, the company already has a good reputation for its environmental performance; there are many other ways of communi-cating about environmental issues; it is too expensive; it is difficult to gather consistent data from all operations and to select correct indicators; it could damage the reputation of the company, have legal implications or wake up.

Not only internal – and sometimes company-specific – factors but also societal aspects such as credibility and reputation play an important role. It appears that for an increasing and substantial number of companies, the arguments in favor of reporting prevail over those against, particularly for the largest, most visible multinational companies (Kolk, 2004, 2008).

The accounting literature usually adopts one or a mix of several different theo-retical perspectives, including stakeholder theory (Adams, 2002; Freeman, 1984; Matten, Crane, & Chapple, 2003), signaling theory (Clarkson, Li, Richardson, &

Vasvari, 2011; Clarkson, Overell, & Chapple, 2011), legitimacy theory (Deegan, 2002; Tate, Ellram, & Kirchoff, 2010), socio-economic theory (Clarkson, Li, et al., 2011; Clarkson, Overell, et al., 2011; Deegan, 2002; Deegan et al., 2002; Dowling & Pfeffer, 1975; Patten, 1992) and institutional theory (Larrinaga-Gonzalez & Bebbington, 2001) to explain why companies issue sustainability reports (Thorne et al., 2014).

Although we believe that conducing a detailed analysis of each of these theories is beyond the scope of this volume, we opted to provide a concise outline in Table 3.1, which introduces the main features of each framework and the most significant studies on them.

3.1.3 Inside the box of sustainability reporting

Over time, SR has broadened from reporting only on the environment to reporting on social and financial aspects as well ("people, planet, profit"); attention to the organization of and performance in these areas has also grown (Global Reporting

Table 3.1 Main theories used to explain why organizations publish sustainability reports

Theory	Main features	References
Stakeholder theory	Organizations must not only be accountable to investors but also balance a multiplicity of stakeholder expectations and interests that can affect or be affected by the organization's actions. Voluntary social and environmental disclosure is a component of this dialogue between the organization and its stakeholders.	Adams, 2002; Donaldson & Preston, 1995; Freeman, 1984; Freeman, Wicks, & Parmar, 2004; Gray, Owen, & Adams, 1996; Mitchell, Agle, & Wood, 1997; Phillips, Freeman, & Wicks, 2003
Institutional theory	The decision to initiate the sustainability reporting process depends on many organizational dynamics and on a variety of regulative, normative and cognitive drivers that are strictly connected to the local context within which the organization is rooted. Enterprises are influenced and shaped by other social institutions.	Adams, 2002; Adams, Larrinaga-González, Adams, & McNicholas, 2007; Gray, 2010; Larrinaga, 2007; Larrinaga-Gonzalez & Bebbington, 2001; Milne, Kearins, & Walton, 2006
Signaling theory	Organizations voluntarily publish sustainability reports to highlight their values, goals and outcomes with regard to diverse social, environmental and ethical issues. Organizations with good financial, social and environmental outcomes are thus motivated to disclose their performance in order to avoid adverse selection problems.	Clarkson, Li, et al., 2011; Clarkson, Overell, et al., 2011; Morris, 1987; Thorne, et al., 2014

Legitimacy theory	Organizations issue social reports to reduce their external costs or diminish the pressures imposed by external stakeholders or regulators. The voluntary disclosure of sustainability reports is adopted for strategic reasons rather than for responsibility to the community and can be used to influence (or manipulate) stakeholder perceptions of their image.	Castello & Lozano, 2011; Deegan, 2002; Gray, Kouhy, & Lavers, 1995; Gray & Milne, 2002; Guthrie & Parker, 1989; Tate, et al., 2010
Socio-economic theory	The organization and its voluntary disclosure practices must be analyzed within a social and political context since the institutional framework helps illuminate their behavior. Problems can emerge when there is a disparity between community values and the organization's values and impacts. By using external accountability mechanisms, voluntary disclosure regarding sustainability issues can strengthen an organization's social legitimacy, improving its image and perception among external stakeholders and the local community. The manipulation of an organization's image (greenwashing or bluewashing*) is perceived as being easier to accomplish than improving the organization's levels of sustainability performance, supply chain structure, or value system.	Clarkson, Li, et al., 2011; Clarkson, Overell, et al., 2011; Deegan, 2002; Deegan et al.,, 2002; Dowling & Pfeffer, 1975; Laufer, 2003; Patten, 1992

Note: * As reported by Laufer (2003), the emergence of the terms "greenwashing" (a deceptive promotion of the perception that an organization's products, aims or policies are environmentally friendly) and "bluewashing" (washing through the reputation of the United Nations) reflects increasing apprehension that at least some organizations creatively manage their reputation with the public, financial community and regulators to hide deviance, deflect attributions of fault, obscure the nature of a problem or allegation, reattribute blame, ensure the entity's reputation and, finally, to appear to hold a leadership position.

Initiative, 2002; Kolk, 2008). Likewise, the number of constituencies and potential readers of sustainability reports has widened to cover external and internal stakeholders, including shareholders. Sometimes also labeled CSR reporting, sustainability reporting plays a role in how companies account for and report their CSR, a concept that is considered to embody companies' economic, legal, ethical and philanthropic responsibilities to society in general and to their range of stakeholders in particular (Bagnoli, 2004; Carroll, 1999; Kolk, 2008; Whetten, Rands, & Godfrey, 2002).

Similar to CSR, sustainability reporting encompasses the economic, legal, ethical, and philanthropic expectations placed on organizations by society at a given point in time (Carroll, 1991). According to Carroll (1991), meeting economic responsibilities toward shareholders, employees, consumers and suppliers is the first layer of CSR and is a requirement for all organizations. A second layer is also required by society, as corporations seeking to be socially responsible must abide by the law. The third layer of ethical responsibility obliges corporations to do what is right, just and fair, even when they are not compelled to do so by the legal system. In other words, ethical responsibilities consist of society's general expectations beyond economic and legal requirements (Carroll, 1991). Finally, the fourth level of CSR – the tip of the pyramid – examines the philanthropic responsibilities that are not expected or required from corporations, making them less important than the other three categories (Crane & Matten, 2004).

Following Lamberton (2005), we discuss here five main themes that are common in every approach to sustainability accounting and reporting:

- SR is based on the contemporary definition of sustainable development provided by the World Commission for Environment and Development (1987), which includes economic, environmental and social dimensions without providing particular guidance regarding how these competing elements are prioritized (probably because the latter topic is more a policy matter rather than a reporting issue);
- Because it is a complex and multi-dimensional concept, sustainability is not directly measurable and requires a set of various indicators to enable the assessment of performance in its multiple objectives;
- Although certain forms of environmental accounting rely on monetary units to measure environmental and social impacts, an increasing trend that is evident in the guidelines provided by the GRI (Global Reporting Initiative, 2013c) is the use of multiple units of measurement to assess performance in the three dimensions of sustainability. Financial units of measurement – the preferred choice for measuring economic performance – are not necessarily suitable for capturing social and ecological impacts (Bellucci, Bagnoli, Biggeri, & Rinaldi, 2012; Lamberton, 2005; Liberatore, 2001). Qualitative tools, such as narratives describing an organization's social and environmental outcomes, form a critical component of sustainability accounting (Lamberton, 2005; Lehman, 1999);
- Given the three dimensions of sustainability, SR inherently becomes a process that reaches across the accounting, social and ecological disciplines and requires cooperation between them;
- Most of the various approaches to sustainability accounting draw on traditional accounting principles and/or practices, including the capital maintenance concept used in sustainable cost and natural resource inventory accounting, full cost accounting, inventory accounting and the valuation of environmental assets and liabilities.

One of the biggest challenges in SR is determining the standards for sustainability information that are as rigorous as those for financial information:

> Without standards, it is difficult for companies to know exactly how to measure and report on some dimensions of sustainability performance. Without standards, the investment community cannot make meaningful "apples-to-apples" comparisons of performance among companies and over time. The ability to make such comparisons is an essential requirement for building sustainability performance information into financial models, with the eventual aim of turning them into more robust business models. Performance comparisons are also of interest to companies that want to be able to benchmark their performance against a set of competitors or peers defined in various ways.
>
> (Eccles et al., 2012)

The literature argues that the simultaneous pursuit of economic, environmental and social sustainability is rapidly becoming a strategic priority for enterprises across sectors and geographical regions (Arevalo et al., 2011; Evans, 2012). We believe that this evolution has involved a reorientation of reporting to increase the emphasis on the most material aspects of performance, including both narrative and quantitative metrics. At the same time, the pursuit of comparability among reports issued by different organizations has begun to produce results, including improved standardization.

As reported by KPMG (2015), the most frequently adopted guidelines for preparing voluntary sustainability reports are those provided by the GRI.[2] The GRI was established in 1997 by various companies and organizations belonging to the Coalition for Environmentally Responsible Economies to develop globally applicable guidelines for reporting on economic, environmental and social performance, initially for corporations and eventually for all businesses and governmental and non-governmental organizations (Global Reporting Initiative, 2002).

> The Global Reporting Initiative . . . is a long-term, multi-stakeholder, international process whose mission is to develop and disseminate globally applicable Sustainable Reporting Guidelines . . . These Guidelines are for voluntary use by organisations for reporting on the economic, environmental, and social dimensions of their activities, products and services.
>
> (Global Reporting Initiative, 2002)

The main reason for initiating the GRI project was the lack of guidelines on what a voluntary SR should contain; therefore, there was no option to compare reports from different companies (Hedberg & Von Malmborg, 2003). The GRI guidelines draw on the accepted three-dimensional definition of sustainability using a series of performance indicators to measure each of the economic, environmental and social dimensions and a set of integrated indicators capturing multiple dimensions (Lamberton, 2005). Additionally, anyone can become a stakeholder in the GRI and leave comments on the work on these guidelines as it progresses. Stakeholders are encouraged to develop the guidelines, and the GRI encourages companies that use the guidelines to communicate with their stakeholders (Lamberton, 2005). The first version of the guidelines was released in 1999, and in 2013, the latest version, GRI-G4, was released.

3.1.4 The critical perspective on sustainability reporting

Skeptics note that despite abundant public rhetoric on CSR and sustainability, the degree to which companies actually implement CSR principles in their on-the-ground operations is questionable, and the results obtained to date in terms of the transparency and comparability of non-financial information in financial statements are not considered satisfactory (Clarke & Gibson-Sweet, 1999; Deegan et al., 2002). The main question here is whether CSR is motivated primarily by the need to integrate sustainability issues into a company's strategic objectives or the need to manage reputation, legitimacy issues or regulatory compliance (Clarke & Gibson-Sweet, 1999; Gray, 2010). The critical perspective on SR argues that the concept of sustainability and the associated use of accounting have been deliberately simplified and oriented toward supporting firms' business interests (Gray, 2010; Tregidga, Kearins, & Milne, 2013). The critical literature points out that firms are oriented toward sustainability to pursue their own self-interest and not to protect natural capital or to increase well-being (Passetti, Cinquini, Marelli, & Tenucci, 2014).

Some authors are concerned that mandating reporting would promote form and rhetoric over substance and commitment, and thus, it would be more beneficial for companies to be strongly encouraged to voluntarily engage in sustainability reporting rather than being forced to do so (Ioannou & Serafeim, 2014). It is clear that to date, despite decades of attention to corporate responsibility and SR, companies have failed to make much headway in assessing their real impacts on society. Of course, such assessments are extremely challenging (Crane & Matten, 2016).

Since recent years have also seen an increase in the practice of SR (Deegan et al., 2002), there is much critical discussion about whether sustainability reports are what they claim to be and what a "true" sustainability report should include (Deegan, 2002). Gray (2010) highlights that the literature increasingly establishes that most business reporting on sustainability actually has little if anything to do with sustainability (Beder, 2002; Gray & Milne, 2002; Milne et al., 2006).

> In essence, there is no sustainability reporting in the public domain, anywhere in the world. This is because it is exceptionally difficult, if not impossible . . . most organisations in pursuit of growth and profit are likely increasing their throughput, and, consequently, their ecological footprints – understandably something which company executives are not keen to recognise or publicise. So the real danger we face is that there is lot of talk about something which nobody is doing, can do or wants to do – sustainability reporting. This term, though, is used interchangeably with something which everybody could do – triple bottom line reporting – but virtually nobody is doing! And what are

organisations doing? Well most of them are doing nothing at all and free-riding on the backs of the few leading reporters who have yet to even reach the foothills of real triple bottom line reporting. So the message is, there is an awful lot of talk and very little action. Don't believe what you read, and social and environmental accountability will remain a "nice idea" until there is substantive legislation requiring it of all large organisations.

(Gray & Milne, 2002)

Recent research has shown that many corporations claim that their operations are sustainable; these claims are often stimulated by strategic and self-interested definitions of sustainability (Luke, 2013). For instance, corporations have argued that they strive for sustainability and hence are sustainable (Ihlen, 2009). Indeed, some corporations have indicated that they have been sustainable since their inception (Ihlen & Roper, 2014). The *topos* of ethical heritage has been recognized in the wider CSR discourse and has been considered a way to strengthen legitimacy and reputation (Balmer, Blombäck, & Scandelius, 2013; Luke, 2013). Similar definition issues apply for CSR, whose scope risks being too broad to become relevant for corporations (Van Marrewijk, 2003). The variations and overlaps in terminology, definitions and conceptual models hamper academic debate (Göbbels, 2002).

The literature notes that because social and environmental reporting emerged in the late 1980s (Milne, 2013) by following through on their claims, corporations should have had a sufficient chance by now to make the world more sustainable (Luke, 2013). It seems important to continue the discussion and critique of corporations' understanding of sustainability and the aspects of sustainability to which they draw attention (Luke, 2013).

Although many organizations have embraced the sustainability rhetoric in their external reporting and mission statements (Newton & Harte, 1997), these reports may serve as "veils" that hide activities (Deegan, 2002) and that serve the sole purpose of reconstructing eroded legitimacy (Gond, Grubnic, Herzig, & Moon, 2012). Clarke and Gibson-Sweet (1999) question whether CSR is motivated primarily by the need to integrate sustainability issues into a company's strategic objectives or to manage reputation and legitimacy issues (see socio-economic theory and the concept of greenwashing in Section 3.1.2). Recently, Slack (2012) documented a paradox between a rhetorical infrastructure that is often "vast and well-established", reflecting companies' public relation strategies, and CSR's low degree of integration into the firms' operating processes.

This skeptical view is nurtured by a lack of study on the intra-organizational impact of sustainability (Bebbington, 2007; Gond et al., 2012) and on the role of management control systems in supporting sustainability within organizations (Durden, 2008). The situation is compounded by apprehensions regarding the ability of any strategic move toward sustainability to alter organizational practices (Hopwood, 2009). Lasting attempts to integrate sustainability within strategy, beyond external reporting, discourse and mission statements, should be reflected within formal control mechanisms at some stage (Gond et al., 2012).

The skepticism cited above is far from groundless, and this type of rhetoric – in which narratives on CSR and sustainability are separate from companies' objectives, business models and strategy – hampers more genuine attempts to integrate sustainability and society's and academia's perceptions of sustainability. In this view, a *real* commitment to CSR should encompass the value creation logic adopted by a company: its business model.

It can be concluded that corporate sustainability has become a topic on which companies offer information and thereby strive to increase transparency and accountability (Kolk, 2008). However, as reported by Castello and Lozano (2011), additional research from both theoretical and empirical standpoints is necessary to understand the different processes initiated by firms to achieve further legitimacy and to determine whether a firm's engagement in CSR is authentic or simply a façade. At the same time, from a more practical point of view, we believe there is room for improving the quality of sustainability reporting, with particular reference to its relevance and materiality. In the future, sustainability accounting research will continue to display the essential quality of diversity while attempting to increase in coverage, depth and quality (Lamberton, 2005).

On one hand, regardless of the report format, sustainability sections in annual reports in many cases continue to be separate but included; the same applies to sections related to sustainability in corporate governance (De Villiers, Rinaldi, & Unerman, 2014; Kiron, Kruschwitz, Haanaes, & Velken, 2012; Kolk, 2008). On the other hand, linking and simultaneously reporting corporate governance and sustainability may offer new opportunities for integrative approaches in addition to the accounting itself, as described by Sherman, Steingard, and Fitzgibbons (2002). It is also important to consider the level of detail of the information given because forms of reporting that include social, ethical and environmental aspects, brand and reputation issues and the ethical dimensions of remuneration and auditing are voluntary to some extent and not within the disclosure requirements for risk and control management (Kolk, 2008).

It is interesting to note, however, that the overwhelming majority of "sustainability reports" still focus on more traditional – but no less important – reporting topics (Kolk, 2004), including those related to health and safety, employee relationships, and philanthropy and charitable contributions. Many studies have shown that the most common social performance indicators included in reports also focus largely on health and safety (frequency of accidents/injuries), followed by community spending and workforce composition (Kolk, 2004).

We believe that there is room for improving both the number of areas covered in sustainability reporting and the quality of this reporting. In the next sections of this volume, we will focus on stakeholders' role in improving the materiality and relevance of sustainability reports.

3.2 The topic of materiality and its relevance for sustainability reporting

3.2.1 The materiality principle

In the previous sections, we have seen how on a general level, an increasing consensus is being reached on large enterprises' responsibility to report not only on their financial performance but also on their social and environmental outcomes. Nonetheless, this is a very general statement: on which elements do organizations need to report in order to provide stakeholders with a relevant and comprehensive sustainability report? In this section, we will attempt to provide additional insights on the answer to this question, which is based, among other considerations, on the materiality principle.

In fact, at the core of preparing a sustainability report is the process of identifying material aspects. According to the materiality principle, material aspects are those that reflect the organization's significant economic, environmental and social impacts or that substantively influence stakeholders' assessments and decisions (Global Reporting Initiative, 2013c). A benefit of using a concept such as materiality in the context of financial, social and environmental issues is that it helps emphasize a business-centric view and narrow the broad universe of social and environmental information to items that help inform investors and other stakeholders about a business's ability to create and sustain value (Eccles et al., 2012).

> Organizations are faced with a wide range of topics on which they could report. Relevant topics are those that may reasonably be considered important for the organization's economic, environmental and social dimensions or for influencing the decisions of stakeholders, and, therefore, potentially merit inclusion in the report. Materiality is the threshold at which aspects become sufficiently important that they should be reported.[3]
>
> (Global Reporting Initiative, 2013c)

The guidelines provided by GRI argue that reports should emphasize information on performance regarding the most material aspects. Other relevant topics can be included but should be given less prominence in a report, and the process by which the relative priority of aspects was determined should be explained.

In addition to guiding the selection of aspects to report, the materiality principle also applies to the use of indicators. When disclosing performance data, varying degrees of comprehensiveness and detail can be provided in a report.

> Overall, decisions on how to report data should be guided by the importance of the information for assessing the performance of the organization, and facilitating appropriate comparisons. Reporting on material aspects may involve disclosing information used by external stakeholders that differs from the information used internally for day-to-day management purposes. However, such information does indeed belong in a report, where it may inform assessments or decision-making by stakeholders, or support engagement with stakeholders that may result in actions that significantly influence performance or address key topics of stakeholder concern.
>
> (Global Reporting Initiative, 2013c)

Materiality is a traditional reporting concept associated with the fair representation of data (Edgley et al., 2015). The first definitions of materiality were proposed in the context of financial reporting since the first reports issued disclosed mainly financial information (Messier Jr, Martinov-Bennie, & Eilifsen, 2005). A piece of information is considered to be material if its omission or misstatement would influence the economic decisions made by the report's users, which, in the case of financial reports, are mainly investors (Mio, 2013).

Thus, materiality, a cornerstone concept in accounting, determines the importance of an item for information users (Lee, 1984). By law, companies are required to project a true and fair view in their financial statements, but the precise meaning of "true and fair" is sometimes unclear, and materiality complements this fuzzy requirement (Edgley et al., 2015): it helps to illuminate important errors or omissions in the data but allows a tolerable degree of flexibility in judgments (Brennan & Gray, 2005). In financial reporting, materiality functions as a threshold that determines significant errors or omissions relevant to decision making and thus benefits shareholders (Edgley et al., 2015; Lo, 2010; Mio, 2013).

The International Accounting Standards Board (2010) provides a definition of materiality for the accounting field. Paragraph QC11 of Chapter 3 "Qualitative characteristics of useful financial information" (International Accounting Standards Board, 2010) in the Conceptual Framework describes the concept of materiality as follows:

> Information is material if omitting it or misstating it could influence decisions that users make on the basis of financial information about a specific reporting entity. In other words, materiality is an entity-specific aspect of relevance based on the nature or magnitude, or both, of the items to which the information relates in the context of an individual entity's financial report. Consequently, the Board cannot specify a uniform quantitative threshold for materiality or predetermine what could be material in a particular situation.

The assumption that an item in question is material in some sense is implicit in every decision to render an event into a financial datum, to classify a transaction, or to dispute a controversial accounting treatment (Frishkoff, 1970; Unerman & Zappettini, 2014). Frishkoff (1970) define materiality in accounting as "the relative, quantitative importance of some piece of financial information, to a user, in the context of a decision to be made".

In the context of financial information, the quantitative threshold is very important because it allows materiality to be assessed by comparing specific financial performance items, such as assets or revenues. This approach is particularly useful to investors, who are interested in understanding the impact of material issues on a company's financial capital (Mio, 2013).

Materiality is among a number of accounting concepts that have been adopted in SR, such as understandability, relevance and faithful representation (Edgley et al., 2015). While the concept of a threshold is also important in sustainability reporting, it is concerned with a wider range of impacts and stakeholders. In sustainability reporting, materiality is not limited to aspects that have a significant financial impact on the organization (Global Reporting Initiative, 2013c):

Determining materiality for a sustainability report also includes considering economic, environmental and social impacts that cross a threshold in reflecting the ability to meet the needs of the present without compromising the needs of future generations. These material aspects often have a significant financial impact in the short term or long term on an organization. They are therefore also relevant for stakeholders who focus strictly on the financial condition of an organization.

(Goertz & Mahoney, 2012)

In the context of non-financial information, "materiality requires that the Assurance Provider states whether the Reporting Organization has included in the report the information about its sustainability performance required by its stakeholders for them to be able to make informed judgments, decisions and actions" (AccountAbility, 2008b, p. 11). Therefore, the definition of materiality in the non-financial information context is quite similar to that used in the financial context; however, it focuses on "stakeholders" rather than investors and on "judgments, decisions and actions" rather than investment decisions (Fasan & Mio, 2017).

3.2.2 SR standards and materiality

Besides the guidance proposed by the Global Reporting Initiative (2013b, 2013c), much of which is cited at the beginning of this section, the other two main international standards that offer advice on materiality are the *International Integrated Reporting Council (*IIRC) Guidelines[4] and AccountAbility AA1000. GRI and these latter standards feature specific sections on materiality in their main guidelines documents.

The IIRC argues that an aspect is material if it is of such relevance and significance that it can substantively influence the assessments and decisions of the organization's highest governing body or change the assessments and decisions of intended users with regard to the organization's ability to create value over time (IIRC, 2013a, 2013b, 2013c; Mio, 2013).

The intended users of integrated reporting are the providers of financial capital because this reporting supports these providers' financial capital allocation (Busco, Frigo, Quattrone, & Riccaboni, 2014; IIRC, 2013b). Additionally, investors must also be involved in determining the most important factors (Mio, 2013): in fact, the IIRC argues that when determining whether or not a matter is material, senior management and those charged with governance should consider whether the matter substantively affects or has the potential to substantively affect the organization's strategy, its business model, or one or more of the capitals it uses or affects (IIRC, 2013b). This argument is coherent with the definition of materiality provided by the IIRC and elucidated above.

However, the Integrated Reporting (IR) framework also encourages companies to engage with other stakeholder groups. Stakeholders' interests and concerns are used as a source to evaluate the effects on capitals (IIRC, 2013b). Following Mio

(2013), the process of determining materiality according to the IR framework consists of three elements: relevance, importance and prioritization:

- Relevance means identifying relevant matters for inclusion in an integrated report. This identification should be based on the potential value that the matter can create.
- Importance is evaluated either by the magnitude of the effect and/or its likelihood of occurrence. Prioritizing matters is the final step.
- Prioritization is the responsibility of the senior management and of those charged with governance to accept the filters and processes in place to identify the material matters (IIRC, 2013b).

AccountAbility (2008a) established a standard for sustainability disclosure under its AA1000 framework and determined criteria that should be met when tackling the issue of materiality (Mio, 2013). AccountAbility is a non-profit global consultancy organization – a multi-stakeholder network that promotes accountability in reporting (Bagnoli, 2004; Edgley et al., 2015). In particular, this framework proposes a five-step test to determine materiality (AccountAbility, 2008a):

> This is aimed at providing companies with some more information . . . The first test is "direct short-term financial impacts". Some non-financial performance indicators (such as carbon emission) may have a financial impact in the short term and, for this reason, need to be disclosed. The second test is "policy-related performance", requiring the disclosure of those issues that do not have any impact on short-term financial performance but that are related to policies the company has agreed upon. The third test is "business peer-based norms". According to this test, information that the company's competitors deem to be material ought to be considered material by the company as well. The fourth test is "stakeholder behaviour and concerns", which considers issues that will impact stakeholders' behaviour as material. This test is fairly similar to the definitions proposed following the user utility theory, and is probably the least insightful of the five tests proposed by (AccountAbility, 2008a), because it does not add much to the indications provided by the materiality definitions discussed above. Finally, the fifth test ("societal norms") requires companies to disclose issues or matters that are embedded in regulations or that will likely become regulated in the future.
>
> (Mio, 2013)

Materiality determines the relevance and significance of an issue to an organization and its stakeholders (AccountAbility, 2008a). A material issue influences the decisions, actions and performance of an organization or its stakeholders; consequently, stakeholders must understand which material issues are relevant to the organization's sustainability performance (AccountAbility, 2008a; Edgley et al., 2015).

While the GRI guidelines framework is mostly "principles-based", the AccountAbility (2008a) framework is more "process-based" and focuses on the company's relationship with its stakeholders. As argued by Mio (2013), on one hand, this process-based approach can be effective because it focuses on the company's peculiarities to the highest extent; on the other hand, it can lack standardization in the outcomes of the process.

Finally, since materiality is a context-specific concept and because it is difficult to determine a set of rules that can apply in all circumstances, another way to address the assessment of the standardization of materiality is the creation of sector-specific standards. As argued by Eccles et al. (2012), developing sector-specific guidelines on what sustainability issues are material to that sector and the key performance indicators (KPIs) for reporting on them would significantly improve companies' ability to report on their social and environmental performance.

> Even such global issues as climate change are much more important in some industries than others. By replacing high-level topic-based guidance . . . with guidance that identifies the sustainability issues that are material to a sector and how best to report on them, companies will have much clearer guidance on what and how to report. For some industries, climate change will make the list; for others, it may not, although some companies in that industry may still choose to report on it because of their particular strategy or to meet the information demands of a specific stakeholder group.
>
> (Eccles et al., 2012)

Moreover, on the European and national levels, there are country-specific features and guidelines that must be taken into account. In the European context – and particularly in Italy – the topic of CSR has been historically analyzed in light of other traditional management accounting and control mechanisms that can verify a company's compliance with business ethics constraints (Manetti, 2006). Although the GRI, AccountAbility and the IIRC are now acclaimed producers of standards and guidelines, the European tradition on business ethics should not be undervalued. Germany, for example, has been characterized by its application of the *"Mitbestimmung"* principle, one of the first examples of multi-stakeholder governance, which opened governance bodies to include workers' representatives (Manetti, 2006); France was the first country to introduce an obligation – albeit a mild one – for larger companies to disclose social reports (Manetti, 2006).

Moreover, Italy has a long tradition of social and environmental reporting. The GBS (Gruppo di studio per il Bilancio Sociale) was the first and most frequently adopted Italian standard for social reporting. The Italian *"bilancio sociale"* encompasses three fundamental sections: corporate identity and the production and distribution of added value and social performance (Bagnoli, 2004; Bagnoli & Megali, 2009; Manetti, 2006). This tool is based on the notion that it is no longer sufficient to report only on the ability to generate profit; while this ability is necessary, for an enterprise seeking public legitimization, it is no longer a sufficient condition on its own (Bagnoli, 2004). A firm's social responsibility represents the attempt to respond to specific calls from the external environment (Terzani, 1989). Terzani (1989) defines *"bilancio sociale"* as a tool that can provide information on a specific enterprise's objectives and achievements in terms of social responsibility.

It is important to note that the topic of firms' social responsibility is deeply rooted in the Italian accounting tradition: many important authors (Ferrero, 1968; Masini, 1960; Onida, 1965; Zappa, 1927, 1957) consider this issue to be a crucial dimension of business institutions. Zappa (1927, 1957) notes that the ontological aim of the "*azienda*" is to "meet human needs": these human needs go beyond simple economic needs (Signori & Rusconi, 2009). Therefore, the *azienda*, as a social institution, is founded and operated by human beings and aims at achieving an ethical life (Onida, 1954). Not all the legal and ethical restrictions necessary to reconcile the *azienda*'s interests with those of society at large are detrimental to the goals of the *azienda*; instead, they are factors that favor consolidation and lasting prosperity (Onida, 1954; Signori & Rusconi, 2009). Additionally, Masini (1960, 1964) emphasizes humankind in its material and spiritual entirety (Signori & Rusconi, 2009). As highlighted by Cafferata (2009) and Ruisi (2014), the topic was further elaborated beginning in the 1980s by academics in the field of accounting and entrepreneurship (Coda, 1985; Giunta, 2008; Sorci, 1986) and social and environmental accounting (Bagnoli, 2004; Bandettini, 1981; Catturi, 2002, 2006; Matacena, 1984, 2008; Rebora, 1981; Rusconi, 1988; Rusconi & Signori, 2007; Terzani, 1984; Vermiglio, 1984).

3.2.3 How to assess materiality for sustainability reporting

The previous section provided a definition of the materiality principle and an overview of the main standards that provide guidance on materiality for sustainability reporting. We now focus on ways to practically assess materiality.

The GRI guidelines (Global Reporting Initiative, 2013c) claim that a combination of internal and external factors should be used to determine whether an aspect (of reporting guidelines) is material for the organization and its stakeholders, including factors such as the organization's overall mission and competitive strategy, concerns expressed by stakeholders, broader social expectations and the organization's influence on upstream entities (such as supply chains) and downstream (such as customers) entities. Assessments of materiality should also consider the basic expectations expressed in the international standards and agreements with which the organization is expected to comply (Global Reporting Initiative, 2013c).

These internal and external factors should be considered when evaluating the importance of information for conveying significant economic, environmental and social impacts or for stakeholder decision making (Global Reporting Initiative, 2013c). A range of established methodologies may be used to assess the significance of impacts.[5] In general, "significant impacts" refer to impacts that are a subject of established concern for expert communities or that have been identified using established tools such as impact assessment methodologies or life cycle assessments (Global Reporting Initiative, 2013c). Impacts that are considered important enough to require active management or engagement by the organization are likely to be considered significant.

Some authors (Tuttle, Coller, & Plumlee, 2002) and standards (International Accounting Standards Board, 2010) attribute predominant importance to thresholds in determining materiality (Mio, 2013). This way of operating is particularly effective (because it simplifies the materiality assessment process) for audit firms, which do not have a deep knowledge of the company and of its operations; additionally, audit firms must rely on quantitative methods to proxy for materiality because they can rely only on accounting numbers (Mio, 2013).

However, as we previously claimed in the text, such quantitative thresholds employed to define financial materiality cannot be easily and completely employed for non-financial information for various reasons (Guthrie & Parker, 1990). In this respect, we agree with the five-points argument by Mio (2013):

> First, non-financial information captures a wider concept of firm value as compared to financial information. Therefore, when materiality is assessed, the relationship between the issue to be assessed and firm value as represented by non-financial information is more difficult to determine, as non-financial pieces of information present many intersection levels in their definition. Second, even if the impact of a certain issue on the firm value can be determined, in the field of non-financial information it is not possible to employ a unique threshold, because the issues considered may have an impact on different capitals. Non-financial information is often relevant for many stakeholders, which have different and non-aligned interests (Berthelot, Cormier, & Magnan, 2003; Brammer & Pavelin, 2004; Guthrie & Parker, 1990). To rely only on financial capital would be a satisfactory approach only for one specific category of stakeholder (investors). Third, non-financial information cannot always be expressed in monetary terms. Fourth, non-financial information is often long- term oriented, meaning there may be some issues that are material despite not having an immediate impact on the item employed as a threshold. The long-term impact may be evaluated, but necessarily relying on models, which would need to make strong assumptions. Fifth, non-financial information is often derived from a life-cycle approach, therefore in order to properly assess it, information about events and phenomena that are external to the company would be needed.
>
> (Mio, 2013)

While non-financial information refers to items that are not often traded on a market, financial information refers to a market in which goods and services are exchanged and often have well-defined prices (Busco et al., 2014). In contrast, aspects represented by non-financial information cannot be "priced" in a market generally because an efficient market for these aspects does not exist. In other words, is it possible to set a quantitative threshold for how many fatalities in a workplace are tolerable? What is the value of a fatality in terms of the firm's loss of reputation? From a non-ethical standpoint, it is impossible to answer those questions – at least by relying on an active market (Busco et al., 2014).

More precisely, quantitative thresholds may be determined even for non-financial information, but their calculation would have to rely on such heavy assumptions that would make the threshold too discretionary, and these assumptions would affect both values and methodology. Since a quantitative value does not exist, it is not possible to apply the thresholds as in the context of financial information, making it more difficult to separate material from non-material information.

(Mio, 2013)

Hence, in assessing materiality, an organization could face the issue of choosing between time-consuming and costly impact evaluations on one hand and the exclusion of very important outcomes concerning intangible aspects on the other. Given the methodological difficulties in setting standardized thresholds, we believe that stakeholders' involvement in determining material aspects is of the utmost importance. The involvement of every group of stakeholders could be the most straightforward way to produce comprehensive, relevant and material sustainability reports (AccountAbility, 2008a, 2008b, 2015; Bebbington, 2007; Global Reporting Initiative, 2013b, 2013c).

3.2.4 The external assurance of sustainability reporting

There is a growing need for quality checks in sustainability reporting. The popularity of sustainability reporting and the increased prevalence of sustainability reports have been accompanied by mounting interest in these reports' accuracy (Kolk & Perego, 2010): external assurance (or verification) can provide both report readers and managers with increased confidence in the quality of sustainability performance data, increasing the likelihood that the data will be relied on and used for effective decision making (Global Reporting Initiative, 2013a). Stakeholders are demanding more transparency, and companies themselves are under increasing competitive and regulatory pressure to demonstrate a commitment to corporate responsibility (Corporate Register, 2008).

While external assurance of sustainability reporting shares similarities with external audits of financial reporting, these two types of reporting also exhibit important differences (Global Reporting Initiative, 2013a). It is clear that financial reporting is intended to measure financial outcomes, and there are long-established procedures for financial accounting; in contrast, sustainability reporting covers diverse topics, and the issues that are most critical to manage, measure and disclose vary by sector and even by company (Global Reporting Initiative, 2013a). As seen previously in the text, sustainability disclosures often involve a mix of quantitative and qualitative information, quantitative sustainability disclosures are not usually measured in monetary units, and internal control systems and data collection processes may not be as developed as systems and processes for historical financial information (Global Reporting Initiative, 2013a).

Assurance makes reports more credible and improves stakeholder confidence in the information provided. Seeking independent assurance also demonstrates one's commitment to corporate responsibility since the process opens up the company to scrutiny of its management systems. It also provides a mechanism to drive improvements in such systems, and thereby increases their performance.

(Corporate Register, 2008)

Consequently, organizations seek assurance for a variety of reasons. We can identify both internal and external benefits of assurance, which are often aimed at building trust and confidence in the areas of governance, management and stakeholder relations (Global Reporting Initiative, 2013a; Kolk & Perego, 2010). The main benefits of assurance, as described in different publications and summarized by the Global Reporting Initiative (2013a), include those shown in Table 3.2.

Table 3.2 Motivations for the assurance of SR

Benefit	Description	References
Increased recognition, trust and credibility	An assured report can provide an organization's stakeholders with a greater sense of confidence in disclosures. Among other factors, it reflects the seriousness with which the reporter approaches sustainability reporting. Investors, rating agencies and other analysts increasingly seek assurance when making investment and rating decisions.	Corporate Register, 2008; Kolk & Perego, 2010; KPMG, 2013, 2015; Simnett, Vanstraelen, & Chua, 2009
Reduced risk and increased value	Data quality continues to be a significant issue for reporters and report users. In this context, it is not unusual for large companies to issue restatements of sustainability disclosures. Disclosures that are considered robust and credible are more likely to be relied on, thus increasing the value of reporting.	KPMG, 2013, 2015; Global Reporting Initiative, 2013c
Improved board and CEO-level engagement	With increased interest in sustainability disclosures and their importance for driving improvements in organizational strategy, performance and reputation, sustainability issues are advancing to the boardroom. Disclosures and data that are believed to be trustworthy and credible are more likely to be used for internal decision making.	Corporate Register, 2008; Global Reporting Initiative, 2013a

(continued)

Table 3.2 (continued)

Benefit	Description	References
Strengthened internal reporting and management systems	Internal robust reporting systems and controls play an important role in managing sustainability performance and impacts. External assurance can help confirm that internal systems and controls are robust and can identify any necessary improvements.	Corporate Register, 2008
Improved stakeholder communication	Assurance processes may involve the review of a reporter's stakeholder engagement processes. Some organizations use their reporting processes and/or sustainability reporting as the basis for ongoing dialogue with stakeholders. Both of these steps can help promote mutual communication and understanding.	AccountAbility, 2008b; Corporate Register, 2008; Global Reporting Initiative, 2013a; Manetti & Toccafondi, 2011; O'Dwyer & Owen, 2005; Simnett et al., 2009

Source: Global Reporting Initiative (2013a).

From a practical standpoint, the difficulties in defining thresholds for non-financial information have led assurance providers to focus mainly on the assurance of stakeholder engagement and of the materiality determination process rather than on the definition of a threshold (Mio, 2013). As seen previously in the text, in recent years, the literature has clearly indicated the need to increase stakeholder involvement and participation in SR processes (Manetti & Toccafondi, 2011). Primarily, it has been noted that SR quality is closely tied to that of stakeholder engagement (Thomson & Bebbington, 2005). Moreover, as argued by Manetti and Toccafondi (2011), experts have supported the thesis that greater stakeholder involvement in SR and SR assurance processes can bring significant benefits to corporations because of increased reporting credibility and a greater ability to interact with the outside environment and the internal organization structure in decision-making processes (Gray, 2000; Gray et al., 1996; Owen, Swift, & Hunt, 2001). In conclusion, we believe that it is necessary to reinforce stakeholder engagement mechanisms during both the SR and the SR assurance processes in order to guarantee the materiality and relevance of information disclosed in reports and assurance statements (Bebbington, 2007).

Notes

1 In this volume, we will use the acronym SR to refer to both sustainability accounting and sustainability reporting. Moreover, SR and the reporting practices that complement CSR activities will be used as synonyms.

2 Another relevant practice is integrated reporting, which is presented in Section 2.2.2 of this volume.
3 However, it must be noted that beyond this threshold, not all material aspects are of equal importance, and the emphasis within a report should reflect the relative priority of these material aspects.
4 For an overview of the IIRC guidelines, see Section 2.2 of this volume.
5 For a review of the main impact evaluation methodologies, see Khandker, Koolwal, and Samad (2010).

References

AccountAbility. (2008a). *AA1000 AccountAbility principles standard 2008*. New York: AccountAbility.
AccountAbility. (2008b). *AA1000 assurance standard 2008*. New York: AccountAbility.
AccountAbility. (2015). *AA1000 stakeholder engagement standard 2015*. New York: AccountAbility.
Adams, C. A. (2002). Internal organisational factors influencing corporate social and ethical reporting: Beyond current theorising. *Accounting, Auditing & Accountability Journal*, *15*(2), 223–250.
Adams, C. A., Larrinaga-González, C., Adams, C. A., & McNicholas, P. (2007). Making a difference: Sustainability reporting, accountability and organisational change. *Accounting, Auditing & Accountability Journal*, *20*(3), 382–402.
Arevalo, J. A., Castello, I., de Colle, S., Lenssen, G., Neumann, K., Zollo, M., . . . Lenssen, G. (2011). Introduction to the special issue: Integrating sustainability in business models. *Journal of Management Development*, *30*(10), 941–954.
Bagnoli, L. (2004). *Quale responsabilità sociale per l'impresa?* (Vol. *21*). Milano: FrancoAngeli.
Bagnoli, L., & Megali, C. (2009). Measuring performance in social enterprises. *Nonprofit and Voluntary Sector Quarterly*, *40*(1), 149–165.
Balmer, J. M., Blombäck, A., & Scandelius, C. (2013). Corporate heritage in CSR communication: A means to responsible brand image? *Corporate Communications: An International Journal*, *18*(3), 362–382.
Bandettini, A. (1981). Responsabilità sociale dell'impresa. AA. VV., Bilancio d'esercizio e amministrazione delle imprese. *Studi in onore di Pietro Onida*. Milano: Giuffrè.
Barth, R., & Wolff, F. (2009). *Corporate social responsibility in Europe: Rhetoric and realities*. Cheltenham: Edward Elgar Publishing.
Bebbington, J. (2001). Sustainable development: a review of the international development, business and accounting literature. *Univ of Aberdeen Acct, Finance & Mgmt Working Paper, 00-17*. doi:http://dx.doi.org/10.2139/ssrn.257434
Bebbington, J. (2007). Changing organizational attitudes and culture through sustainability accounting. In J. Unerman, J. Bebbington, & B. O'Dwyer (Eds), *Sustainability Accounting and Accountability* (pp. 226–242). London: Routledge.
Beder, S. (2002). *Global spin: The corporate assault on environmentalism*. Totnes: Green Books.
Bellucci, M., Bagnoli, L., Biggeri, M., & Rinaldi, V. (2012). Performance measurement in solidarity economy organizations: The case of fair trade shops in Italy. *Annals of Public and Cooperative Economics*, *83*(1), 25–59. doi:10.1111/j.1467-8292.2011.00453.x
Berthelot, S., Cormier, D., & Magnan, M. (2003). Environmental disclosure research: Review and synthesis. *Journal of Accounting Literature*, *22*, 1.

Brammer, S., & Pavelin, S. (2004). Voluntary social disclosures by large UK companies. *Business Ethics A European Review, 13*(2-3), 86–99.

Brennan, N. M., & Gray, S. J. (2005). The impact of materiality: Accounting's best kept secret. *Asian Academy of Management Journal of Accounting and Finance, 1*, 1–31.

Busco, C., Frigo, M. L., Quattrone, P., & Riccaboni, A. (2014). *Integrated reporting*. Dordrecht: Springer.

Cafferata, R. (2009). Il cantiere aperto della responsabilità sociale dell'impresa. *Impresa Progetto-Electronic Journal of Management, 1*. https://www.impresaprogetto.it/sites/ impresaprogetto.it/files/articles/ip_1-09_saggio_cafferata.pdf

Carroll, A. B. (1991). The pyramid of corporate social responsibility: Toward the moral management of organizational stakeholders. *Business horizons, 34*(4), 39–48.

Carroll, A. B. (1999). Corporate social responsibility evolution of a definitional construct. *Business & society, 38*(3), 268–295.

Castello, I., & Lozano, J. M. (2011). Searching for new forms of legitimacy through corporate responsibility rhetoric. *Journal of Business Ethics, 100*(1), 11–29. doi:10.1007/ s10551-011-0770-8

Catturi, G. (2002). *Sviluppo sostenibile e nuove attività del professionista economico-contabile*. Università di Siena, Facoltà di economia.

Catturi, G. (2006). *L'azienda universale: Piste di riflessione*. Padova: Cedam.

Ciappei, C., & Ninci, D. (2006). *Etica di impresa: Considerazioni teoriche ed evidenze cliniche*. Firenze: Firenze University Press.

Clarke, J., & Gibson-Sweet, M. (1999). The use of corporate social disclosures in the management of reputation and legitimacy: A cross sectoral analysis of UK Top 100 Companies. *Business Ethics: A European Review, 8*(1), 5–13.

Clarkson, P. M., Li, Y., Richardson, G. D., & Vasvari, F. P. (2011). Does it really pay to be green? Determinants and consequences of proactive environmental strategies. *Journal of Accounting and Public Policy, 30*(2), 122–144.

Clarkson, P. M., Overell, M. B., & Chapple, L. (2011). Environmental reporting and its relation to corporate environmental performance. *Abacus, 47*(1), 27–60.

Coda, V. (1985). Valori imprenditoriali e successo dell'impresa. *Finanza, Marketing e Produzione, 2*, 23–56.

Corporate Register. (2008). *The CSR assurance statement report*. London: Corporate Register.

Crane, A., & Matten, D. (2004). Business ethics: A European perspective: Managing corporate citizenship and sustainability in the age of globalization. Oxford: Oxford University Press.

Crane, A., & Matten, D. (2016). Engagement required: The changing role of the corporation in society. In D. Barton, D. Horvath, & M. Kipping (Eds), *Re-imagining capitalism: Building a responsible, long-term model*. Oxford: Oxford University Press.

De Villiers, C., Rinaldi, L., & Unerman, J. (2014). Integrated reporting: Insights, gaps and an agenda for future research. *Accounting, Auditing & Accountability Journal, 27*(7), 1042–1067. doi:10.1108/AAAJ-06-2014-1736

Deegan, C. (2002). Introduction: The legitimising effect of social and environmental disclosures-a theoretical foundation. *Accounting, Auditing & Accountability Journal, 15*(3), 282–311.

Deegan, C., Rankin, M., & Tobin, J. (2002). An examination of the corporate social and environmental disclosures of BHP from 1983–1997: A test of legitimacy theory. *Accounting, Auditing & Accountability Journal, 15*(3), 312–343.

Donaldson, T., & Preston, L. E. (1995). The stakeholder theory of the corporation: Concepts, evidence, and implications. *Academy of Management Review*, *20*(1), 65–91.

Dowling, J., & Pfeffer, J. (1975). Organizational legitimacy: Social values and organizational behavior. *Pacific Sociological Review*, *18*(1), 122–136.

Durden, C. (2008). Towards a socially responsible management control system. *Accounting, Auditing & Accountability Journal*, *21*(5), 671–694.

Eccles, R. G., Krzus, M. P., Rogers, J., & Serafeim, G. (2012). The need for sector-specific materiality and sustainability reporting standards. *Journal of Applied Corporate Finance*, *24*(2), 65–71.

Edgley, C., Jones, M. J., & Atkins, J. (2015). The adoption of the materiality concept in social and environmental reporting assurance: A field study approach. *The British Accounting Review*, *47*(1), 1–18.

Elkington, J. (1999). The link between accountability and sustainability: Theory put into practice. Paper presented at the Conference on the Practice of Social Reporting for Business, ISEA, January, 19, Commonwealth Conference Centre, London.

Epstein, E. M. (2007). The good company: Rhetoric or reality? Corporate social responsibility and business ethics redux. *American Business Law Journal*, *44*(2), 207–222. doi:10.1111/j.1744-1714.2007.00035.x

Evans, T. L. (2012). *Occupy education: Living and learning sustainability* (Vol. 22). New York: Peter Lang.

Fasan, M., & Mio, C. (2017). Fostering stakeholder engagement: The role of materiality disclosure in integrated reporting. *Business Strategy and the Environment*, *26*(3), 288–305.

Ferrero, G. (1968). *Istituzioni di economia d'azienda*. Milano: Giuffrè.

Freeman, R. E. (1984). *Strategic management: A stakeholder approach*. Boston: Pitman.

Freeman, R. E., Wicks, A. C., & Parmar, B. (2004). Stakeholder theory and "the corporate objective revisited". *Organization Science*, *15*(3), 364–369.

Frishkoff, P. (1970). An empirical investigation of the concept of materiality in accounting. *Journal of Accounting Research*, *8*, 116–129.

Giunta, F. (2008). *Economia aziendale*. Padova: Cedam.

Global Reporting Initiative. (2002). *Sustainability reporting guidelines 2002*. Amsterdam: Global Reporting Initiative.

Global Reporting Initiative. (2013a). *The external assurance of sustainability reporting*. Amsterdam: Global Reporting Initiative.

Global Reporting Initiative. (2013b). *Implementation manual*. Amsterdam: Global Reporting Initiative.

Global Reporting Initiative. (2013c). *Reporting principles and standard disclosure*. Amsterdam: Global Reporting Initiative.

Göbbels, M. (2002). Reframing corporate social responsibility: The contemporary conception of a fuzzy notion. Journal of Business Ethics, *44*, 95–105.

Goertz, G., & Mahoney, J. (2012). *A tale of two cultures: Qualitative and quantitative research in the social sciences*. Princeton: Princeton University Press.

Gond, J. P., Grubnic, S., Herzig, C., & Moon, J. (2012). Configuring management control systems: Theorizing the integration of strategy and sustainability. *Management Accounting Research*, *23*(3), 205–223. doi:10.1016/j.mar.2012.06.003

Gray, R. (2000). Current developments and trends in social and environmental auditing, reporting and attestation: A review and comment. *International Journal of Auditing*, *4*(3), 247–268.

Gray, R. (2010). Is accounting for sustainability actually accounting for sustainability . . . and how would we know? An exploration of narratives of organisations and the planet. *Accounting Organizations and Society, 35*(1), 47–62. doi:10.1016/j.aos.2009.04.006

Gray, R., & Milne, M. (2002). Sustainability reporting: who's kidding whom? *Chartered Accountants Journal of New Zealand, 81*(6), 66–70.

Gray, R., Kouhy, R., & Lavers, S. (1995). Corporate social and environmental reporting: A review of the literature and a longitudinal study of UK disclosure. *Accounting, Auditing & Accountability Journal, 8*(2), 47–77.

Gray, R., Owen, D., & Adams, C. (1996). *Accounting & accountability: Changes and challenges in corporate social and environmental reporting.* Upper Saddle River: Prentice Hall.

Guthrie, J., & Parker, L. D. (1989). Corporate social reporting: A rebuttal of legitimacy theory. *Accounting and Business Research, 19*(76), 343–352.

Guthrie, J., & Parker, L. D. (1990). Corporate social disclosure practice: A comparative international analysis. *Advances in Public Interest Accounting, 3*, 159–175.

Hedberg, C. J., & Von Malmborg, F. (2003). The global reporting initiative and corporate sustainability reporting in Swedish companies. *Corporate Social Responsibility and Environmental Management, 10*(3), 153–164.

Hopwood, A. G. (2009). Accounting and the environment. *Accounting, Organizations and Society, 34*(3), 433–439.

Ihlen, Ø. (2009). The oxymoron of 'sustainable oil production': The case of the Norwegian oil industry. *Business Strategy and the Environment, 18*(1), 53–63.

Ihlen, Ø., & Roper, J. (2014). Corporate reports on sustainability and sustainable development: 'We have arrived'. *Sustainable Development, 22*(1), 42–51.

IIRC. (2013a). *Business model–background paper for < IR>.* Retrieved from http://integratedreporting.org//wp-content/uploads/2013/03/Business_Model.pdf

IIRC. (2013b). The international <IR> framework. London: IIRC.

IIRC. (2013c). *Materiality–background paper for < IR>.* Retrieved from http://integratedreporting.org//wp-content/uploads/2013/03/IR-Background-Paper-Materiality.pdf

International Accounting Standards Board. (2010). *The conceptual framework for financial reporting 2010.* London: IFRS.

Ioannou, I., & Serafeim, G. (2014). The consequences of mandatory corporate sustainability reporting: Evidence from four countries. *Harvard Business School Research Working Paper, 11–100.* Harvard: Harvard Business School.

Khandker, S. R., Koolwal, G. B., & Samad, H. A. (2010). *Handbook on impact evaluation: Quantitative methods and practices.* Washington: World Bank Publications.

Kiron, D., Kruschwitz, N., Haanaes, K., & Velken, I. V. S. (2012). Sustainability nears a tipping point. *MIT Sloan Management Review, 53*(2), 69.

Kolk, A. (2004). A decade of sustainability reporting: Developments and significance. *International Journal of Environment and Sustainable Development, 3*(1), 51–64. doi:10.1504/IJESD.2004.004688

Kolk, A. (2008). Sustainability, accountability and corporate governance: Exploring multinationals' reporting practices. *Business Strategy and the Environment, 17*(1), 1–15.

Kolk, A., & Perego, P. (2010). Determinants of the adoption of sustainability assurance statements: An international investigation. *Business Strategy and the Environment, 19*(3), 182–198.

KPMG. (2013). *The KPMG Survey of Corporate Responsibility Reporting 2013.* Amsterdam: KPMG.

KPMG. (2015). *Currents of change: The KPMG Survey of Corporate Responsibility Reporting 2015.* Amsterdam: KPMG.

Laine, M. (2010). Towards sustaining the status quo: Business talk of sustainability in Finnish corporate disclosures 1987–2005. *European Accounting Review, 19*(2), 247–274. doi:10.1080/09638180903136258

Lamberton, G. (2005). Sustainability accounting: A brief history and conceptual framework. *Accounting Forum, 29*(1), 7–26. doi:10.1016/j.accfor.2004.11.001

Larrinaga, C. (2007). Sustainability reporting: Insights from neo-institutional theory. In J. Unerman, J. Bebbington, & B. O'Dwyer (Eds), *Sustainability accounting and accountability* (pp. 150–167). London: Routledge.

Larrinaga-Gonzalez, C., & Bebbington, J. (2001). Accounting change or institutional appropriation? A case study of the implementation of environmental accounting. *Critical Perspectives on Accounting, 12*(3), 269–292.

Laufer, W. S. (2003). Social accountability and corporate greenwashing. *Journal of Business Ethics, 43*(3), 253–261.

Lee, T. A. (1984). *Materiality: A review and analysis of its reporting significance and auditing implications*. London: Auditing Practices Committee of the Consultative Committee of Accounting Bodies.

Lehman, G. (1999). Disclosing new worlds: A role for social and environmental accounting and auditing. *Accounting, Organizations and Society, 24*(3), 217–241.

Liberatore, G. (2001). *Pianificazione e controllo delle aziende di trasporto pubblico locale: problematiche di misurazione della performance*. Milano: FrancoAngeli.

Lo, K. (2010). Materiality and voluntary disclosures. *Journal of Accounting and Economics, 49*(1), 133–135.

Lopatta, K., Jaeschke, R., & Chen, C. (2017). Stakeholder engagement and corporate social responsibility (CSR) performance: International evidence. *Corporate Social Responsibility and Environmental Management, 24*(3), 199–209.

Luke, T. W. (2013). Corporate social responsibility: An uneasy merger of sustainability and development. *Sustainable Development, 21*(2), 83–91. doi:10.1002/sd.1558

Manetti, G. (2006). Il triple bottom line reporting: Dal coinvolgimento degli stakeholder alle verifiche esterne (Vol. 30). Milano: FrancoAngeli.

Manetti, G., & Toccafondi, S. (2011). The role of stakeholders in sustainability reporting assurance. *Journal of Business Ethics, 107*(3), 363–377. doi:10.1007/s10551-011-1044-1

Masini, C. (1960). *L'organizzazione del lavoro nell'impresa* (Vol. 1). Milano: Giuffrè.

Masini, C. (1964). *La struttura dell'impresa*. Milano: Giuffrè.

Matacena, A. (1984). *Impresa e ambiente: Il bilancio sociale*. Bologna: Clueb.

Matacena, A. (2008). *Responsabilità sociale delle imprese e accountability: Alcune glosse*. Milano: Diapason.

Matten, D., Crane, A., & Chapple, W. (2003). Behind the mask: Revealing the true face of corporate citizenship. *Journal of Business Ethics, 45*(1), 109–120. doi:10.1023/a:1024128730308

Messier Jr, W. F., Martinov-Bennie, N., & Eilifsen, A. (2005). A review and integration of empirical research on materiality: Two decades later. *Auditing: A Journal of Practice & Theory, 24*(2), 153–187.

Milne, M. J. (2013). Phantasmagoria, sustain-a-babbling and the communication of corporate social and environmental accountability. In J. L. Davison, & R. Craig (Eds), *The Routledge companion to accounting communication* (pp. 135–153). London: Routledge.

Milne, M. J., Kearins, K., & Walton, S. (2006). Creating adventures in wonderland: The journey metaphor and environmental sustainability. *Organization, 13*(6), 801–839.

Mio, C. (2013). Materiality and assurance: Building the link. In C. Busco, M. L. Frigo, A. Riccaboni, & P. Quattrone (Eds), *Integrated reporting* (pp. 79–94). Dordrecht: Springer.

Mitchell, R. K., Agle, B. R., & Wood, D. J. (1997). Toward a theory of stakeholder identification and salience: Defining the principle of who and what really counts. *Academy of Management Review, 22*(4), 853–886. doi:10.2307/259247

Morris, R. D. (1987). Signalling, agency theory and accounting policy choice. *Accounting and Business Research, 18*(69), 47–56.

Newton, T., & Harte, G. (1997). Green business: Technicist kitsch? *Journal of Management Studies, 34*(1), 75–98.

Nielsen, C. (2010). Conceptualizing, analyzing and communicating the business model. *Department of Business Studies, Aalborg University, Working Paper, 2*, 1–24. Aalborg: Aalbord University.

O'Dwyer, B., & Owen, D. L. (2005). Assurance statement practice in environmental, social and sustainability reporting: A critical evaluation. *The British Accounting Review, 37*(2), 205–229.

Onida, P. (1954). *L'azienda: primi principi di gestione e di organizzazione.* Milano: Giuffrè.

Onida, P. (1965). *Economia d'azienda.* Torino: Unione tipografico-editrice torinese.

Owen, D. L., Swift, T., & Hunt, K. (2001). Questioning the role of stakeholder engagement in social and ethical accounting, auditing and reporting. *Paper presented at the Accounting Forum.* http://connection.ebscohost.com/c/articles/5326647/questioning-role-stakeholder-engagement-social-ethical-accounting-auditing-reporting

Passetti, E., Cinquini, L., Marelli, A., & Tenucci, A. (2014). Sustainability accounting in action: Lights and shadows in the Italian context. *The British Accounting Review, 46*(3), 295–308.

Patten, D. M. (1992). Intra-industry environmental disclosures in response to the Alaskan oil spill: A note on legitimacy theory. *Accounting, Organizations and Society, 17*(5), 471–475.

Phillips, R., Freeman, R. E., & Wicks, A. C. (2003). What stakeholder theory is not. *Business Ethics Quarterly, 13*(04), 479–502.

Rebora, G. (1981). *Comportamento d'impresa e controllo sociale.* Milano: Etas Libri.

Ruisi, M. (2014). *La dimensione etico-valoriale nel governo delle aziende.* http://riviste. paviauniversitypress.it/index.php/ea/article/viewFile/1719/1796

Rusconi, G. (1988). *Il bilancio sociale d'impresa: Problemi e pospettive.* Milano: Giuffrè.

Rusconi, G., & Signori, S. (2007). Responsabilità sociale e azienda non profit: Quale declinazione. *Impresa sociale, 76*(1), 39–58.

Sherman, W. R., Steingard, D. S., & Fitzgibbons, D. E. (2002). Sustainable stakeholder accounting beyond complementarity and towards integration in environmental accounting. *Research in corporate sustainability: The evolving theory and practice of organizations in the natural environment.* https://books.google.it/books?hl=it&lr=&id=KEYUy7pxiFMC&oi=fnd&pg=PA257&dq=Sustainable+stakeholder+accounting+beyond+complementarity+and+towards+integration+in+environmental+accounting&ots=v4V6EeCg55&sig=9JsMjcIONnFa0GigbxHK3pW2oeM#v=onepage&q=Sustainable%20stakeholder%20accounting%20beyond%20complementarity%20and%20towards%20integration%20in%20environmental%20accounting&f=false

Signori, S., & Rusconi, G. (2009). Ethical thinking in traditional Italian Economia Aziendale and the stakeholder management theory: The search for possible interactions. *Journal of Business Ethics, 89*(3), 303–318.

Simnett, R., Vanstraelen, A., & Chua, W. F. (2009). Assurance on sustainability reports: An international comparison. *The Accounting Review, 84*(3), 937–967.

Slack, K. (2012). Mission impossible? Adopting a CSR-based business model for extractive industries in developing countries. *Resources Policy, 37*(2), 179–184.

Sorci, C. (1986). I valori imprenditoriali nei rapporti con i proprietari del capitale. In AA. VV. (Ed.), *Valori imprenditoriali e successo* aziendale (pp. 39–58). Milano: Giuffrè.

Tate, W. L., Ellram, L. M., & Kirchoff, J. F. (2010). Corporate social responsibility reports: A thematic analysis related to supply chain management. *Journal of Supply Chain Management, 46*(1), 19–44.

Terzani, S. (1984). Responsabilità sociale dell'azienda. *Rivista Italiana di Ragioneria e di Economia aziendale, 8*, 286–299.

Terzani, S. (1989). *Introduzione al bilancio di esercizio* (Quinta edizione. ed.). Padova: Cedam.

Thomson, I., & Bebbington, J. (2005). Social and environmental reporting in the UK: A pedagogic evaluation. *Critical Perspectives on Accounting, 16*(5), 507–533.

Thorne, L., Mahoney, L. S., & Manetti, G. (2014). Motivations for issuing standalone CSR reports: A survey of Canadian firms. *Accounting, Auditing & Accountability Journal, 27*(4), 686–714.

Tregidga, H., Kearins, K., & Milne, M. (2013). The politics of knowing "organizational sustainable development". *Organization & Environment.* http://journals.sagepub.com/doi/abs/10.1177/1086026612474957

Tuttle, B., Coller, M., & Plumlee, R. D. (2002). The effect of misstatements on decisions of financial statement users: An experimental investigation of auditor materiality thresholds. *Auditing: A Journal of Practice & Theory, 21*(1), 11–27.

UNEP. (1998). *The non-reporting report.* London: UNEP.

Unerman, J., & Zappettini, F. (2014). Incorporating materiality considerations into analyses of absence from sustainability reporting. *Social and Environmental Accountability Journal, 34*(3), 172–186.

Van Marrewijk, M. (2003). Concepts and definitions of CSR and corporate sustainability: Between agency and communion. *Journal of Business Ethics, 44*(2), 95–105. doi:10.1023/a:1023331212247

Vermiglio, F. (1984). *Il bilancio sociale nel quadro evolutivo del sistema d'impresa.* Brescia: Grafo Editore.

Whetten, D. A., Rands, G., & Godfrey, P. (2002). What are the responsibilities of business to society. *Handbook of strategy and management.* http://marriottschool.net/emp/daw4/Responsibilities%20of%20Business%20to%20Society%202002.pdf

World Commission for Environment and Development. (1987). *Our common future.* Oxford: Oxford University Press.

Zappa, G. (1927). *Tendenze nuove negli studi di ragioneria.* Milano: Istituto Editoriale Scientifico.

Zappa, G. (1957). *Le produzioni nell'economia delle imprese.* Milano; Giuffrè.

4 A theory of stakeholder engagement

4.1 Stakeholder theory

4.1.1 An introduction to the stakeholder approach

In the previous chapters, we argued that enterprises – especially large ones – currently have an extended role in society. These new responsibilities have increased corporations' willingness to integrally report on their financial, social and environmental outcomes. When deciding the topics on which to report, enterprises are called to select from a wide set of aspects related to the triple bottom line. This selection is oriented by the principle of materiality, according to which material aspects are aspects that reflect the organization's significant economic, environmental and social impacts or that substantively influence stakeholders' assessments and decisions. Using the materiality principle in the sustainability reporting (SR) context helps illustrate items that inform investors and other stakeholders about a business's ability to create and sustain value.

Since it is often impossible or very difficult to set thresholds for non-financial or non-market aspects to assess their materiality, we highlight the centrality of the stakeholder engagement process. An analysis of stakeholders' interests, in fact, can help define the spectrum of financial, social and environmental aspects for which the organization must be accountable.

To further analyze the role of stakeholder engagement in sustainability reporting, this chapter will provide a theoretical framework based on stakeholder theory and review the main tools and methodologies for undertaking stakeholder engagement.

In the last 30 years, the stakeholder approach and its uneasy coexistence with the goal of shareholder value maximization has increased in prominence in organization and accounting studies (Lopatta, Jaeschke, & Chen, 2017; Sundaram & Inkpen, 2004). Scholars usually credit Freeman's (1984) pioneering work that linked stakeholders with strategic management as the starting point (e.g., Mitchell, Agle, & Wood, 1997). Stakeholder theory is an organizational and management approach that was originally elaborated by Freeman (1984), who points out that managers must not only satisfy the expectations of the company's shareholders or contractors but also recognize the interests of various stakeholders (Scherer,

Palazzo, & Baumann, 2006). In other words, a common theme in the literature is that firms should treat stakeholders as their ends and should attend to the interests of all stakeholders, not just shareholders (Jawahar & McLaughlin, 2001). Crucially, in light of stakeholder theory, organizations must be accountable to all relevant stakeholders and not simply to owners and managers.

> Stakeholder theory is managerial in that it reflects and directs how managers operate rather than primarily addressing management theorists and economists. The focus of stakeholder theory is articulated in two core questions (Freeman, 1984). First, it asks, what is the purpose of the firm? This encourages managers to articulate the shared sense of the value they create, and what brings its core stakeholders together. This propels the firm forward and allows it to generate outstanding performance, determined both in terms of its purpose and marketplace financial metrics. Second, stakeholder theory asks, what responsibility does management have to stakeholders? This pushes managers to articulate how they want to do business—specifically, what kinds of relationships they want and need to create with their stakeholders to deliver on their purpose.
>
> (Freeman, Wicks, & Parmar, 2004)

Stakeholder theory is rooted in strategic management (e.g. Clarkson, 1995; Edward Freeman, Rusconi, Signori, & Strudler, 2012; Freeman, 1984; Frooman, 1999), but in the past 20 years, it has also been found in the fields of organization theory (e.g. Donaldson & Preston, 1995; Jones, 1995; Rowley, 1997), business ethics (e.g. Phillips & Reichart, 2000; Starik, 1995), and accounting theory (Thorne, Mahoney, & Manetti, 2014). Stakeholder theory also figures prominently in the study of social, environmental and sustainability issues (Moratis & Brandt, 2017; Wood, 1991a, 1991b). Moreover, in the last decade, the topic has gained traction among scholars who study sustainable development (Sharma & Henriques, 2005; Steurer, Langer, Konrad, & Martinuzzi, 2005).

Freeman (1984) offers a rational approach to strategic management, urging firms to recognize stakeholders in order to achieve better results and improve general performance. Whereas the traditional "shareholder view" (see Section 2.1.2 of this volume) suggests that companies have a fiduciary duty to prioritize shareholders' expectations, Freeman's stakeholder approach argues that several other groups and individuals should be involved in the process of managing an organization, including employees, customers, suppliers, financiers, the community, governmental and non-governmental organizations (NGOs), political groups and trade unions. These stakeholder groups have the right to not be treated as a means to an end, and therefore, they must participate in determining the future direction of the firm in which they have a stake (Evan & Freeman, 1988; Miles, 2012; Stieb, 2009). In this initial work, Freeman (1984) intends to offer a pragmatic approach to strategy that urged organizations to be cognizant of stakeholders in order to achieve superior performance (Laplume, Sonpar, & Litz, 2008). Freeman and McVea (2001) argue that the stakeholder framework does not rely on a single overriding management objective for all decisions. In contrast, the stakeholder approach rejects the very idea of maximizing a single-objective function as a useful way to think about management strategy; rather, stakeholder management is an ongoing task of balancing and integrating multiple relationships and multiple objectives (Sundaram & Inkpen, 2004). A major role of corporate management in light of stakeholder theory is to assess the importance of meeting stakeholder demands in order to achieve the firm's strategic objectives: as the level of stakeholder power increases, the importance of meeting stakeholder demands increases (Roberts, 1992).

As suggested in Figure 4.1 and as previously indicated in the text, one of the cornerstones of stakeholder theory is the notion that the organization itself should be considered a combination of stakeholders and that the purpose of the organization should be to manage these stakeholders' interests, needs and viewpoints (Friedman & Miles, 2006).[1]

> In so doing, a particular group of stakeholders – (top-level) managers – are thought of as the focal group, charged with fulfilling the role of stakeholder management. The concept was elaborated by (Evan & Freeman, 1988) as the following two principles:
>
> 1   Principle of corporate legitimacy. The corporation should be managed for the benefit of its stakeholders: its customers, suppliers, owners, employees, and local communities. The rights of these groups must be ensured, and, further, the groups must participate, in some sense, in decisions that substantially affect their welfare.
> 2   The stakeholder fiduciary principle. Management bears a fiduciary relationship (. . .) to stakeholders and to the corporation as an abstract entity. It must act in the interests of the stakeholders as their agent, and it must act in the interests of the corporation to ensure the survival of the firm, safeguarding the long-term stakes of each group.
>
> (Friedman & Miles, 2006)

Figure 4.1 From an input-output model to the stakeholder model

Source: Our elaboration of Donaldson and Preston (1995).

If the original conception of the relationship between the stakeholder and the corporation followed a "hub and spoke" approach, in the last decade, models of interactive relations – often defined as forms of "stakeholder thinking" – have been developed. In these models, management and stakeholders agree to a management approach oriented toward transparency and accountability (Andriof & Waddock, 2002; Manetti, 2011).

Stakeholder theory has been at the core of the scientific debate in management and accounting studies for over 30 years, beginning with the first formulation of the "stakeholder approach" by Freeman (1984). However, despite its increasing popularity among academics and non-academics, stakeholder theory still faces a number of critiques. As reported by Friedman and Miles (2006), a further indicator of the popularity of the stakeholder approach has been the recent proliferation of literature that broadly contests the concept and reiterates the view that promoters of the stakeholder concept have specifically attempted to replace (Argenti, 1993, 1997; Jensen, 2001; Marcoux, 2000, 2003; Sternberg, 1997, 2000; Sundaram & Inkpen, 2004). According to Laplume et al. (2008), "stakeholder theory is timely yet adolescent, controversial yet important". It is timely because it affects "the dominant institutions of our time", often highlighting misconduct or environmental wrongdoing by firms. At the same time, the theory is "adolescent" because its empirical validity has yet to be established (Jones, 1995). Obviously, stakeholder theory is debated because it questions the traditional idea that profits are the primary measure of firm success, a phenomenon that (Jensen, 2001) calls a "single-valued objective". Many of those who have contributed to developing the stakeholder concept have done so within debates with those who promote the chief rival vision of the corporation and the role of its top managers: the shareholder model, which is based on ownership (Friedman & Miles, 2006).

> The objective of the corporation is to maximize stockholder (*shareholder, ndr*) value expressed either as maximizing long-run profits, growth, or dividends (though how long this long run should be is debatable). Friedman (1970) argued that this is the "one and only social responsibility of business" as long as companies keep to the rules of the capitalist game, i.e. "engage in open and free competition without deception or fraud".
>
> (Friedman & Miles, 2006)

However, this shareholder view appears to be losing prominence to the view that businesses have wider responsibilities and that these responsibilities are best expressed in terms of the stakeholder approach (Friedman & Miles, 2006). In other words, stakeholder theory is relevant precisely because it seeks to address not only organizations' economic and financial performance but also how they affect the societies in which they operate. Additionally, Laplume et al. (2008) believe that despite stakeholder theory's detractors (cfr. Margolis & Walsh, 2003), the theory's emergence is also a product of its emotional resonance and its ability to move people (Weick, 1999). Thus, Freeman (2000) claims that stakeholder theory emphasizes the "emergence of concerns with 'vision and values,' and 'a sense of purpose' in the mainstream conversations about business". Even detractors such as Jensen (2001) acknowledge that "stakeholder theory taps into the deep emotional commitment of most individuals to the family and tribe". In this sense, stakeholder theory should be given priority in the study of behavioral economics and deserves to be a focus of present and future academic research.

4.1.2 The various approaches to stakeholder theory

Stakeholder theory is a multifaceted concept. In this section, to provide additional insights on this theory, we follow Donaldson and Preston (1995), who argue that stakeholder theory features three distinct categories of analysis: descriptive, instrumental and normative.

The first approach to stakeholder theory involves studying how managers and stakeholders actually behave and how they view their actions and roles (Friedman & Miles, 2006). This approach has been labeled the descriptive approach to stakeholder theory. From a descriptive point of view, stakeholder theory is used to explain the characteristics and behaviors of companies and other organizations, including how they are managed (Brenner & Molander, 1977), how boards of directors address the needs and demands of multiple constituencies (Wang & Dewhirst, 1992), how a company creates and implements various management strategies and how these processes affect the nature of the organization itself (Clarkson, 1991; Halal, 1990; Kreiner & Bhambri, 1988). In other words, from this perspective, the theory is used to empirically describe, and sometimes to explain, specific corporate characteristics and behaviors (Donaldson & Preston, 1995).

The second approach involves studying how managers should act if they are willing to further their own interests or what theorists traditionally conceive as the organization's interests, usually viewed as (long-run) profit maximization or the maximization of stockholder value (Friedman & Miles, 2006). This strategic approach is generally based on what has been called instrumental stakeholder theory, which proposes that if managers treat stakeholders in accordance with the stakeholder concept, the organization will be more successful or will be more likely to be sustainable (Friedman & Miles, 2006; Sundaram & Inkpen, 2004). The instrumental approach attempts to identify the potential or effective connections that exist between stakeholder management and the achievement of the organization's goals and aims. These connections include the links between better stakeholder management and profitability, as well as the enhancement of an organization's reputation within the community. In particular, instrumental stakeholder theory views the firm as a nexus of contracts (Jensen & Meckling, 1976) and addresses a firm's ability to increase its competitive advantage by minimizing its contracting costs. In his discussion of instrumental stakeholder theory, Jones (1995) argues that if firms contract with their stakeholders on the basis of mutual trust and cooperation, they will have a competitive advantage over firms that do not (Sundaram & Inkpen, 2004). A firm minimizes these contracting costs by developing trusting relations with its various stakeholders (Berman, Wicks, Kotha, & Jones, 1999). Mitchell et al. (1997) state that "stakeholder theory . . . holds the key to more effective management". Engaging in socially responsible behaviors has become a primary mechanism through which a firm may foster strong relationships with stakeholders (Barnett & Salomon, 2012). Donaldson and Preston (1995) argue that "corporations practicing stakeholder management will, other things being equal, be relatively successful in conventional performance terms".

Finally, the normative approach presumes that organizations have a duty to identify and involve stakeholders who have specific interests with the organization, identifying the "moral or philosophical guidelines for the operation and management of the corporation" (Donaldson & Preston, 1995). According to Phillips (1997), stakeholder engagement is based on the "moral" assumption that the firm has an obligation to its stakeholders: "stakeholder status as here conceived indicates the presence of an additional obligation over and above that due others simply by virtue of being human" (Phillips, 1997). The normative approach refers to firms' extended responsibilities. An example of a normative argument is that "the interests of key stakeholders must be integrated into the very purpose of the firm, and stakeholder relationships must be managed in a coherent and strategic fashion" (Freeman & McVea, 2001). Clarkson (1995), for instance, argues that "the economic and social purpose of the corporation is to create and distribute wealth and value to all its primary stakeholder groups, without favoring one group at the expense of others".

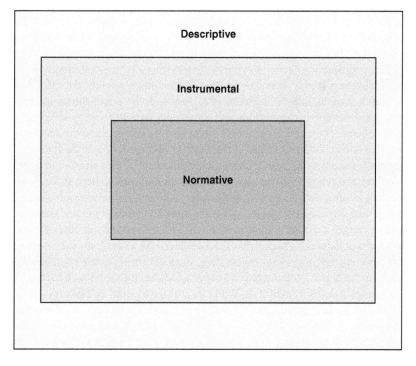

Figure 4.2 Three aspects of stakeholder theory
Source: Donaldson and Preston (1995).

According to Donaldson and Preston (1995), the three aspects of stakeholder theory are nested within each other, as suggested in Figure 4.2.

> The external shell of the theory is its descriptive aspect; the theory presents and explains relationships that are observed in the external world. The theory's descriptive accuracy is supported, at the second level, by its instrumental and predictive value; if certain practices are carried out, then certain results will be obtained. The central core of the theory is, however, normative. The descriptive accuracy of the theory presumes the truth of the core normative conception, insofar as it presumes that managers and other agents act as if all stakeholders' interests have intrinsic value. In turn, recognition of these ultimate moral values and obligations gives stakeholder management its fundamental normative base.
>
> (Donaldson & Preston, 1995)

Drawing inspiration from the proposals of Donaldson and Preston (1995), some scholars believe that stakeholder theory is primarily a moral theory and that much of the extant research focuses on finding moral bases to support stakeholder theory's major ideas (Boatright, 1994; Donaldson & Preston, 1995; Goodpaster, 1991). In accordance with the normative point of view, stakeholder theory implies that various stakeholders create specific duties and obligations that companies must address. Recently, supporters of the normative approach have attempted to classify the relational models between organizations and stakeholders by assuming a gradual growth of stakeholder involvement and participation (Andriof & Waddock, 2002; Svendsen, 1998). First, an organization identifies and maps its stakeholders, distinguishing if possible between primary parties (those who are strategic in the middle to long terms) and secondary parties (stakeholders who do not affect the organization's sustainability) (Clarkson, 1995). Second, the organization attempts to manage stakeholders' expectations and the claims they support in accordance with their salience (Mitchell et al., 1997) while also balancing these various positions through a stakeholder management process (O'Dwyer, 2005). In the final step, organizations attempt to engage primary stakeholders in various decision-making processes, allowing them to participate in organizational management and governance, sharing information, dialoguing and creating a model of mutual responsibility. The stakeholder engagement phase, unlike the stakeholder mapping and management phase, creates a dynamic context of interaction, mutual respect, dialogue and change – not a unilateral management of stakeholders. As a result, the main feature of stakeholder engagement is not encouraging the mere involvement of stakeholders in order to "mitigate" or manage their expectations but rather creating a network of mutual responsibility (Andriof & Waddock, 2002; Manetti & Bellucci, 2016; Manetti, Bellucci, & Bagnoli, 2017; Polonsky, Giraud Voss, Voss, & Moorman, 2005; Unerman & Bennett, 2004). Jones and Wicks (1999) and Freeman (1999) explicitly reject the notion that it is possible to separate the branches of stakeholder theory, arguing that all the branches overlap with each other. Thus, stakeholder theory is simultaneously descriptive, instrumental and normative.

Regardless of the preferred approach to stakeholder theory, the theory requires addressing the question of which groups of stakeholders deserve or require management's attention (Sundaram & Inkpen, 2004). In the following sections, we will focus on the process of defining and classifying stakeholders.

4.1.3 Defining stakeholders

We believe that at this point, it is important to take a step back and raise a crucial question: what do we precisely mean by the term "stakeholder"? The earliest definition of the term is often credited to an internal memo produced in 1963 by the Stanford Research Institute: "those groups without whose support the organization would cease to exist" (Freeman, 1984; Friedman & Miles, 2006; Mitchell et al., 1997). Similar definitions have been advocated by Bowie (1988), Freeman and Reed (1983) and Näsi (1995). Freeman et al. (2004) also use this definition in a modified form: "those groups who are vital to the survival and success of the organization". This definition, which is entirely organization-centric, is stringent in the sense that it excludes categories of agents that other definitions include (Friedman & Miles, 2006). For example, in works commonly regarded as seminal stakeholder texts – at least in academic circles – stakeholders are defined as "any group or individual who can affect or is affected by the achievement of the organization objectives" (Freeman, 1984; Friedman & Miles, 2006).

For the purpose of this volume, we will adopt this latter definition provided by Freeman (1984), although we recognize the need for a compromise between a very broad and a very narrow approach to the delineation of the appropriate range of relevant stakeholders. We appreciate this definition because, despite being one of the broadest in literature, it leaves the notion of "stakes" and the field of possible stakeholders open, giving full discretion to the organization in identifying stakeholders (this phase will be covered in detail in Section 4.2.2).

According to Bryson (2004), in this definition, the term refers to persons, groups or organizations that must somehow be taken into account by leaders, managers and front-line staff. This definition is intentionally broad: Freeman aimed to develop a literary device that questions the emphasis on shareholders (Sundaram & Inkpen, 2004). Clearly, such a broad definition raises some practical concerns.

> This definition is much broader than that of the Stanford Research Institute. The symmetrical phrase "can affect or is affected by" opens the idea that "outside" individuals or groups may consider themselves to be stakeholders of an organization, without the organization considering them to be stakeholders. A group or individuals may consider themselves to be affected by the achievement of organization objectives without "insiders" in the organization noticing or acknowledging these affects.
>
> (Friedman & Miles, 2006)

The topic of stakeholder identification is still debated.

> How should a manager identify the important stakeholders and on what basis should other stakeholders be classified as unimportant? Who should determine the criteria that distinguish important and unimportant stakeholders – The board? The CEO? The stakeholders themselves? In attempting to answer these questions, Mitchell et al. (1997) reviewed the literature and developed a list of 27 different definitions of stakeholders. The definitions were sorted along dimensions such as basis for legitimacy, power dependence, and urgency.
>
> (Sundaram & Inkpen, 2004)

Although Mitchell et al. (1997) develop a theory of stakeholder identification and salience, they conclude that the attempt to define relevant stakeholders along these dimensions may be complex (Sundaram & Inkpen, 2004).

> Jones (1995) makes clear that the term stakeholder applies not only to groups such as customers or employees, but also to subgroups of customers (e.g., buyers of over-the-counter medicine versus buyers of shampoo) and employees (e.g., shopworkers and middle managers) who might have distinct and competing interests, thus implying that some stakeholders are more important than others. In contrast to such a hierarchy, Clarkson (1995) argues that the interests of all legitimate stakeholders have intrinsic value and that no particular interests should dominate those of the others.
>
> (Sundaram & Inkpen, 2004)

There is a clear relationship between definitions of stakeholders and the identification of stakeholders: the most common way to classify stakeholders is to consider groups of people with a distinct relationship with corporations (Friedman & Miles, 2006). The most common and simple groups of stakeholders considered include the following:

- Shareholders;
- Customers;
- Suppliers;
- Employees
- Local communities.

As we stated above:

> a key issue is whether stakeholders are confined to those that are crucial for the achievement of corporate objectives or if they are merely any entity affected by corporate actions, especially if the latter includes alternative actions corporations could have taken in order to achieve their objectives, but were not chosen. The latter can lead to a very wide definition of stakeholders.

Freeman and Reed (1983) and Freeman (2004) actually label these definitions separately: narrow and wide. Freeman's stakeholder-enabling principle, based on the narrow definition, was stated to apply only to "stakeholders defined as employees, financiers, customers, and communities".

(Friedman & Miles, 2006)

It is clear that if one is willing to adopt a broad approach to stakeholder identification, one can consider almost every subject and group of subjects to be affected in some way by at least one activity that large enterprises carry out to achieve their goals. Following the argument by Friedman and Miles (2006), many types of individuals or groups have been considered to be possible stakeholders in addition to the main one listed above, including:

- Managers;[2]
- Stakeholder representatives (such as trade unions or trade associations of suppliers);
- NGOs or "activists" (who have been considered individually or as stakeholder representatives);
- Competitors;
- Government(s), regulators and other policy makers;
- Financiers other than stockholders (creditors, bondholders, debt providers);
- Media;
- The public in general;
- The environment and other non-human aspects of the Earth;
- Business partners;
- Academics;
- Future generations;
- Past generations (particularly the memory of the organization's founders).

The number of identifiable categories of stakeholder groups depends on the narrowness or broadness of the approach adopted and is inversely proportional to the broadness of the way these groups are defined. For example:

> the category of employees, for example, can usefully be defined more finely as white-collar and blue-collar, trade unionists and non-trade unionists, permanent or temporary, full-time or part-time, or in terms of which plant or section they work in. Different subcategories of employees may have different interests, identities, claims, and other characteristics. Strategically, organizations may clearly treat different subcategories of employees differently based on differential power. Normatively, the line of legitimacy may run between different employee categories, rather than between the crude category of employees compared with other crude groupings.

(Friedman & Miles, 2006)

An advantage of using finer stakeholder categories is that they are likely to embrace more homogeneous groupings of people; at the same time, a limitation in considering finer categories is that the likelihood of overlap among interests and actions will increase (Friedman & Miles, 2006).

The following sections of this volume will study stakeholder engagement on two different but complementary levels: theory and practice. We will provide a theoretical framework for stakeholder engagement and a review of the tools supporting stakeholder engagement.

4.2 The process of stakeholder engagement

4.2.1 The phases of stakeholder engagement

In this section, we will begin to analyze the definition of stakeholder engagement from a theoretical standpoint and the role of stakeholder engagement in relation to strategies and reporting.

We believe that stakeholder involvement is important because it provides crucial data and information that can be useful both to effectively manage an organization and to determine the most relevant and material topics to be covered in the organization's integrated or sustainability reports. In fact, as argued by Friedman and Miles (2006), large enterprises have many reasons to devote resources to stakeholder engagement:

> business case motives are most frequently linked to the attainment of maximizing long-term profits through strategies either to forestall government regulation or for risk management. Effective risk management can lead to damage limitation and reduction of financial penalties for acting unethically, whether directly through lawsuits or clean-up costs or indirectly through the deterioration of relationships. Employee relations are most commonly highlighted, as poor relations can result in declining productivity, creativity, and loyalty as well as recruitment and staff retention problems. The development of a close stakeholder network can provide corporations with valuable information about external events, market conditions, technological advances, or consumer trends, which can help corporations anticipate, understand, and respond to external changes more efficiently and effectively (Svendsen, 1998). Where stakeholders feel they are being ignored, or that their claims are not being met, dissatisfaction is often expressed through protest. Stakeholder engagement cannot only diffuse protest but is also credited with leading to more effective solutions (Neligan, 2003).
>
> (Friedman & Miles, 2006)

Building on Garriga and Melé (2013), we define stakeholder engagement as the attempt to integrate groups with a stake in the firm into managerial decision making. Thus, a stakeholder engagement plan includes the systematic analysis and implementation of actions designed to involve stakeholders.

Certain studies differentiate the concept of stakeholder engagement from the concept of stakeholder management (Manetti, 2011; Manetti & Toccafondi, 2011; Moratis & Brandt, 2017; Svendsen, 1998; Waddock, 2008), defining the latter as the mere administration of stakeholders' interests and expectations in an instrumental way. Stakeholder management is essentially stakeholder relationship management because the company manages its relationships with stakeholders, not the actual stakeholder groups (Friedman & Miles, 2006).

Stakeholder theory scholars have attempted to classify the relational models between corporations and stakeholders by assuming different gradual paths of stakeholder involvement (Manetti, 2011; Svendsen, 1998; Waddock, 2008). We opt to summarize the overall stakeholder engagement process in the following three phases:

1   Stakeholder identification and analysis. First, organizations must identify and analyze the characteristics of each group of stakeholders, understanding how these groups can affect and/or are affected by the organization. Moreover, in this phase, it is necessary to study how stakeholder engagement affects the enterprise's risk management. We refer to these steps as the "Stakeholder identification and analysis" phase.

2   Interaction with stakeholders. Second, corporations try to manage stakeholders' expectations and the social and economic issues that they support and begin to find a way to balance their positions (Manetti, 2011). This phase includes the implementation of a stakeholder engagement strategy and interaction with stakeholders. Corporations involve their stakeholders in decision-making processes, making them participants in business management, information sharing, dialogue and the creation of a model of mutual responsibility (Manetti, 2011).

3   Evaluation and reporting. The third phase is not necessarily intended to be a final stage. Its steps include measuring stakeholder engagement performance and outcomes and reporting data to use in the consequent redefinition of the process: thus, these operations are to be performed during the whole process and are useful in further developing the next iterations of stakeholder engagement activities.

The path of these phases is illustrated in Figure 4.3 and is analyzed in detail in the following sections. As Figure 4.3 shows, the three phases are reciprocally interconnected and all steps form a path whose endpoint helps reinitiate the process with new data and information.

4.2.2 Phase 1: Stakeholder identification and analysis

The first stage of stakeholder engagement is to identify the stakeholders with which an organization wants to interact. In other words, the questions to ask include, "which are the relevant stakeholders?" and "are there difference in terms of relevance between stakeholder groups that should affect the interaction with them?". In this and the following subsections, we will analyze how the most relevant academic literature addresses the issue of stakeholder identification and engagement.

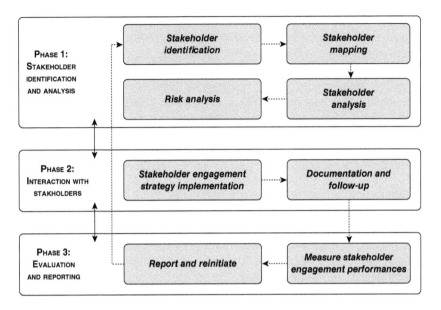

Figure 4.3 The components of stakeholder engagement

As we noted earlier, a main component of stakeholder engagement is the identification and prioritization of stakeholders (Carroll, 1999; Clarkson, 1995; Donaldson & Preston, 1995; Manetti, 2011). Mitchell et al. (1997) argue that stakeholder theory attempts to articulate the fundamental question of which groups of stakeholders deserve or require management attention and which do not. Much of stakeholder theory is concerned with identifying different ways to segment the range of possible stakeholders in order to distinguish different ways in which corporations should deal with stakeholders in each segment (Friedman & Miles, 2006).

An organization's managers must first know what kind of stakeholders exist and, second, who or what factors matter most. Mitchell et al. (1997) wrote a seminal paper on the theory of stakeholder identification and salience.

These authors begin their analysis by adopting Freeman's definition of a stakeholder: "any group or individual who can affect or is affected by the achievement of the organization's objectives" (1984). They begin with a broad definition so that no potential or actual stakeholders are excluded from analysis arbitrarily or *a priori*, and we agree with this conception. On the basis of this definition, they develop a theory of stakeholder identification from various theoretical literatures, such as agency, resource dependence and transaction cost theories, which are particularly helpful in explaining why power plays such an important role in the attention that managers give to stakeholders.

We then propose that classes of stakeholders can be identified by their possession or attributed possession of one, two, or all three of the following attributes: (1) the stakeholder's power to influence the firm, (2) the legitimacy of
the stakeholder's relationship with the firm, and (3) the urgency of the stakeholder's claim on the firm. This theory produces a comprehensive typology of
stakeholders based on the normative assumption that these variables define the
field of stakeholders: those entities to whom managers should pay attention.

(Mitchell et al., 1997)

Thus, Mitchell et al. (1997) propose that managers should identify a subject as
a stakeholder if that subject features at least power, legitimacy or urgency. A
stakeholder will present higher salience with respect to managers if it features two
or all of these attributes. In other words, stakeholder salience will be positively
related to the cumulative number of stakeholder attributes – power, legitimacy
and urgency – that managers perceive to be present (Mitchell et al., 1997).

Power is the ability to bring about the outcomes one desires (Salancik &
Pfeffer, 1974). Suchman (1995) defines legitimacy as "a generalized perception
or assumption that the actions of an entity are desirable, proper, or appropriate
within some socially constructed system of norms, values, beliefs, and definitions". Additionally, Mitchell et al. (1997) define urgency as the degree to which
stakeholder claims call for immediate attention and salience as the degree to
which managers prioritize competing stakeholder claims.

This analysis allows and justifies identification of entities that should be considered stakeholders of the firm, and it also constitutes the set from which
managers select those entities they perceive as salient. According to this
model, then, entities with no power, legitimacy, or urgency in relation to the
firm are not stakeholders and will be perceived as having no salience by the
firm's managers.

(Salancik & Pfeffer, 1974)

Figure 4.4 provides an outline of the different stakeholder groups that can be
defined using this identification approach.

The low salience classes (areas 1, 2, and 3), which we term "latent" stakeholders, are identified by their possession or attributed possession of only one of the
attributes. The moderately salient stakeholders (areas 4, 5, and 6) are identified
by their possession or attributed possession of two of the attributes, and because
they are stakeholders who "expect something," we call them "expectant" stakeholders. The combination of all three attributes (including the dynamic relations
among them) is the defining feature of highly salient stakeholders (area 7).

(Mitchell et al., 1997)

Now, citing Mitchell et al. (1997), we will provide a brief description of these
classes of stakeholders. Dormant stakeholders possess the power to impose their

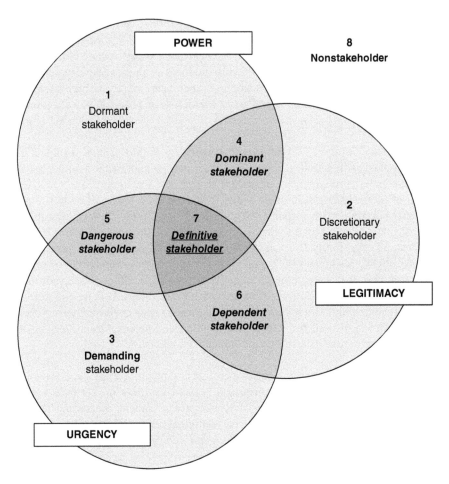

Figure 4.4 Stakeholder identification in Mitchell et al. (1997)
Source: Mitchell et al. (1997).

will on a firm, but because they do not have a legitimate relationship or an urgent claim, their power remains unused (e.g., these stakeholders include potential buyers of the company).

> Dormant stakeholders have little or no interaction with the firm. However, because of their potential to acquire a second attribute, management should remain cognizant of such stakeholders, as the dynamic nature of the stakeholder-manager relationship suggests that dormant stakeholders will become more salient to managers if they acquire either urgency or legitimacy.
>
> (Mitchell et al., 1997)

While discretionary stakeholders possess legitimacy, they have no power to influence the firm and no urgent claims.[3] Demanding stakeholders are those with urgent claims but without power or legitimacy.

Dominant stakeholders are both powerful and legitimate, and therefore, their influence on the firm is assured. These stakeholders are dominant in terms of the legitimate claims they have on the firm and their ability to act on these claims. Usually, these stakeholders will have a formal mechanism in place that acknowledges the importance of their relationship with the firm. Dependent stakeholders lack power but have urgent legitimate claims and depend upon others (other stakeholders or the firm's managers) for the power needed to carry out their will. Mitchell et al. (1997) suggest that a stakeholder without legitimacy but with urgency and power will be coercive and possibly violent, making the stakeholder literally "dangerous" to the firm.

Finally, by definition,

> a stakeholder exhibiting both power and legitimacy already will be a member of a firm's dominant coalition. When such a stakeholder's claim is urgent, managers have a clear and immediate mandate to attend to and give priority to that stakeholder's claim.
>
> (Mitchell et al., 1997)

It is important to note that this model of stakeholder identification depicts a dynamic situation in which stakeholders can move from one sector to another by losing or gaining attributes over time.

> Further, this model enables a more systematic sorting by managers of stakeholder-manager relationships as these relationships attain and relinquish salience in the dynamics of ongoing business. In addition, our three-attribute model permits managers to map the legitimacy of stakeholders and therefore to become sensitized to the moral implications of their actions with respect to each stakeholder.
>
> (Mitchell et al., 1997)

In the academic literature, this framework is among the best-regarded ways to approach the topic of stakeholder identification and analysis. Many authors have addressed this topic. For example, Bryson (2004) focuses specifically on stakeholder analyses, arguing that they can either help the organization perform better directly or help create an "authorizing environment" (Moore, 1995) that will indirectly improve organizational performance – for example, by changing the organization's externally imposed mandates, funding sources, decision-making protocols and accountability mechanisms. Moore (1995) and Bryson (2004) claim that attention to stakeholders is important throughout the strategic management process because organizations' success – and certainly their survival – often depends on satisfying key stakeholders according to their definition of what is valuable (Bryson, 2004; Moore, 1995).

Because attention to stakeholders is so important, stakeholder analyses become important. If they can help public organizations better fulfill their purposes, then there is much to commend them. Said differently, I would hypothesize that strategic management processes that employ a reasonable number of competently done stakeholder analyses are more likely to be successful.

(Bryson, 2004)

Donaldson and Preston (1995) argue that it is important to distinguish between influencers and stakeholders: some actors in the firm may be both influencers and stakeholders (e.g., stockholders), some may be recognizable as stakeholders but have no influence (e.g., job applicants), while others may have influence but no stake (e.g., the media) (Friedman & Miles, 2006). Clarkson (1995) argues that is important to use different methodologies to distinguish between primary stakeholders (who determine the very survival of the corporation) and secondary stakeholders (who affect or are affected by the corporation but do not affect its sustainability) (Manetti, 2011). For example, Bryson (2004) presents 15 stakeholder identification and analysis techniques. In practice, among these methods, stakeholder mapping enables managers and organizations to map stakeholders in a chart whose horizontal axis represents the stakeholder group's level of interest in the company's success (from negative to positive attitudes) and the vertical axis represents the group's actual or potential influence on the company (from low to high influence). Another kind of stakeholder analysis maps stakeholders in terms of their influence on the company (from no to high influence) and the impact the company has on them (from low to high impact).

This kind of stakeholder analysis helps determine the appropriate level of engagement for every category of stakeholders, which, ranging from lower to higher, include informing, consulting, involving, collaborating and empowering. These analyses are then usually complemented with a social risk analysis. In brief, risk assessment is based on tools that consider the likelihood and the magnitude of possible consequences for every risk associated with every stakeholder. For every risk, there is usually a person responsible for preparing a plan to minimize and address it. All the activities performed in the stakeholder identification and analysis phase serve to gather the data necessary to define the next phase, which includes the implementation of a stakeholder engagement strategy.

4.2.3 Phase 2: Interaction with stakeholders

This phase, unlike the first phase, includes a mutual commitment among stakeholders and the company to resolving issues and may affect the relationships between the corporation and its general and specific environment (Manetti, 2011). Actual engagement activities occur in this phase. This involvement process "creates a dynamic context of interaction, mutual respect, dialogue and change, not a unilateral management of stakeholders" (Andriof & Waddock, 2002). Phillips (1997) argues that in ideal conditions, the interaction with stakeholders draws on a mutually beneficial and just cooperation scheme that is based on the idea of a "social contract"[4] (Rawls, 1971). The concept of the reciprocity of rights and duties implies overcoming a vision focused on shareholders' interests, alleging that stakeholder expectations are managed in a strategic manner to create value in the medium to long term (Jonker & Foster, 2002; Manetti, 2011), as simple stakeholder management would imply.

> In this perspective, relations between stakeholders and corporations are based on the principles of reciprocity, interdependence, and power (Andriof & Waddock, 2002) as a network that interprets the relationship as two-way rather than one-way (Rowley, 1997). The main feature of SE [stakeholder engagement], therefore, is not the mere involvement of stakeholders to "mitigate" or manage their expectations (stakeholder management), but to create a network of mutual responsibility (Andriof & Waddock, 2002). Stakeholders are also participants in business management through the submission of questions and issues deemed important that generate positive or negative impact on corporations, influencing managerial decisions. Their main responsibility is therefore to avoid making matters that might cause unintended negative externalities on the corporation, other organizations or local communities (Andriof & Waddock, 2002). If, on the contrary, the negative effects of the mentioned subjects were known and based on ethical relevant issues, stakeholders would still have fulfilled their fiduciary duties to the company.
>
> (Manetti, 2011)

If stakeholders have responsibilities and rights, their interest in the relationship with the corporation goes beyond the scope of mere satisfaction of their ambitions and expectations (Manetti, 2011). Therefore, as petitioners with legitimate expectations, stakeholders assume the role of moral agents (Jones, Wicks, & Freeman, 2002) with the responsibility to consider the corporation's and other parties' rights and interests and to promote effective and ethical relationships (Manetti, 2011).

A great deal of empirical research has been conducted on these topics. As reported by Garriga and Melé (2013), the literature includes studies on how to determine the best practices to incorporate stakeholder relations (Bendheim, Waddock, & Graves, 1998) and stakeholder salience to managers, as shown in the previous section (Agle, Mitchell, & Sonnenfeld, 1999; Mitchell et al., 1997); the impact of stakeholder management on financial performance (Berman et al., 1999); the influence of stakeholder network structural relations (Rowley, 1997) and how managers can successfully balance the competing demands of various stakeholder groups (Ogden & Watson, 1999).

In their seminal paper, Emshoff and Freeman (1978) present two basic principles that underpin stakeholder engagement (Garriga & Melé, 2013). The first principle is that the central goal of stakeholder engagement is to achieve the maximum overall cooperation between the entire system of stakeholder groups and to meet the corporation's objectives; the second principle states that the most efficient strategy for managing stakeholder relations involves efforts that simultaneously deal with issues affecting multiple stakeholders (Garriga & Melé, 2013).

Table 4.1 Clarkson principles for stakeholder engagement

Principle 1	Managers should acknowledge and actively monitor the concerns of all legitimate stakeholders and should take their interests into account appropriately in decision making and operations.
Principle 2	Managers should listen to and openly communicate with stakeholders about their respective concerns and contributions and about the risks that they assume as a result of their involvement with the corporation.
Principle 3	Managers should adopt processes and modes of behavior that are sensitive to the concerns and capabilities of each stakeholder constituency.
Principle 4	Managers should recognize the interdependence of efforts and rewards among stakeholders and should attempt to achieve a fair distribution of the benefits and burdens of corporate activity among them while taking into account their respective risks and vulnerabilities.
Principle 5	Managers should work cooperatively with other entities, both public and private, to ensure that risks and harms arising from corporate activities are minimized and, when they cannot be avoided, appropriately compensated.
Principle 6	Managers should altogether avoid activities that might jeopardize inalienable human rights (e.g., the right to life) or give rise to risks that, if clearly understood, would be patently unacceptable to relevant stakeholders.
Principle 7	Managers should acknowledge the potential conflicts between (a) their own role as corporate stakeholders and (b) their legal and moral responsibilities for the stakeholders' interests and should address such conflicts through open communication, appropriate reporting and incentive systems, and, where necessary, third party review.

Source: Clarkson Centre for Business Ethics (1999).

The interaction with stakeholders considers different heavily interconnected activities. The Clarkson Centre for Business Ethics (1999) developed a list of principles that summarize the key features of stakeholder engagement (Table 4.1) and defined stakeholder engagement as the process of effectively eliciting stakeholder views on their relationship with the organization.

The Clarkson principles are highly respected in the literature as a model of best practices (Friedman & Miles, 2006). The first principle arises from a need to recognize the existence of multiple and diverse stakeholder interests: only legitimate interests are considered, as defined by stakeholders that have explicit or implied contracts with the firm and those whose well-being has been impacted by the firm (Clarkson Centre for Business Ethics, 1999; Friedman & Miles, 2006). Two-way dialogue, the second principle, is a prerequisite for good stakeholder management (Friedman & Miles, 2006). The third principle attempts to increase managers' awareness that stakeholders differ with respect to their involvement with the organization.

Governance mechanisms have created official arenas for some stakeholders to engage through formal processes, such as annual general meetings (AGMs) and union representation. Others require an unofficial approach, such as through direct contact, advertising, or press releases. Two points are raised: regardless of the means of engagement a consistent message should be delivered; and extreme caution should be taken when dealing with stakeholders that have a limited capacity to interpret complex situations and options (Clarkson Centre for Business Ethics, 1999).

(Friedman & Miles, 2006)

The fourth principle highlights the need to balance the risks and rewards between different stakeholders and to make the distribution of benefits apparent to all parties (Friedman & Miles, 2006). The fifth principle seeks to promote cooperation and joint corporate action to reduce harmful externalities on the premise that individual action is inadequate (Friedman & Miles, 2006). The sixth principle relates to the need to avoid activities that endanger basic rights (Friedman & Miles, 2006). The seventh principle requires managers to recognize their own conflicts of interest and to encourage practices intended to regulate them. This step should lead to greater credibility and thereby increase trust in the organization (Friedman & Miles, 2006).

In general, the first issue that needs to be addressed when a stakeholder engagement plan is initiated refers to the explicit or implicit nature of the approach that a company wants to follow.

Many corporations undertake explicit stakeholder management associated with official procedures, policies, and allocated lines of responsibility, without adopting a comprehensive approach founded on the principles of participation, empowerment, and inclusion. The explicit nature of this approach can also afford greater corporate legitimacy. Some organizations have created "community relations" or CSR positions or even departments in order to highlight their commitment to stakeholder management. However, such practices do not necessarily reflect a high level of stakeholder synthesis. The focus of stakeholder management may be as a strategic tool for competitive advantage, which is not deeply embedded and could be abandoned with changed competitive environments.

(Friedman & Miles, 2006)

A second issue is related to how organizations balance their approach to stakeholders. In fact, organizations often use more resources to manage their relations with primary stakeholders (employees or customers) (Friedman & Miles, 2006). This unbalanced approach risks disregarding important stakeholders for the sake of opportunism.

Third and finally, many organizations have no genuine commitment to stakeholder engagement: fiduciary duties to shareholders and legal – not moral – obligations are the driving factors, and therefore, stakeholder management exists only to resolve conflicts, such as boycotts, protests and strikes, which can negatively impact short-term shareholder value (Friedman & Miles, 2006).

This issue is one among many reasons why it is important to assess and report on the quality of stakeholder engagement. This topic will be analyzed in the next subsection.

4.2.4 Phase 3: Evaluation and reporting

The evaluation phase of stakeholder engagement is not necessarily intended to be the final stage. Its steps include measuring stakeholder engagement performance and outcomes and reporting data that are useful for the consequent redefinition of the process. Thus, these operations should be performed during the whole process and are useful in further developing subsequent iterations of stakeholder management activities.

The activities in this phase are useful for collecting all documents related to the engagement efforts and their results. In fact, staff in charge of stakeholder engagement must ensure that there is a data management system in place to follow up with the implementation plan. This system may contain both qualitative (transcripts of focus group sessions, etc.) and quantitative (the number of meetings, participants, etc.) information. The latter information is internally useful, while qualitative data usually provide the most important information for the organization.

Here, the key points include the need to assess the quality of stakeholder engagement and the willingness to report on the outcome of this engagement to contribute to new iterations of the loop. AccountAbility (2015) defines stakeholder engagement as high quality when it:

- clearly defines its scope;
- has an agreed-upon decision-making process;
- focuses on issues material to the organization and/or its stakeholders;
- creates opportunities for dialogue;
- is integral to organizational governance;
- is transparent and has a process appropriate to the stakeholders engaged;
- is timely;
- is flexible and responsive;
- adds value both for the organization and its stakeholders.

The academic literature includes a broad range of works on these topics. Strong, Ringer, and Taylor (2001) survey customers, stockholders and employees of financial institutions to identify management behaviors that lead to stakeholders' satisfaction with their involvement. These authors suggest that the factors critical to satisfaction across stakeholder groups are the timeliness of communication, the honesty and completeness of the information and the empathy and equity of the treatment received from management. There are several common-sense aspects of effective dialogue, such as the willingness to learn for each other and the flexibility to ensure the implementation of good ideas (Friedman & Miles, 2006). Zöller (1999) suggests that effective dialogues require symmetrical communication, the transparency of benefits and risks, unbiased facilitation, inclusivity and an early start to facilitating change, if needed.

Zadek and Raynard (2002) suggest three dimensions of quality: procedural quality, responsiveness quality and the quality of outcomes.

Procedural quality encapsulates how the engagement was undertaken and whether it was consistent with the declared purpose. The terms of engagement, the parameters for discussion, and the areas that are negotiable or not relevant should all be clearly understood and shared by all parties. Most engagement is restricted to operational issues and therefore precludes stakeholders from having a say in terms of the broader structures and policies that impact them . . . Quality characteristics include the existence of formalized procedures, the facility for stakeholders to initiate engagement, and the assurance that stakeholders are empowered to raise the issues of most concern to them . . . The legitimacy of engagement is also important in assessing quality. Stakeholders should be selected in an unbiased and comprehensive fashion, with some verification process included to ensure that all relevant parties are represented and that participants represent the interests of those they claim to speak on behalf of.

(Friedman & Miles, 2006)

Neligan (2003), for example, identifies four dimensions of procedural quality: access to timely and accurate information, the terms of engagement, the legitimacy of engagement and procedures for redress. Second, responsiveness quality relates to whether an organization responds in a coherent and responsible manner and the way stakeholder views are addressed.

Were recommendations forwarded to the relevant decision-makers? Did the organization have the competencies to understand stakeholder concerns? How might they be addressed in practice? Was there evidence of organizational learning through the engagement and of putting such learning into practice in policies and decisions? Were corporate responses consistent with general policy statements such as represented in budgets and staff performance reviews?

(Friedman & Miles, 2006)

Third and most importantly, tangible evidence of the extent to which the organization adjusts its policies and practices in line with stakeholder engagement or evidence of stakeholder satisfaction indicates the level of outcome quality: quality stakeholder engagement must involve mechanisms that link engagement with decision making (Friedman & Miles, 2006; Zadek & Raynard, 2002). The quality of outcomes is important for understanding whether stakeholder engagement is only a façade or if is truly used as a tool for supporting and enhancing corporate strategies.

Ethics also plays a relevant role in the quality of the stakeholder engagement process. Weiss (2014) recommends constructing a matrix of stakeholder moral responsibilities that distinguishes legal, economic, ethical and voluntary corporate responsibilities for each stakeholder group. Managers can implement stakeholder involvement, be proponents of best practices and engage in optimal stakeholder activities such as effective constructive dialogue, but ignore ethics when generating policy (Friedman & Miles, 2006). Ethics are an important element to consider throughout the whole process.

Arnstein (1969) proposes a "ladder of citizen participation" that measures public involvement in strategy creation, with eight categories ranging from a paternalistic system to a more participatory system. On the lower rungs of non-participation lie manipulation and therapy, the middle section of the ladder includes degrees of tokenism (informing, consulting and placating), and the higher rungs are degrees of citizen power (partnership, delegated power and citizen control) (Friedman & Miles, 2006). Friedman and Miles (2006) build on this model and elaborate a 12-level model of stakeholder management and engagement, which is shown in Figure 4.5.

We believe the model shown in Figure 4.5 focuses on two very important elements: stakeholders' level of influence (knowing about decisions; being heard before decisions; having an influence on decisions; forming or agreeing to decisions) and the style of dialogue (mono-way; two-way; multi-way) for each level of engagement.

> Besides reviewing lies the step of reporting the results and the quality of the process. Communicating to stakeholders on the value and impact of engagement should go beyond providing feedback to stakeholders who participated in specific engagements. The organisation should publicly report on the aggregate of its engagement activities together with overall outcomes and impact, to show the scope and breadth of its outreach, and to demonstrate how its engagements contribute value to its strategy and operations.
>
> (AccountAbility, 2015)

Reporting on stakeholder engagement may include defining the stakeholder groups engaged, the approach to stakeholder engagement and the methods used, the frequency of engagement, the primary issues and concerns raised through engagement and the organization's response to the engagement outcomes. Organizations should integrate reporting on stakeholder engagement with other appropriate forms of public organizational reporting, such as sustainability reports, annual or financial reports, website reports and social media reports (AccountAbility, 2015).

4.3 Stakeholder engagement for sustainability reporting

4.3.1 Stakeholders' role in sustainability reports

How sustainability reports address the stakeholders' importance and their role in and for sustainability reports are two different but intertwined issues. As shown in the previous section, the stakeholder literature argues that stakeholders who are important, primary (Clarkson, 1995; Freeman, 1984), or salient in terms of their power, legitimacy and urgency as perceived by managers (Mitchell et al., 1997)

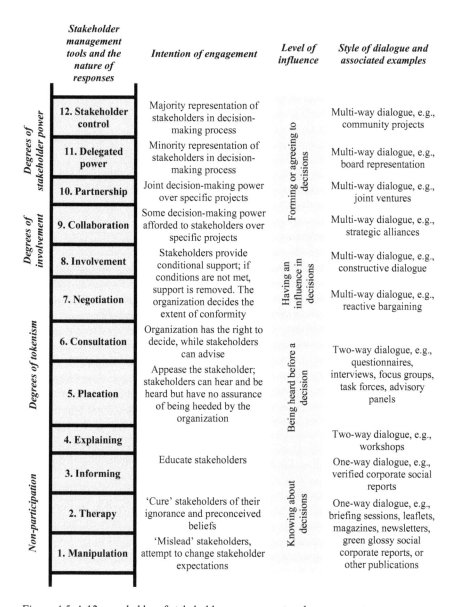

Stakeholder management tools and the nature of responses	Intention of engagement	Level of influence	Style of dialogue and associated examples
12. Stakeholder control	Majority representation of stakeholders in decision-making process	Forming or agreeing to decisions	Multi-way dialogue, e.g., community projects
11. Delegated power	Minority representation of stakeholders in decision-making process		Multi-way dialogue, e.g., board representation
10. Partnership	Joint decision-making power over specific projects		Multi-way dialogue, e.g., joint ventures
9. Collaboration	Some decision-making power afforded to stakeholders over specific projects		Multi-way dialogue, e.g., strategic alliances
8. Involvement	Stakeholders provide conditional support; if conditions are not met, support is removed. The organization decides the extent of conformity	Having an influence in decisions	Multi-way dialogue, e.g., constructive dialogue
7. Negotiation			Multi-way dialogue, e.g., reactive bargaining
6. Consultation	Organization has the right to decide, while stakeholders can advise	Being heard before a decision	Two-way dialogue, e.g., questionnaires, interviews, focus groups, task forces, advisory panels
5. Placation	Appease the stakeholder; stakeholders can hear and be heard but have no assurance of being heeded by the organization		
4. Explaining			Two-way dialogue, e.g., workshops
3. Informing	Educate stakeholders	Knowing about decisions	One-way dialogue, e.g., verified corporate social reports
2. Therapy	'Cure' stakeholders of their ignorance and preconceived beliefs		One-way dialogue, e.g., briefing sessions, leaflets, magazines, newsletters, green glossy social corporate reports, or other publications
1. Manipulation	'Mislead' stakeholders, attempt to change stakeholder expectations		

Degrees of stakeholder power — *Degrees of involvement* — *Degrees of tokenism* — *Non-participation*

Figure 4.5 A 12-rung ladder of stakeholder management and engagement
Source: Friedman and Miles (2006).

influence organizational strategies (Sharma & Henriques, 2005). Stakeholder influences can be direct or indirect, depending on the resource dependence (Pfeffer & Salancik, 1978) between the focal firm and the stakeholder (Frooman, 1999) or based on the focal firm's position in the stakeholder network (Rowley,

1997; Sharma & Henriques, 2005). Stakeholders who do not control resources critical to the focal firm's operations or who do not have the attributes of saliency (Mitchell et al., 1997) may be able to influence the focal firm only indirectly via other stakeholders (Frooman, 1999; Rowley, 1997; Sharma & Henriques, 2005). Several stakeholders who were once considered to be secondary by managers, such as local communities, NGOs and international regimes, are currently more salient in assessments of the social and ecological impacts of a business (Sharma & Henriques, 2005).

Furthermore, stakeholder engagement has been of paramount importance in the evolution of corporate reporting in the sense that systematic engagement with key stakeholders has enabled corporations to question, and then challenge, a number of factors that may have been taken for granted previously (Busco, Frigo, Quattrone, & Riccaboni, 2014). Moreover, in the context of sustainability reporting, the principles of relevance and materiality indicate that stakeholder engagement will help determine what information and data should be included in a report (Gray, 2000). In fact, all the major international standards and guidelines for SR require stakeholder engagement to obtain a complete and useful document for the intended users (AccountAbility, 2008a; Global Reporting Initiative, 2013a, 2013b; Manetti, 2011). Beyond giving a general framework of corporation activities as planned and carried out by managers, a sustainability report should communicate information that is truly useful for stakeholders (Global Reporting Initiative, 2013a, 2013b; Manetti, 2011).

In recent decades, much research at both national and international levels has collected empirical evidence of unprecedented levels of stakeholder dialogue in SR, but it has questioned the sincerity of these practices and their impact on sustainability reports (Downey, 2002; Manetti, 2011; Owen, Swift, & Hunt, 2001; UNEP, 1998). Engagement and dialogue with stakeholders are increasingly recognized as crucial elements of preparing a SR, although there is a shortage of evidence in social and environmental reports that such engagement and dialogue actually occurs (ACCA, 2005) and produces relevant outcomes.

Notwithstanding the democratizing potential of corporate social reporting standards, as claimed by the Global Reporting Initiative (GRI) and AccountAbility, for example, severe reservations have been expressed in the academic accounting literature regarding the real degree of the participatory role played by stakeholders in the process (Cooper & Owen, 2007). The literature has suggested that the prevailing stakeholder engagement practices have little to do with extending accountability and result only in exercises in stakeholder management and corporate spin (Cooper & Owen, 2007; O'Dwyer & Owen, 2005; Owen et al., 2001). In particular, this argument led some authors to claim that SR has often been used by corporations as a legitimating tool to change stakeholders' expectations (Campbell, 2003; Swift, 2001) even though it has often been found ineffective (O'Dwyer, 2002).

For example, Manetti (2011) studies the quality of stakeholder engagement in the process of social and sustainability reporting, including considering the dual process that should, in theory, characterize relations between corporations and stakeholders. The author noted an opportunistic and strategic approach to stakeholder theory, as management can believe it is essential to involve stake-holders in order to reach the social consensus necessary for economic success in the long term while also failing to acknowledge stakeholders' legitimate interests. Therefore, we can conclude that in practice to date, sustainability reporting can use stakeholder engagement both as a legitimization device or as a tool to effec-tively manage stakeholders' expectations.

Manetti (2011) shares the application of Arnstein's ladder of citizen participa-tion (introduced in Section 4.2.4) to sustainability reports with Cummings (2001), who notes that for her sample of 13 British or multinational companies, man-agers reported that approaches to stakeholder dialogue are mixed and matched depending on the stakeholder groups concerned, their physical location and the relevant issue at hand. Cummings conducts her research using semi-structured interviews with representatives of the corporations included in the sample. The use of structured techniques to monitor the opinions and expectations of company stakeholders constitutes levels 3 and 4 of Arnstein's ladder; when panels or small groups of stakeholder representatives are nominated (e.g., in focus groups, round tables, community forums, etc.) and engage in dialogue with management, levels 5 and 6 of the ladder are reached; and when consultation techniques, such as tel-ephone interviews, one-to-one conversations and dedicated hotlines, are applied, the company can be ranked between levels 4 and 6 (Manetti, 2011).

> The author points out that, in the vast majority of cases in the companies studied, SE is limited to levels 1–5 on the Arnstein's Ladder. Her research identified only one case of partnership (level 6) using bi-directional commu-nication and no companies at all on levels 7 and 8. Cumming emphasis that the higher levels of the Ladder cannot be found in the sample, owing to the problem of balancing different expectations among stakeholders. In particu-lar, to reach the eighth level, companies would have to redefine their statutes, sometimes violating the principal that is commonly found in company law of safe- guarding, as a priority, the investors and shareholders. As far as the sev-enth level is concerned, only companies particularly inclined towards good social responsibility practices could envisage delegating decision-making to stakeholders.
>
> (Manetti, 2011)

Clarkson (1995) argues that transferring corporate social responsibilities to busi-ness objectives is best undertaken using a stakeholder perspective – more spe-cifically, by transferring intangible social and environmental issues into tangible stakeholder interests (Sharma & Henriques, 2005). However, companies are cur-rently far more likely to consult stakeholders in an opportunistic manner in order to build consensus for what they are already doing rather than genuinely engaging stakeholders in a two-way conversation that involves them in meaningful decision making about what constitutes performance and how it should be assessed (Crane & Matten, 2016; Manetti, 2011). As O'Dwyer and Owen (2005) note, many aca-demic researchers have been critical of key features of the emerging practice of sustainability reporting, given its tendencies toward managerialism at the expense of accountability and transparency to stakeholder groups (Crane & Matten, 2016). Analyses suggest that while improvements are evident, significant deficiencies in many core quality indicators persist (Crane & Matten, 2016; Manetti, 2011; O'Dwyer & Owen, 2005). As shown in the second and third chapters of this volume, it is clear that to date, despite decades of attention to corporate responsibility and sustainability reporting, companies still have a long way to go to improve their process of assessing and reporting their economic, social and environmental impacts on society (Crane & Matten, 2016). Of course, such assessments are extremely challenging.

Stakeholder theory can be used to transform social and environmental responsibilities not only into business objectives but also into clear objectives and indicators on which organizations need to report. In other words, dialogue with stakeholder groups is essential for sustainability reporting because it enables organizations to create truly material and relevant reports about the true creation of value for all stakeholders. As an example, Mark Bristow, the chief executive of Randgold Resources, claims in the 2015 sustainability report of the company that "It [has been] 20 years since Randgold was first incorporated as an Africa-focused gold mining and exploration business with a vision to create long-term value for all stakeholders".[5] The company also claims:

> we have a wide range of policies, processes and people in place to ensure we identify and manage the risks and opportunities that sustainability factors present to our business, and to ensure we engage effectively and transparently with all our stakeholders.[6]

Similar claims on the centrality of relationships with stakeholders also appear with increasing frequency on corporations' websites:

> Effective engagement is a prerequisite to our establishing mutually-beneficial relationships with stakeholders. These relationships, we believe, are essential in maintaining our social licence to operate. AngloGold Ashanti has a wide range of stakeholders. Relationships with communities, government and regulators, employees, both individually and through affiliations such as organised labour, community-based organisations (CBOs) and non-governmental organisations (NGOs) are some of the most critical to our business. Engagement takes place at a group level with stakeholders whose interests require them to have an overview of the business as a whole, such as investors, employees, organised labour unions, the media, regulatory authorities and certain government and civic organisation representatives . . . Engagement begins from early stages of exploration and continues through to closure.[7]

Chapter 5 will focus on how sustainability reports address the topic of stakeholder engagement and the role of stakeholder engagement in assessing materiality, but these examples, which are currently very commonly found in large enterprises' reports, provide initial insights on what corporations publicly claim about their relationships with stakeholders.

Thus, many companies underline the importance of partnerships and interactions with their stakeholders. In interacting with their stakeholders, companies can use several instruments. Most frequently mentioned in reports are staff surveys and community panels/forums; moreover, to reflect different stakeholder views, it has become common to include stakeholder statements in reports (Kolk, 2004).

> Some companies give detailed information about opinion polls and surveys among their employees. Employee perceptions on a variety of issues, including safety, health and environment, ethics, accountability, diversity, personal respect and open, two-way communications, are presented . . . The stakeholder statements included in the reports can originate from internal and external stakeholders.
>
> (Kolk, 2004)

As argued by Kolk (2004) in a study of worldwide trends in sustainability practices in recent decades, certain companies provide information about the circulation of reports and the feedback they have received in their public communication efforts. "In some cases, readers' opinions on the previous report are presented on a separate 'environmental communication sheet' enclosed in the report. On the back of the form, stakeholders are invited to give their view on the current report" (Kolk, 2004).

Influential standards and guidelines that increasingly inform cutting edge reporting practices, notably the GRI and AccountAbility's AA1000, unequivocally suggest that the "business case" for CSR can enable a gradual empowerment of stakeholders (Cooper & Owen, 2007). The former, for example, notes that:

> a primary goal of reporting is to contribute to an ongoing stakeholder dialogue. Reports alone provide little value if they fail to inform stakeholders or support a dialogue that influences the decisions and behaviour of both the reporting organisation and its stakeholders.
>
> (Global Reporting Initiative, 2002)

As argued by AccountAbility (2015), a quality reporting process is governed by the principle of accountability, which is itself underpinned by the principle of inclusivity: inclusivity concerns the reflection, at all stages of the reporting process over time, of the aspirations and needs of all stakeholder groups. Stakeholder views are obtained through an engagement process that allows stakeholders to express themselves without fear or restriction (AccountAbility, 2015). The principle of inclusivity embraces accountability to all stakeholder groups.

4.3.2 Achieving materiality in sustainability reporting through stakeholder engagement standards

AccountAbility provides a specific standard for supporting high-quality stakeholder engagement. The AA1000 Stakeholder Engagement Standard (AA1000SES) is a generally applicable framework for assessing, designing, implementing and communicating stakeholder engagement (AccountAbility, 2015). This standard builds on and is consistent with the AA1000 AccountAbility Principles Standard (AccountAbility, 2008a) and the principle of inclusivity, materiality and responsiveness.

Stakeholder engagement is a tool that organizations can use to achieve inclusiveness. In AA1000SES, stakeholder engagement is defined as:

> the process used by an organisation to engage relevant stakeholders for a clear purpose to achieve agreed outcomes. It is now also recognised as a fundamental accountability mechanism, since it obliges an organisation to involve stakeholders in identifying, understanding and responding to sustainability issues and concerns, and to report, explain and answer to stakeholders for decisions, actions and performance.
>
> Stakeholder engagement must have a purpose. It is essential to first think about why the organisation is engaging and what needs to be achieved. No stakeholder engagement should be initiated without defining a purpose. There are two broad categories of purpose: strategy and operations. That is, stakeholder engagement takes place to develop or improve strategy or to help identify and address operational issues. Building trust-based relationships is inherent to both strategic and operational stakeholder engagement. The purpose may be associated with ongoing activities, such as aiming to ensure that the organisation has a good understanding of stakeholder views or to foster positive stakeholder relationships, or it may be associated with a specific project or need, such as to inform a materiality-determination process.
>
> (AccountAbility, 2015)

More concisely, stakeholder engagement is not only a tool for discussing material issues with stakeholders but also a process in which the interaction with stakeholders is crucial to defining what is material from a participatory perspective. AA1000SES also provides recommendations for how to report on the stakeholder engagement process and how this process can benefit annual or integrated sustainability reports since "quality stakeholder engagement can help to determine material issues for sustainability management and reporting".

AccountAbility (2008b) also issued an Assurance Standard, which further underlines the importance of stakeholder accountability credentials in the reporting process for promulgating the principles of materiality, completeness and responsiveness (Cooper & Owen, 2007). The materiality principle requires the assurance[8] provider to state whether the reporting organization has included in its report information stakeholders need to be able to make informed judgments, decisions and actions, while the completeness principle calls for an evaluation of the extent to which the organization can identify and understand material aspects of performance (Cooper & Owen, 2007). Moreover, the responsiveness principle requires that the assurance provider evaluate whether the reporting organization has responded to stakeholder concerns, policies and relevant standards and adequately communicated these responses in its report (AccountAbility, 2008b; Cooper & Owen, 2007).

Additionally, the International Integrated Reporting Council (IIRC) (2013) provides guidance on the materiality determination process and on the way to disclose material aspects in integrated reporting. In particular, the Technical Task Force of the IIRC established a Technical Collaboration Group (TCG) to prepare the Materiality Background Paper for <IR> (IIRC, 2013). The process of materiality determination is similar to that provided by GRI, which is described later in this section. Stakeholder engagement plays a crucial role, and Appendix 1 of the Materiality Background Paper for <IR> recommends referring to the previously described AA1000 Stakeholder Engagement Standard for specific guidance and states that AA1000SES "provides a principles-based, open-source framework for quality stakeholder engagement and . . . it can be used as a 'stand-alone' standard, or as a mechanism to achieve the stakeholder requirements of other standards".

GRI-G4, the new version of the guidelines provided by the GRI (see Chapter 3) also has a clear focus on materiality.

> G4 has an increased emphasis on the need for organizations to focus the reporting process and final report on those topics that are material to their business and their key stakeholders. This "materiality" focus will make reports more relevant, more credible and more user-friendly. This will, in turn, enable organizations to better inform markets and society on sustainability matters.
>
> (Global Reporting Initiative, 2013b)

In its guidelines, the GRI provides guidance on how to perform a materiality assessment with stakeholders. At the core of preparing a sustainability report is a focus on the process of identifying material aspects based, among other factors, on the materiality principle; material aspects are those that reflect the organization's significant economic, environmental and social impacts or substantively influence stakeholders' assessments and decisions (Global Reporting Initiative, 2013b). This approach is consistent with the adoption of four principles that describe the process to be applied to identify the content that a report should cover by considering the organization's activities, impacts and its stakeholders' substantive expectations and interests (Global Reporting Initiative, 2013b):

1 Stakeholder inclusiveness: the organization should identify all its stakeholders and explain how it has responded to their reasonable expectations and interests.
2 Sustainability context: the report should present the organization's performance in the wider context of sustainability (see Section 2.3 of this volume).
3 Materiality: the report should cover aspects that reflect the organization's significant economic, environmental and social impacts or substantively influence stakeholders' assessments and decisions.
4 Completeness: the report should include coverage of material aspects and their boundaries to a sufficient degree to reflect all the significant economic, environmental and social impacts and to enable stakeholders to assess the organization's performance in the reporting period.

All these principles, which inspire the entire procedure of elaborating a report in compliance with GRI guidelines, are extremely relevant for the purpose of this volume. Henceforth, Table 4.2 describes the points of GRI-G4 guidelines that directly refer to stakeholder engagement. In particular, these standard disclosures provide an overview of the organization's stakeholder engagement during the reporting period (however, these standard disclosures do not need to be limited to engagement that was conducted to prepare the report) (Global Reporting Initiative, 2013b).

Moreover, Table 4.3 outlines the process to be followed to define the content of reports in accordance with the GRI-G4 guidelines in light of materiality and stakeholder inclusiveness principles.

Table 4.2 Aspects of the GRI G4 guidelines directly concerned with stakeholder engagement

Aspect	Instructions	Further guidance from the GRI Implementation Manual
G4-24	Provide a list of stakeholder groups engaged by the organization.	Examples of stakeholder groups are civil society; customers; employees, other workers, and their trade unions; local communities; shareholders and providers of capital; suppliers.
G4-25	Report the basis for the identification and selection of stakeholders with whom to engage.	The report should describe the organization's process for defining its stakeholder groups and for determining the groups with which to engage and not to engage.
G4-26	Report the organization's approach to stakeholder engagement, including the frequency of engagement by type and by stakeholder group and an indication of whether any of the engagement was undertaken specifically as part of the report preparation process.	This step may include surveys (such as supplier surveys), focus groups, community panels, corporate advisory panels, written communication, management or union structures, and other vehicles.
G4-27	Report key topics and concerns that have been raised through stakeholder engagement and how the organization has responded to those key topics and concerns, including through its reporting. Report the stakeholder groups that raised each of the key topics and concerns.	n.a.

Source: Global Reporting Initiative (2013a, 2013b).

Table 4.3 Process for defining reporting content using the principles of materiality and stakeholder inclusiveness in the GRI G4 guidelines

Step 1 - Identification	*Step 3 - Validation*
• Consider the GRI Aspects list and other topics of interest • Apply the Principles of Sustainability Context and Stakeholder Inclusiveness: Identify the Aspects and other relevant topics based on the relevant economic, environmental and social impacts related to all the organization's activities, products, services, and relationships or on the influence they have on stakeholders' assessments and decisions • Identify where the impacts occur: within or outside the organization • List the Aspects and other topics considered relevant and their Boundaries	• Apply the Principles of Completeness and Stakeholder Inclusiveness: Assess the list of material Aspects against Scope, Aspect Boundaries and Time to ensure that the report provides a reasonable and balanced representation of the organization's significant economic, environmental and social impacts and enables stakeholders to assess the organization's performance • Approve the list of identified material Aspects with the relevant internal senior decision maker • Prepare systems and processes to gather the information needed to be disclosed • Translate the identified material Aspects into Standard Disclosures – DMA and Indicators – to report against • Determine what information is available and explain that for which it still needs to establish management approaches and measurements systems
Step 2 - Prioritization	*Step 4 - Review*

• Apply the Principles of Materiality and Stakeholder Inclusiveness: Assess each Aspect and other topic considered relevant for
 	
  ○ the significance of the organization's economic, environmental and social impacts
  ○ the influence on stakeholder assessments and decisions
 	
• Identify the material Aspects by combining the assessments
• Define and document thresholds (criteria) that render an Aspect material
• For each material Aspect identified, decide the level of coverage, the amount of data and narrative explanation to be disclosed
• List the material Aspects to be included in the report, along with their Boundaries and the level of coverage
	• Apply the Principles of Sustainability Context and Stakeholder Engagement: Review the Aspects that were material in the previous reporting period
	• Use the result of the review to inform Step 1 (Identification) for the next reporting cycle

Source: Global Reporting Initiative (2013a, 2013b).

As Table 4.3 shows in detail, to begin the process of defining a report's content, the organization is required to identify an initial set of material topics (or "Aspects" in GRI guidelines) (Step 1). The next step in defining the content to be included in a report refers to the prioritization of relevant topics from Step 1 in order to identify those that are material and therefore deserve to be reported (Step 2). This step is followed by the validation phase, where the principles of completeness and stakeholder inclusiveness are used to finalize the content of the report together with stakeholders (Step 3). The main outcome of these first three steps is a list of material topics. Finally, after the report is published, it is important that the organization undertakes a review of its report (Step 4). This review can occur as the organization prepares for the next reporting cycle (Global Reporting Initiative, 2013a).

All these steps should implement the principle of stakeholder inclusiveness. In other words, stakeholder engagement is considered a decisive component of the process of identifying material topics and material impacts. Both in the GRI and AccountAbility guidelines, the aspects that the organization, in response to its stakeholders' expectations and interests, deems to be material drive sustainability reporting and its content (AccountAbility, 2008a, 2015; Global Reporting Initiative, 2013b). In conclusion, genuine, quality stakeholder engagement represents a crucial step for organizations aiming to disclose truly relevant sustainability reports.

4.3.3 Dialogic accounting and stakeholder engagement

In the last decade, many scholars have collected empirical evidence regarding unprecedented levels of stakeholder dialogue in social, environmental or sustainability reporting while also questioning the sincerity and the impact of these practices on sustainability reports (ACCA, 2005; Bellucci & Manetti, 2017; Downey, 2002; Manetti & Bellucci, 2016; UNEP, 1998). According to sustainability reporting guidelines 4.0 from the GRI:

> The organization should identify its stakeholders, and explain how it has responded to their reasonable expectations and interests. Stakeholders can include those who are invested in the organization as well as those who have other relationships to the organization. The reasonable expectations and interests of stakeholders are a key reference point for many decisions in the preparation of the report.
>
> (Global Reporting Initiative, 2013b)

Again:

> Organizations are faced with a wide range of topics on which they could report. Relevant topics are those that may reasonably be considered important for reflecting the organization's economic, environmental and social impacts, or influencing the decisions of stakeholders, and, therefore, potentially merit inclusion in the report.
>
> (Global Reporting Initiative, 2013b)

Not only is stakeholder engagement clearly at the very core of SR, but SR itself has the characteristics of a dialogic process that examines accountability relationships between stakeholders and organizations (Gray, 1997). A dialogic system, in fact, extends beyond notions of communication and refers to iterative mutual learning processes that are designed to promote transformative action. According to Brown (2009), dialogic processes inform accountability relationships between stakeholders and organizations (Gray, 1997). For this reason, previous studies on SR focused on enhancing the levels of democratic interaction (Boyce, 2000; Brown, 2009; Dey, 2003; Gray, 1997; Gray & Bebbington, 2001; Medawar, 1976; Morgan, 1988) and, most recently, on attempts to create new dialogic accounting practices and technologies that can promote stakeholder engagement and interaction at every level (Bebbington, Brown, & Frame, 2007; Bebbington, Brown, Frame, & Thomson, 2007; Bellucci & Manetti, 2017; Frame & Brown, 2008; Thomson & Bebbington, 2005). Thomson and Bebbington (2005) claim that stakeholder engagement is of utmost importance in SR, arguing that it should address conflicts among stakeholders, recognize diverse viewpoints and explicitly manage power dynamics. They maintain that monologic accounting should be replaced by an accounting approach that can consider and balance the community's different perspectives and expectations (Gray, 1997).

Critical studies have problematized the analysis of engagement, the participatory and governance processes that draw on deliberative-agonistic democracy principles and the authentic engagement process (Brown, 2009; Brown & Dillard, 2015; Passetti, Bianchi, Battaglia, & Frey, 2017). They have revealed the importance of democratizing the process of exchange and of reducing the power asymmetry among agents, stressing the importance of openly involving stakeholders in organizational decision making (Bebbington, Brown, Frame, et al., 2007; Brown & Dillard, 2014; Passetti et al.; Vinnari & Dillard, 2016). According to Brown (2009), Brown and Dillard (2013) and Dillard and Yuthas (2013), many CSR tools over the years have been proposed as a means to promote democratic interaction (Bebbington & Gray, 2001; Boyce, 2000; Dey, 2003; Gray, 1997; Medawar, 1976; Morgan, 1988). In the past decade, these have included attempts to promote explicitly dialogic accounting technologies and forms of engagement (Bebbington, Brown, & Frame, 2007; Bebbington, Brown, Frame, et al., 2007; Bellucci & Manetti, 2017; Frame & Brown, 2008; Thomson & Bebbington, 2005) that use online social media and social networks. These new tools of dialogic communication have created new possibilities for organizations to connect with their stakeholders by allowing them to receive real-time feedback about organizational announcements and engage in conversations. Although one-way communication is still the most common form of messaging strategy adopted by organizations on social media (Waters & Jamal, 2011; Xifra & Grau, 2010), attempts to develop interactions among corporations and users are becoming increasingly popular (Rybalko & Seltzer, 2010).

In a dialogic accounting framework, the outcomes of stakeholder engagement processes generally include:

1   a deliberative, general consensus (Laughlin, 1987, 2007) based on Habermas' "ideal speech situation" — communication among stakeholders in undistorted conditions (Habermas, 1984, 1987, 1991) that can be built in a "public sphere", "a discursive arena that is home to citizen debate, deliberation, agreement and action" (Dahlberg, 2005; Villa, 1992) regarding what information and data should be disclosed in the report. When applied to the corporate arena, the result of "an open, honest and unbiased ideal speech situation debate among all stakeholders should therefore lead to the acceptance by all stakeholders of a democratically determined consensus view of corporate responsibilities" (Unerman & Bennett, 2004, p. 691);

2   a collection of divergent socio-political views in an agonistic perspective, highlighting the unavoidable values and assumptions associated with different accounts and recognizing the need for multiple engagements between different actors across various political spaces (Brown & Dillard, 2013; Gray & Milne, 2002; O'Dwyer, 2005). This perspective involves an understanding of SR that is much broader than formal organization-centric reports and recognizes the need for multiple engagements between different actors across various political spaces (Gray & Milne, 2002; O'Dwyer, 2005) based on an agonistic model of democratic participation (Brown, 2009; Brown & Dillard, 2013; Dillard & Brown, 2012; Dillard & Roslender, 2011).

In the democratic deliberative approach, stakeholder engagement is necessary for defining the general consensus among diverse stakeholders or within a specific category. Proponents of the agonistic approach, meanwhile, suggest that stakeholder engagement helps synthesize the different points of view among various interest groups.

4.4 A review of stakeholder engagement tools

4.4.1 The nature of stakeholder engagement

Stakeholder analyses have long had important practical implications for many disciplines. As reported by Bryson (2004):

> Barbara Tuchman in her sobering history *The March of Folly: From Troy to Vietnam* (2009) recounts a series of disastrous misadventures that followed in the footsteps of ignoring the interests of, and information held by, key stakeholders. She concludes "Three outstanding attitudes – obliviousness to the growing disaffection of constituents, primacy of self-aggrandizement, and the illusion of invulnerable status – are persistent aspects of folly". The story continues with Paul Nutt's *Why Decisions Fail* (2002), a careful analysis of 400 strategic decisions. Nutt finds that half of the decisions "failed" – that is they were not implemented, only partially implemented or otherwise produced poor results – in large part because decision makers failed to attend to interests and information held by key stakeholders. Other quantitative and

qualitative studies report broadly similar findings with respect to the importance of paying attention to stakeholders (Bryson & Bromiley, 1993; Bryson, Bromiley, & Jung, 1990; Burby, 2003; Margerum, 2002).

In other words, the failure to attend to the information and concerns of stakeholders is clearly a kind of flaw in thinking or action that too often and too predictably leads to poor performance, outright failure or even disaster (Bryson, 2004).

While Chapters 2 and 3 provided a literature review on the extended responsibilities of corporations and the issues underlying the topic of sustainability, and the first part of Chapter 4 introduced a theoretical framework based mainly on stakeholder theory, we now focus on what stakeholder engagement means in practice. For this purpose, we will introduce here a general and not exhaustive description of a set of tools that can support the second phase (see Section 4.2.3 of this volume) of the stakeholder engagement process. A study of companies' reported utilization of these tools in engaging their stakeholders is part of the empirical analysis illustrated in the last chapter of this volume.

SE is now accepted as integral to an organization's sustainability and success (AccountAbility, 2015). As stated previously in the text, the following is one possible definition of stakeholder engagement:

> the process used by an organisation to engage relevant stakeholders for a clear purpose to achieve agreed outcomes. It is now also recognised as a fundamental accountability mechanism, since it obliges an organisation to involve stakeholders in identifying, understanding and responding to sustainability issues and concerns, and to report, explain and answer to stakeholders for decisions, actions and performance.
>
> (AccountAbility, 2015)

It is important, however, to understand the difference between good-quality and poor-quality engagement (Manetti, 2011). High-quality stakeholder engagement can help give those who have a right to be heard the opportunity to be considered in decision-making processes and, moreover, help illustrate material issues for sustainability management and reporting.

> Stakeholder engagement takes place to develop or improve strategy or to help identify and address operational issues. Building trust-based relationships is inherent to both strategic and operational stakeholder engagement. The purpose may be associated with ongoing activities, such as aiming to ensure that the organisation has a good understanding of stakeholder views or to foster positive stakeholder relationships, or it may be associated with a specific project or need, such as to inform a materiality-determination process.
>
> (AccountAbility, 2015)

The empirical analysis illustrated in Chapter 5 will provide insights on these two functions (definition of strategies and determination of materiality), contributing to an understanding of the reported role of stakeholder engagement for companies operating in the mining sector.

Another question arises at this point: what tools can companies use to support stakeholder engagement and, in particular, these two functions? In their annual reports, many companies currently underline the importance of partnerships and interaction with their stakeholders (Kolk, 2004; Moratis & Brandt, 2017). Companies can use several instruments to interact with their stakeholders. The instruments organizations can use to involve stakeholders also depend on the level and type of involvement they aim to achieve.

> In determining level(s) of engagement, the owners of the engagement define the nature of the relationship they have or aim to develop with their stakeholders. Engagement may take place at more than one level. The owners of the engagement may choose to engage with the stakeholders in one segment of its stakeholder map at one level and with stakeholders in another segment of the stakeholder map at another. The level of engagement may also change over time as relationships deepen and mature. The method of engagement should be selected to best meet the needs, capacity and expectations of the relevant stakeholders. More than one method may be selected for any given engagement. Different methods may be used concurrently or sequentially.
>
> (AccountAbility, 2015)

Consequently, we opted to organize this review of tools of stakeholder engagement in three parts. Every part is based on the level of engagement the organization can typically achieve through the different methodologies. This classification builds on the models of stakeholder engagement quality developed by Arnstein (1969)[9] and Friedman and Miles (2006). Our three-level model, which is supported by AccountAbility (2015), will be implemented in the empirical analysis illustrated in the next chapter; the analysis will provide insights on the most recurrent levels of engagement reported in sustainability reports.

Table 4.4 provides, a list of preferred methods for each level of stakeholder engagement. The first level is represented by simple "information", with one-way dialogue and no real opportunity for stakeholder engagement to influence decisions. The second level is "consultation", including monitoring and information gathering in a truly two-way perspective. Third, "empowerment" requires a proactive stakeholder role, which can occur through alliances and the appointment of representatives in the governing bodies.

Although presenting every aspect of each method is beyond the scope of our volume, the following sections will highlight the key features of the most important approaches to each desired level of engagement.

4.4.2 Information

The promise of this level is, "We will keep you informed" (Bryson, 2004). Standard tools such as websites, bulletins, newsletters and presentations of reports are often used by organizations to inform their stakeholders. If a company aims

Table 4.4 Levels of stakeholder engagement and supporting methodologies

Level	Examples of preferred methods of engagement
1) Information Simple information on stakeholders gathered by the organization: one-way dialogue and no opportunity for stakeholder engagement to influence decisions (*1st-4th rungs in Friedman and Miles's model*)	• Media • Websites • Social media • Reports • Bulletins and newsletters • Speeches and presentations
2) Consultation Consultation of stakeholders by the organization: information gathering and basic involvement (*5th-6th rungs in Friedman and Miles's model*)	• Focus groups and workshops • Surveys • Interviews • Social media • Field visits and public meetings with Q&AS
3) Empowerment Proactive role of stakeholders, decision-making alliances and appointment of representatives in the governing bodies (*7th-12th rungs in Friedman and Miles's model*)	• Joint ventures, partnerships and collaborations • Advisory panels • Specific online interaction tools • Multi-stakeholder forums • Social media

only to inform stakeholders without creating a truly two-way interaction, the company remains at the first level of stakeholder engagement.

Corporations may release information to stakeholders to increase their openness and transparency (Friedman & Miles, 2006). However, one could argue whether this level, which does not encompass real forms of interaction, can be considered a type of stakeholder engagement. If we look at the definition given in the previous section, the key feature of stakeholder engagement is its purpose. In light of this definition, a company aiming to engage stakeholders in order to keep them informed still represents a legitimate form of stakeholder engagement. At the same time, we believe that many doubts emerge when we analyze the potential of stakeholder engagement to create an interaction directed toward the definition of strategies and to a materiality assessment; this potential is dispersed if an organization aims only to inform their stakeholders without collecting their opinions or ideas.

At this level, we commonly find tools that do not encompass the possibility or opportunity for a reply, such as bulletins, newsletters and presentations of reports, which are designed to communicate in a mono-directional way. Instead of supporting an accounting approach that can consider and balance the community's various perspectives and expectations, these tools support a monologic (Gray, 1997) form of accounting. These tools are useful if a company is willing to disclose a certain message but is not interested in gathering any comments or opinions about this message or its general strategies.

At the same time, certain tools can be used in both a mono-directional way and a multi-directional way. In these cases, the company's orientation when pursuing a particular level of engagement or another matters. A clear example of a tool featuring this binary orientation is represented by a company's official website. A website can simply represent a showcase for the company's products and services or provide a platform through which stakeholders can comment, interact and submit their opinions. In fact, among the instruments and techniques for stakeholder engagement, a leading and crucial role is played by online interaction, which includes the organization's social media, social networks, blogs, websites and other Internet-enabled technologies (Kent, Taylor, & White, 2003; Park & Reber, 2008; Rybalko & Seltzer, 2010; Unerman & Bennett, 2004). Once again, however, the owner of the stakeholder engagement process determines whether these tools will be used for consulting (or even empowering) stakeholders or just for informing them. As shown later in the text, websites and social media increasingly represent powerful and innovative tools for supporting stakeholder engagement, but the organization can determine if and how to exploit these tools' potential to create a conversation with stakeholders.

4.4.3 Consultation

This level promises, "We will work with you to ensure your concerns are considered and reflected in the alternatives considered, and provide feedback on how your input influenced the decision" (Bryson, 2004). Stakeholder engagement is considered the process of effectively eliciting stakeholder views on their relationship with the organization (Friedman & Miles, 2006). Surveys, focus groups, interviews and social media are frequently mentioned in reports as methods for supporting this level of stakeholder engagement. These tools are usually used to gain more than simple information on stakeholders. Stakeholders are usually asked to give their opinions on the materiality of issues in a way that can influence the decision-making process.

Each of the tools featured in this level has its peculiarities. In the frame of stakeholder engagement, surveys are built on a list of questions (which can be open or closed) aimed at gathering specific information from a particular group of stakeholders. Surveys may be conducted by mail, phone, web and face-to-face in the field and are often used to assess views, opinions and feelings; they can be specific or have more widespread objectives. Surveys are typical of this level, as they represent an important tool to collect information through interactions with stakeholders. Stakeholder surveys can lead to a noteworthy level of engagement because the organization uses surveys to actively solicit stakeholder feedback (Friedman & Miles, 2006). Arguably, organizations would not waste precious resources in conducting such activities if the results were not to be actively incorporated into future strategic actions; however, the organization has the right to decide how it uses the feedback (Friedman & Miles, 2006).

Moreover, once the survey structure has been prepared and the sample of respondents defined, surveys are a convenient way to collect information from a large number of respondents and to build a relevant database for subsequent analysis. Consequently, many companies use stakeholder surveys to assess stakeholder needs and expectations (Jackson & Bundgard, 2002). This assessment can be conducted in-house or commissioned to an independent research agency. Surveys can solicit views that would otherwise go unheard and are considered more democratic than other engagement methods (Friedman & Miles, 2006; MacRae Jr & Whittington, 1997).

Corporations have historically used stakeholder surveys for employee and consumer research (Friedman & Miles, 2006). Some companies provide detailed information from opinion polls and surveys conducted with their employees (Kolk, 2004). Surveys can collect information on employees' perceptions of a variety of issues, including safety, health and the environment, ethics, accountability, diversity, personal respect and open, two-way communication (Kolk, 2004). Nonetheless, surveys can represent a powerful tool to consult – in the sense that organizations can collect information and opinions – with both internal and external stakeholders (e.g., consumers) and to determine – in consultation with every group of stakeholders – the issues on which the organization should report.

Interviews are another typical method to consult internal or external stakeholders. Stakeholder interviews can provide detailed information about individuals' perceptions. Interviews also allow for a two-way communication and can reduce or avoid misunderstandings (Friedman & Miles, 2006). While surveys can reach a large number of respondents with a single questionnaire, interviews are more time-consuming; nevertheless, interviews can provide a more tailored, one-on-one experience and collect more specific data. The processes of conducting the interviews, transcribing the interviews and analyzing the transcripts are all very time-consuming (Bryman & Bell, 2015). Interviews can be conducted by phone, online and face-to-face.

There are many levels to the degree of structuration that interviews can have: organizations can opt for either structured interviews with very specific questions following a previously prepared outline or less structured interviews. While the former orientation usually maximizes the reliability and validity of the measurement of key concepts, the latter can provide more insights on what the interviewee considers relevant and important (Bryman & Bell, 2015). Organizations must choose case by case the most suitable approach for each kind of stakeholder they aim to involve and the level of stakeholder engagement they aim to pursue.

Meetings, workshops and focus groups are other methods to collectively engage stakeholders. In particular, the focus group method is a form of group interview that features several participants (in addition to the moderator/facilitator) and that relies on interaction within the group and the joint construction of meaning (Bryman & Bell, 2015). In other words, the interactive aspect of data collection is stressed (Flick, 2009): the hallmark of focus groups is the explicit use of group interaction to produce data and insights that would be less accessible without group interaction (Flick, 2009; Morgan, 1988). Focus groups can be used as a stakeholder engagement method on its own or in combination with other methods – surveys, single interviews, etc. (Flick, 2009; Morgan, 1988). Focus groups emphasize questioning on a fairly tightly defined topic and contain elements of two methods: the group interview, in which several people discuss a number of topics, and the so-called focused interview, in which interviewees are selected because they are known to have been involved in a particular situation (Bryman & Bell, 2015; Merton, Fiske, & Kendall, 1956). Focus groups are usually recorded and transcribed.

Meetings, workshops and focus groups can represent a powerful tool for stakeholder engagement, calling stakeholders to discuss the materiality of certain issues or to provide their opinions or points of view on specific topics. Participant stakeholders can originate from the same groups of stakeholders (e.g., a focus group with employees) or represent a more heterogeneous group, with stakeholders originating from different categories (e.g., workshops with a participant representing each class of salient stakeholders).

As we claimed earlier in the text, we believe that social media can also represent a powerful tool for supporting stakeholder engagement and dialogic accounting. There exists a partial gap in the literature on the role of stakeholder engagement in defining the contents of sustainability reports according to the principles of materiality and relevance of information disclosed and on the specific contribution of social media and web 2.0 in creating a model of authentic dialogic accounting. In light of these considerations, Section 4.4.5 will focus on social media's innovative role in and potential for consulting and engaging stakeholders.

As a result of the consultation process and with the aim of reflecting different stakeholder views, it has become rather common to include stakeholder statements in reports (Kolk, 2004). Reports can include statements from both internal and external stakeholders (Kolk, 2004). A specific portion of the analysis described in Chapter 5 will be devoted to assessing how many reports contain statements or quotes from stakeholders.

4.4.4 Empowerment

This level promises, "We will incorporate your advice and recommendations to the maximum extent possible" (Bryson, 2004). In other words, the third level, "empowerment", involves a proactive role for stakeholders, the creation of alliances and the appointment of representatives in the governing bodies. This third level has different features with respect to others and cannot build on tools and methods of engagement only. Empowerment implies directly involving stakeholders in the decision-making process and creating partnerships and joint initiatives. Through this emancipatory process, the organization shifts from "accounting for" communities and stakeholders to "accounting by" communities and stakeholders (Lombardi, 2016).

Organizations that pursue this level of involvement usually appoint representatives of certain stakeholder groups to governing bodies. Crucially, organizations try not only to engage stakeholders to gather information or opinions but also to form productive alliances with the individuals or organizations that are considered relevant to their activity.

Strategic alliances are collaborative "marriages" between organizations and stakeholders to pursue mutually beneficial goals. Each partner brings a particular (complementary) skill or resource and through joint engagement both parties are expected to benefit. The most common alliances are between corporations and environmental groups (Murphy & Bendell, 1997) and with supply chain partners.

(Friedman & Miles, 2006)

Organizations can engage in joint ventures, social partnerships and joint committees with a range of stakeholders. Suppliers and NGOs are among the most salient classes of stakeholders for alliances because joint ventures with these parties could help improve the decision-making process by providing skills and different, proactive point of views. If stakeholders are informed of and participate in the decision-making process, they are more likely to agree with the outcome, and hence, the public's perception of the decision may increase, leading to a greater degree of public trust (Darnall & Jolley, 2004; Friedman & Miles, 2006). Consequently, stakeholder engagement could be implemented for purely political, strategic or instrumental reasons in order to manage the organization's legitimacy. As shown previously in the text, the instrumental approach attempts to identify the potential or effective connections that exist between stakeholder management and the achievement of the organization's goals and aims, including the links between better stakeholder management and profitability and the enhancement of an organization's reputation within the community. We believe a case-by-case analysis is necessary to understand the true nature of stakeholder engagement.

Organizations may join forces with competitors to lobby at the industry level, or with customers, suppliers, or an environmental group for product development. The difference between partnerships and collaborations or alliances is a matter of degree, with the former involving more substantial joint activities and taking on greater risk.

(Friedman & Miles, 2006)

This behavior can be explained in light of stakeholder theory because organizations may be willing to orient their strategies toward stakeholders' expectations for various reasons. In particular, instrumental stakeholder theory, which views the firm as a nexus of contracts (Jensen & Meckling, 1976), addresses a firm's ability to increase its competitive advantage by minimizing the costs of contracting. Jones (1995), in his discussion of instrumental stakeholder theory, argues that firms that contract with their stakeholders on the basis of mutual trust and cooperation will have a competitive advantage over firms that do not (Sundaram & Inkpen, 2004).

Bridging reduces uncertainties that arise from unpredictable demands and pressures that come from high levels of interdependences among stakeholders, by increasing the level of control each party has over the other's activities. Bridging can also increase organizational flexibility. This style of stakeholder management requires high levels of trust between parties. Social capital must be created, values and norms should be shared, and there should be agreement about rules for cooperation. Such activities can positively result in increased levels of decision-making power being transferred to the stakeholder.

(Friedman & Miles, 2006)

An organization can minimize these costs by developing trusting relationships with its various stakeholders (Berman et al., 1999). Mitchell et al. (1997) state that stakeholder theory holds the key to more effective management: if managers empower stakeholders, the organization will be more successful or more likely to be sustainable (Friedman & Miles, 2006; Sundaram & Inkpen, 2004).

Thus, if the features of the first level, "information", cast some doubt on whether a genuine form of engagement is achieved, this level, "empowerment", concerns activities that go beyond the consultation of stakeholders through surveys and interviews, among other methods, and involve stakeholders in the decision-making process in various ways. The organization is more likely to engage in multi-way discussions if the stakeholder's goals converge with – or are not excessively different from – those of the organization (Friedman & Miles, 2006). The resolution to share a part of the decisional power with one group (or more) of stakeholders may not only introduce new opportunities but also lead the organization to unavoidably expose itself. Therefore, in this level, management needs to tackle managerial issues more than methodological ones, which concern if and how certain stakeholders must be involved in the decision-making process and which are the most effective forms of partnership.

The next section will present the main results of an empirical study in which Manetti and Bellucci (2016) assess whether online interaction through social media represents an effective stakeholder engagement mechanism in order to define the content of sustainability reports.

4.4.5 Social media for stakeholder engagement

Many recent studies have shown an increasing interest in the role social media plays in stakeholder engagement (Agostino & Arnaboldi, 2015; Bellucci & Manetti, 2017; Brainard & Edlins, 2015; Inauen & Schoeneborn, 2014; Kent, 2013; Lee, Oh, & Kim, 2013; Manetti et al., 2017; Perrin, 2015; Ramanadhan, Mendez, Rao, & Viswanath, 2013). In particular, Manetti and Bellucci (2016) explore the utilization of social media (with particular reference to Facebook, Twitter, LinkedIn, YouTube, Google+ and Flickr) as instruments of stakeholder engagement in sustainability reporting in terms of identifying, dialoguing with and engaging as many of the organization's stakeholders as possible (Lovejoy, Waters, & Saxton, 2012; Swift, 2001) while also considering their opinions and expectations, even if they diverge from the organization's point of view. More specifically, Manetti and Bellucci (2016) study the role played by social media in promoting a democratic debate on CSR issues (Unerman & Bennett, 2004) in order to define the contents of social, environmental or sustainability reporting.

We believe that social media and social networks can be powerful mechanisms for reaching and keeping in touch with a large number of stakeholders, thereby guaranteeing an interactive dialogue with them at a very low cost. This Internet-based dialogue can also contribute to creating a process of authentic stakeholder engagement based on a democratic – even if not necessarily convergent – consultation of stakeholder opinions. We believe that this topic is increasingly relevant, as social media is becoming one of the main channels through which organizations promote their activities and communicate with customers, users, communities and other primary stakeholders. Moreover, from an interdisciplinary accounting research perspective, the study by Manetti and Bellucci (2016) aims to explore the link between accounting and social media since issues of accountability have become more prominent and prevalent as corporations and markets have become increasingly mediatized (Jeacle & Carter, 2014).

In the process of answering their exploratory research question, Manetti and Bellucci (2016) run a two-step analysis. First, the authors analyze a sample of 332 sustainability reports to verify the presence of references to social media (placing special emphasis on Facebook, Twitter, LinkedIn, YouTube, Google+ and Flickr) or of disclosures in the stakeholder engagement section on the use of social media. This step aims to illuminate whether the organization has effectively declared its intent to use these online tools for engaging stakeholders. Then, the authors observe and analyze the social media pages of organizations that declared in their reports the use of these tools for interacting with their stakeholders. Using both social media analytics and content analysis, this step aims to study the type of interactions that exist between the organization and its stakeholders through social media.

We believe this study by Manetti and Bellucci (2016) offers at least two significant results. First, they determine whether (and to what extent) organizations effectively use social media to engage stakeholders. Their analysis, in fact, suggests that few organizations use stakeholder engagement through social media as a way to define the content of sustainability reports. Their results show that using social media to interact with stakeholders, retrieve their opinions, and collect data for SR is not yet common among organizations that publish GRI reports. It seems that the use of social media to engage in one-way communication with users (especially customers) and to legitimize the organization's presence within society is a strong and consolidated tendency. However, the authors find a higher level of online interaction with the "community" in regard to more broadly understood CSR topics that are not specifically connected to SR policies and practices.

Second, these authors' analysis of social media pages enables an understanding of the kind of dialogue between organizations and stakeholders that is actually performed: the level of interaction (measured in terms of comments/replies, liking/starring and sharing/retweeting, depending on the social network) is generally very low, with the exception of posts on Facebook, which sometimes result in effective means of dialogue among various parties. However, using a Facebook profile to interact with the community is more often oriented toward a dialogue on CSR topics than toward the definition of SR content. In particular, Manetti and Bellucci (2016) observe several posts concerning very key topics (e.g., the use of renewable resources or the collection of resources in areas at risk of war) on which a high amount of negative feedback is produced. Accordingly, this type of interaction is more strongly oriented toward gathering divergent socio-political views from an agonistic perspective (Brown & Dillard, 2013) than toward adopting a deliberative approach to forge a democratic consensus on how to address specific CSR or SR issues and problems (Unerman & Bennett, 2004, p. 691). In these cases, we can affirm that organizations' tendency to use social media for legitimizing their presence in society (Deegan, 2006) is still strong, but the interaction that arises from initial posts on CSR topics is associated with agonist accounting. Indeed, cases in which the initial post by the organization generates a conversation that could be potentially damaging to the organization's image, as the company is criticized for its activities, for the services or products provided, or for the way in which it manages socially or environmentally sensitive issues, are common. The "tone" and the contents of the replies are unpredictable and, given the nature of social media, difficult for the organization to manage.

Facebook in particular seems to be utilized as a vehicle for synthesizing the different points of view among diverse groups of interest and for recognizing elements of difference, antagonism and divergent socio-political orientations within the online user community. As such, organizations should take these views into account. Regardless, the level of interaction between the organization and its stakeholders on these topics is not particularly high, and after an initial push toward a two-way conversation, communication assumes unidirectional tones because organizations tend not to respond to the comments or provocations of Facebook users.

Additionally, Manetti and Bellucci (2016) determine that messages posted with the aim of interacting with users are not usually targeted toward a specific category of stakeholders but rather are targeted toward the community in general. Social media are still used mainly as mono-directional channels for promoting products, services and activities rather than as platforms through which to interact with stakeholders and to gather relevant data for sustainability reporting.

In conclusion, social media can be used by corporations, public agencies, and non-profit organizations to give a voice to their stakeholders with reference to SR or to CSR topics but without necessarily providing people an effective voice in the decision-making process (Fuchs, 2009). Stakeholders can communicate their ideas, but in their everyday lives, they do not necessarily have transformative institutionalized power over organizations. As a result, the main risk of using social media to engage stakeholders in SR is to provide the illusion that stakeholders can make a difference, whereas in reality, they do not often influence policies. In contrast, the recourse to using social media for this type of involvement is building an illusory mechanism of a democratic decision-making process in SR. However, in accordance with the principle of materiality and the relevance of information disclosed (Global Reporting Initiative, 2013b; Unerman & Bennett, 2004), the different levels of interaction on different topics enable organizations to better define the main relevant topics – in addition to the content and way to communicate such topics – they need to cover in their reports, although in reality, this occurs in few cases.

In light of these considerations, we believe that Manetti and Bellucci (2016) indicate the need to determine whether online mobilization through social media induces social self-expression, information gathering and real changes of opinion among stakeholders, as it does in politics of politics (Bellucci & Manetti, 2017; Bond et al., 2012). There exists evidence that online mobilization helps to change political opinions because it is spread primarily through strong-tie networks that, while often existing offline, have also established an online presence. These findings suggest that online messages might influence a variety of offline behaviors that have implications for our understanding of the role of social media in society (Bond et al., 2012). By adopting a similar approach, contemporary scholars might consider studying how organizations plan, build and organize their online interactive networks and media in order to engage stakeholders in addressing their CSR and SR issues. Moreover, future research might examine the best features of social media for engaging stakeholders in SR and the corresponding impacts on an organization's economic, social and environmental performance. This prospective development could allow us to better understand what types of organizations are more likely to engage in a two-way conversation with stakeholders to define the content of SR.

Notes

1 In Figure 4.1, the arrows between the firm and its stakeholder constituents run in both directions. At the same time, all stakeholder relationships are depicted in the same size and shape and are equidistant from the "black box" of the firm in the center (Donaldson & Preston, 1995): this representation is a simplification, and the points at which the relevance of each group of stakeholders differs will be better analyzed in the next sections.
2 Managers are treated in various ways in the literature. Many authors regard managers as stakeholders with special access to the focal organization's resources; others treat managers as the embodiment of the focal organization's actions and responsibilities (Friedman & Miles, 2006).
3 Discretionary stakeholders are a particularly interesting group for scholars of corporate social responsibility and performance (see Wood, 1991a, 1991b) because they are most likely to be recipients of what Carroll (1979) calls discretionary corporate social responsibility, which he later redefined as corporate philanthropy (Carroll, 1991).
4 A "social contract" – or "social license" for a company – contains the implicit and explicit expectations that society has regarding how an entity should conduct its operations. As reported by Deegan (2002), the social contract idea is not new, as it was discussed by philosophers such as Thomas Hobbes (1588–1679), John Locke (1632–1704) and Jean-Jacques Rousseau (1712–1778). These early thinkers in the field viewed the social contract primarily as a political theory insofar as it explained the supposed relationship between the government and its constituencies (Rawls, 1971). In the modern era, however, the social contract has been extended to include businesses and other institutions (Campbell, 2007).
5 Randgold Resources Sustainability Report 2015, part of Annual Report 2015.
6 Randgold Resources Sustainability Report 2015, part of Annual Report 2015.
7 AngloGoldAshanti website: www.aga-reports.com/14/ir/strategy/stakeholder-engagement
8 See Section 3.2.4 of this volume for a focus on the role of external assurance.
9 This model was initially applied to a different field: citizen participation.

References

ACCA. (2005). Improving stakeholder engagement reporting: An ACCA and the Environment Council workshop. London: ACCA.

AccountAbility. (2008a). *AA1000 AccountAbility principles standard 2008*. New York: AccountAbility

AccountAbility. (2008b). *AA1000 assurance standard 2008*. New York: AccountAbility

AccountAbility. (2015). *AA1000 stakeholder engagement standard 2015*. New York: AccountAbility

Agle, B. R., Mitchell, R. K., & Sonnenfeld, J. A. (1999). Who matters to CEOs? An investigation of stakeholder attributes and salience, corporate performance, and CEO values. *Academy of Management Journal, 42*(5), 507–525.

Agostino, D., & Arnaboldi, M. (2015). A measurement framework for assessing the contribution of social media to public engagement: An empirical analysis on Facebook. *Public Management Review*, 1–19.

Andriof, J., & Waddock, S. (2002). Unfolding stakeholder engagement. In J. Andriof, S. Waddock, B. Husted, & S. Sutherland Rahman (Eds),*Unfolding stakeholder thinking: Theory, responsibility and engagement* (Vol. 17, pp. 17–42). Greenleaf Publishing in association with GSE Research. www.ingentaconnect.com/content/glbj/ust;jsessionid=6nm5sef1glp61.x-ic-live-01#expand/collapse

Argenti, J. (1993). Your organization: What is it for? Challenging traditional organizational aims. New York: McGraw Hill Book.

Argenti, J. (1997). Stakeholders: The case against. *Long Range Planning, 30*(3), 442–445.

Arnstein, S. R. (1969). A ladder of citizen participation. *Journal of the American Institute of Planners, 35*(4), 216–224.

Barnett, M. L., & Salomon, R. M. (2012). Does it pay to be really good? Addressing the shape of the relationship between social and financial performance. *Strategic Management Journal, 33*(11), 1304–1320.

Bebbington, J., & Gray, R. (2001). An account of sustainability: failure, success and a reconceptualization. *Critical Perspectives on Accounting, 12*(5), 557–587.

Bebbington, J., Brown, J., & Frame, B. (2007). Accounting technologies and sustainability assessment models. *Ecological Economics, 61*(2), 224–236.

Bebbington, J., Brown, J., Frame, B., & Thomson, I. (2007). Theorizing engagement: The potential of a critical dialogic approach. *Accounting, Auditing & Accountability Journal, 20*(3), 356–381.

Bellucci, M., & Manetti, G. (2017). Facebook as a tool for supporting dialogic accounting? Evidence from large philanthropic foundations in the United States. *Accounting, Auditing & Accountability Journal, 30*(4), 874–905. doi:10.1108/AAAJ-07-2015-2122

Bendheim, C. L., Waddock, S. A., & Graves, S. B. (1998). Determining best practice in corporate-stakeholder relations using data envelopment analysis: An industry-level study. *Business & Society, 37*(3), 306–338.

Berman, S. L., Wicks, A. C., Kotha, S., & Jones, T. M. (1999). Does stakeholder orientation matter? The relationship between stakeholder management models and firm financial performance. *Academy of Management Journal, 42*(5), 488–506.

Boatright, J. R. (1994). Fiduciary duties and the shareholder-management relation: Or, what's so special about shareholders? *Business Ethics Quarterly, 4*(04), 393–407.

Bond, R. M., Fariss, C. J., Jones, J. J., Kramer, A. D., Marlow, C., Settle, J. E., & Fowler, J. H. (2012). A 61-million-person experiment in social influence and political mobilization. *Nature, 489*(7415), 295–298.

Bowie, N. (1988). The moral obligations of multinational corporations. *Problems of International Justice*, *97*, 113.

Boyce, G. (2000). Public discourse and decision making: Exploring possibilities for financial, social and environmental accounting. *Accounting, Auditing & Accountability Journal*, *13*(1), 27–64.

Brainard, L., & Edlins, M. (2015). Top 10 US municipal police departments and their social media usage. *The American Review of Public Administration*, *45*(6), 728–745.

Brenner, S. N., & Molander, E. A. (1977). Is ethics of business changing. *Harvard Business Review*, *55*(1), 57–71.

Brown, J. (2009). Democracy, sustainability and dialogic accounting technologies: Taking pluralism seriously. *Critical Perspectives on Accounting*, *20*(3), 313–342.

Brown, J., & Dillard, J. (2013). Critical accounting and communicative action: On the limits of consensual deliberation. *Critical Perspectives on Accounting*, *24*(3), 176–190.

Brown, J., & Dillard, J. (2014). Integrated reporting: On the need for broadening out and opening up. *Accounting, Auditing & Accountability Journal*, *27*(7), 1120–1156. doi:10.1108/AAAJ-04-2013-1313

Brown, J., & Dillard, J. (2015). Dialogic accountings for stakeholders: On opening up and closing down participatory governance. *Journal of Management Studies*, *52*(7), 961–985. doi:10.1111/joms.12153

Bryman, A., & Bell, E. (2015). *Business research methods*. Oxford: Oxford University Press.

Bryson, J. M. (2004). What to do when stakeholders matter: Stakeholder identification and analysis techniques. *Public Management Review*, *6*(1), 21–53.

Bryson, J. M., & Bromiley, P. (1993). Critical factors affecting the planning and implementation of major projects. *Strategic Management Journal*, *14*(5), 319–337.

Bryson, J. M., Bromiley, P., & Jung, Y. S. (1990). Influences of context and process on project planning success. *Journal of Planning Education and Research*, *9*(3), 183–195.

Burby, R. J. (2003). Making plans that matter: Citizen involvement and government action. *Journal of the American Planning Association*, *69*(1), 33–49.

Busco, C., Frigo, M. L., Quattrone, P., & Riccaboni, A. (2014). *Integrated reporting*. Dordrecht: Springer.

Campbell, D. (2003). Intra-and intersectoral effects in environmental disclosures: Evidence for legitimacy theory? *Business Strategy and the Environment*, *12*(6), 357–371.

Campbell, J. L. (2007). Why would corporations behave in socially responsible ways? An institutional theory of corporate social responsibility. *Academy of Management Review*, *32*(3), 946–967.

Carroll, A. (1979). A three-dimensional conceptual model of corporate performance. *Academy of Management Review*, *4*, 497–505. https://doi.org/10.2307/257850

Carroll, A. B. (1991). The pyramid of corporate social responsibility: Toward the moral management of organizational stakeholders. *Business Horizons*, *34*(4), 39–48. www.sciencedirect.com/science/article/pii/000768139190005G

Carroll, A. B. (1999). Corporate social responsibility evolution of a definitional construct. *Business & society*, *38*(3), 268–295.

Clarkson Centre for Business Ethics. (1999). *Principles of stakeholder management*. Clarkson Centre for Business Ethics, Joseph L. Rotman School of Management, University of Toronto.

Clarkson, M. B. (1991). Defining, evaluating, and managing corporate social performance: The stakeholder management model. *Research in Corporate Social Performance and Policy*, *12*(1), 331–358.

Clarkson, M. B. (1995). A stakeholder framework for analyzing and evaluating corporate social performance. *Academy of Management Review, 20*(1), 92–117.

Cooper, S. M., & Owen, D. L. (2007). Corporate social reporting and stakeholder accountability: The missing link. *Accounting, Organizations and Society, 32*(7), 649–667.

Crane, A., & Matten, D. (2016). Engagement required: The changing role of the corporation in society. In D. Barton, D. Horvath, & M. Kipping (Eds), *Re-imagining capitalism: Building a responsible, long-term model* (Chapter 9). Oxford: Oxford University Press.

Cummings, J. (2001). Engaging stakeholders in corporate accountability programmes: A cross-sectoral analysis of UK and transnational experience. *Business Ethics: A European Review, 10*(1), 45–52.

Dahlberg, L. (2005). The Habermasian public sphere: Taking difference seriously? *Theory and Society, 34*(2), 111–136.

Darnall, N., & Jolley, G. J. (2004). Involving the public: When are surveys and stakeholder interviews effective? 1. *Review of Policy Research, 21*(4), 581–593.

Deegan, C. (2002). Introduction: The legitimising effect of social and environmental disclosures-a theoretical foundation. *Accounting, Auditing & Accountability Journal, 15*(3), 282–311.

Deegan, C. (2006). Legitimacy theory. In Z. Hoque (Ed.), *Methodological issues in accounting research: Theories and methods* (pp. 161–182). Spiramus.

Dey, C. (2003). Corporate 'silent' and 'shadow' social accounting. *Social and Environmental Accountability Journal, 23*(2), 6–9.

Dillard, J., & Brown, J. (2012). Agonistic pluralism and imagining CSEAR into the future. *Social and Environmental Accountability Journal, 32*(1), 3–16.

Dillard, J., & Roslender, R. (2011). Taking pluralism seriously: Embedded moralities in management accounting and control systems. *Critical Perspectives on Accounting, 22*(2), 135–147.

Dillard, J., & Yuthas, K. (2013). Critical dialogics, agonistic pluralism, and accounting information systems. *International Journal of Accounting Information Systems, 14*(2), 113–119.

Donaldson, T., & Preston, L. E. (1995). The stakeholder theory of the corporation: Concepts, evidence, and implications. *Academy of Management Review, 20*(1), 65–91.

Downey, P. R. (2002). The essential stakeholder dialogue. *Corporate Social Responsibility and Environmental Management, 9*(1), 37–45.

Edward Freeman, R., Rusconi, G., Signori, S., & Strudler, A. (2012). Stakeholder theory (ies): Ethical ideas and managerial action. *Journal of Business Ethics, 109*(1), 1–2.

Emshoff, J. R., & Freeman, R. E. (1978). *Stakeholder management.* Pennsylvania: Wharton Applied Research Center.

Evan, W. M., & Freeman, R. E. (1988). *A stakeholder theory of the modern corporation: Kantian capitalism.* Englewood Cliffs: Prentice Hall.

Flick, U. (2009). *An introduction to qualitative research.* Thousand Oaks: Sage.

Frame, B., & Brown, J. (2008). Developing post-normal technologies for sustainability. *Ecological Economics, 65*(2), 225–241.

Freeman, R. E. (1984). *Strategic management: A stakeholder approach.* Boston: Pitman.

Freeman, R. E. (1999). Divergent stakeholder theory. *Academy of Management Review, 24*(2), 233–236.

Freeman, R. E. (2000). Business ethics at the millennium. *Business Ethics Quarterly, 10*(01), 169–180.

Freeman, R. E. (2004). A stakeholder theory of the modern corporation. In T. L. Beauchamp and N. E. Bowie (Eds), *Ethical theory and business*, 7th edn (pp. 55–64). Upper Saddle River: Pearson/Prentice-Hall.

Freeman, R. E., & McVea, J. (2001). *A stakeholder approach to strategic management*. www.researchgate.net/publication/228320877_A_Stakeholder_Approach_to_Strategic_Management

Freeman, R. E., & Reed, D. L. (1983). Stockholders and stakeholders: A new perspective on corporate governance. *California Management Review*, *25*(3), 88–106.

Freeman, R. E., Wicks, A. C., & Parmar, B. (2004). Stakeholder theory and "the corporate objective revisited". *Organization Science*, *15*(3), 364–369.

Friedman, A. L., & Miles, S. (2006). *Stakeholders: Theory and practice*. Oxford: Oxford University Press on Demand.

Friedman, M. (1970). The social responsibility of business is to increase its profits. *New York Times Magazine*, September 13, *1970*, 122–126.

Frooman, J. (1999). Stakeholder influence strategies. *Academy of Management Review*, *24*(2), 191–205.

Fuchs, C. (2009). Information and communication technologies and society: A contribution to the critique of the political economy of the internet. *European Journal of Communication*, *24*(1), 69–87.

Garriga, E., & Melé, D. (2013). Corporate social responsibility theories: Mapping the territory. In Michalos, A. C., Poff C. M., & Deborah, C, (Eds) *Citation classics from the Journal of Business Ethics* (pp. 69–96). Dordrecht: Springer.

Global Reporting Initiative. (2002). *Sustainability reporting guidelines 2002*. Amsterdam: Global Reporting Initiative.

Global Reporting Initiative. (2013a). *Implementation manual*. Amsterdam: Global Reporting Initiative.

Global Reporting Initiative. (2013b). *Reporting principles and standard disclosure*. Amsterdam: Global Reporting Initiative.

Goodpaster, K. E. (1991). Business ethics and stakeholder analysis. *Business Ethics Quarterly*, *1*(01), 53–73.

Gray, R. (1997). The silent practice of social and environmental accounting and corporate social reporting in companies. In S. Zadek, R. Evans, & P. Pruzan (Eds), *Building corporate accountability: Emerging practices in social and ethical accounting auditing and reporting* (pp. 201–217). London: Earthscan.

Gray, R. (2000). Current developments and trends in social and environmental auditing, reporting and attestation: a review and comment. *International Journal of Auditing*, *4*(3), 247–268.

Gray, R., & Bebbington, J. (2001). *Accounting for the environment*. Thousand Oaks: Sage.

Gray, R., & Milne, M. (2002). Sustainability reporting: Who's kidding whom? *Chartered Accountants Journal of New Zealand*, *81*(6), 66–70.

Habermas, J. (1984). The theory of communicative action 1, reason and the rationalization of society. Boston: Beacon Press.

Habermas, J. (1987). The theory of communicative action 2: Lifeworld and system-A critique of functionalist reason (trans. Thomas McCarthy). Cambridge: Polity.

Habermas, J. (1991). The structural transformation of the public sphere: An inquiry into a category of bourgeois society. Boston: MIT press.

Halal, W. E. (1990). The new management: Business and social institutions for the information age. *Business in the Contemporary World*, *2*(2), 41–54.

IIRC. (2013). *Materiality – background paper for < IR>*. Retrieved from http://integratedreporting.org//wp-content/uploads/2013/03/IR-Background-Paper-Materiality.pdf

Inauen, S., & Schoeneborn, D. (2014) Twitter and its usage for dialogic stakeholder communication by MNCs and NGOs. In R. Tench, W. Sun, & B. Jones (Eds) *Communicating corporate social responsibility: Perspectives and practice (Critical studies on corporate responsibility, governance and sustainability, Volume 6)* (pp. 283–310). Emerald Group Publishing Limited.

Jackson, C., & Bundgard, T. (2002). Achieving quality in social reporting: The role of surveys in stakeholder consultation. *Business Ethics: A European Review, 11*(3), 253–259.

Jawahar, I., & McLaughlin, G. L. (2001). Toward a descriptive stakeholder theory: An organizational life cycle approach. *Academy of Management Review, 26*(3), 397–414.

Jeacle, I., & Carter, C. (2014). Creative spaces in interdisciplinary accounting research. *Accounting, Auditing & Accountability Journal, 27*(8), 1233–1240.

Jensen, M. C. (2001). Value maximization, stakeholder theory, and the corporate objective function. *Journal of Applied Corporate Finance, 14*(3), 8–21.

Jensen, M. C., & Meckling, W. H. (1976). Theory of the firm: Managerial behavior, agency costs and ownership structure. *Journal of Financial Economics, 3*(4), 305–360.

Jones, T. M. (1995). Instrumental stakeholder theory: A synthesis of ethics and economics. *Academy of Management Review, 20*(2), 404–437.

Jones, T. M., & Wicks, A. C. (1999). Convergent stakeholder theory. *Academy of Management Review, 24*(2), 206–221.

Jones, T. M., Wicks, A. C., & Freeman, R. E. (2002). Stakeholder theory: The state of the art. In N. E. Bowie (Ed.), *The Blackwell guide to business ethics* (pp. 19–37). London: Blackwell.

Jonker, J., & Foster, D. (2002). Stakeholder excellence? Framing the evolution and complexity of a stakeholder perspective of the firm. *Corporate Social Responsibility and Environmental Management, 9*(4), 187–195.

Kent, M. L. (2013). Using social media dialogically: Public relations role in reviving democracy. *Public Relations Review, 39*(4), 337–345.

Kent, M. L., Taylor, M., & White, W. J. (2003). The relationship between web site design and organizational responsiveness to stakeholders. *Public Relations Review, 29*(1), 63–77.

Kolk, A. (2004). A decade of sustainability reporting: Developments and significance. *International Journal of Environment and Sustainable Development, 3*(1), 51–64. doi:10.1504/IJESD.2004.004688

Kreiner, P., & Bhambri, A. (1988). Influence and information in organization-stakeholder relationships. In *Academy of management proceedings*, no. 1 (pp. 319–323). Briarcliff Manor: Academy of Management.

Laplume, A. O., Sonpar, K., & Litz, R. A. (2008). Stakeholder theory: Reviewing a theory that moves us. *Journal of Management, 34*(6), 1152–1189.

Laughlin, R. C. (1987). Accounting systems in organisational contexts: A case for critical theory. *Accounting, Organizations and Society, 12*(5), 479–502.

Laughlin, R. C. (2007). Critical reflections on research approaches, accounting regulation and the regulation of accounting. *The British Accounting Review, 39*(4), 271–289.

Lee, K., Oh, W.-Y., & Kim, N. (2013). Social media for socially responsible firms: Analysis of fortune 500's twitter profiles and their CSR/CSIR ratings. *Journal of Business Ethics, 118*(4), 791–806.

Lombardi, L. (2016). Disempowerment and empowerment of accounting: An indigenous accounting context. *Accounting, Auditing & Accountability Journal, 29*(8), 1320–1341. doi:10.1108/AAAJ-08-2015-2167

Lopatta, K., Jaeschke, R., & Chen, C. (2017). Stakeholder engagement and corporate social responsibility (CSR) performance: International evidence. *Corporate Social Responsibility and Environmental Management, 24*(3), 199–209.

Lovejoy, K., Waters, R. D., & Saxton, G. D. (2012). Engaging stakeholders through Twitter: How nonprofit organizations are getting more out of 140 characters or less. *Public Relations Review, 38*(2), 313–318.

MacRae Jr, D., & Whittington, D. (1997). *Expert advice for policy choice: Analysis and discourse.* Washington: Georgetown University Press.

Manetti, G. (2011). The quality of stakeholder engagement in sustainability reporting: empirical evidence and critical points. *Corporate Social Responsibility and Environmental Management, 18*(2), 110–122.

Manetti, G., & Bellucci, M. (2016). The use of social media for engaging stakeholders in sustainability reporting. *Accounting, Auditing & Accountability Journal, 29*(6), 985–1011. doi:10.1108/AAAJ-08-2014-1797

Manetti, G., & Toccafondi, S. (2011). The role of stakeholders in sustainability reporting assurance. *Journal of Business Ethics, 107*(3), 363–377. doi:10.1007/s10551-011-1044-1

Manetti, G., Bellucci, M., & Bagnoli, L. (2017). Stakeholder engagement and public information through social media: A study of Canadian and American public transportation agencies. *The American Review of Public Administration, 47*(8). doi:10.1177/0275074016649260

Marcoux, A. (2000). *Business ethics gone wrong.* Emmitsburg: National Emergency Training Center.

Marcoux, A. M. (2003). A fiduciary argument against stakeholder theory. *Business Ethics Quarterly, 13*(01), 1–24.

Margerum, R. D. (2002). Collaborative planning building consensus and building a distinct model for practice. *Journal of Planning Education and Research, 21*(3), 237–253.

Margolis, J. D., & Walsh, J. P. (2003). Misery loves companies: Rethinking social initiatives by business. *Administrative Science Quarterly, 48*(2), 268–305.

Medawar, C. (1976). The social audit: A political view. *Accounting, Organizations and Society, 1*(4), 389–394.

Merton, R. K., Fiske, M., & Kendall, P. (1956). *The focused interview.* Glencoe: Ballachulish.

Miles, S. (2012). Stakeholder: Essentially contested or just confused? *Journal of Business Ethics, 108*, 285–298.

Mitchell, R. K., Agle, B. R., & Wood, D. J. (1997). Toward a theory of stakeholder identification and salience: Defining the principle of who and what really counts. *Academy of Management Review, 22*(4), 853–886. doi:10.2307/259247

Moore, M. H. (1995). *Creating public value: Strategic management in government.* Harvard: Harvard university press.

Moratis, L., & Brandt, S. (2017). Corporate stakeholder responsiveness? Exploring the state and quality of GRI-based stakeholder engagement disclosures of European firms. *Corporate Social Responsibility and Environmental Management, 24*(4), 312–325

Morgan, G. (1988). Accounting as reality construction: Towards a new epistemology for accounting practice. *Accounting, Organizations and Society, 13*(5), 477–485.

Murphy, D. F., & Bendell, J. (1997). *In the company of partners: Business, environmental groups and sustainable development post-Rio.* Bristol: Policy Press.

Näsi, J. (1995). What is stakeholder thinking? A snapshot of a social theory of the firm. *Understanding Stakeholder Thinking, 19*, 31.

Neligan, C. (2003). Increasing accountability through external stakeholder engagement. London: One World Trust, Houses of Parliament.

Nutt, P. C. (2002). *Why decisions fail*. San Francisco: Barrett-Kohler Publishers.

O'Dwyer, B. (2002). Managerial perceptions of corporate social disclosure: An Irish story. *Accounting, Auditing & Accountability Journal, 15*(3), 406–436.

O'Dwyer, B. (2005). The construction of a social account: A case study in an overseas aid agency. *Accounting, Organizations and Society, 30*(3), 279–296.

O'Dwyer, B., & Owen, D. L. (2005). Assurance statement practice in environmental, social and sustainability reporting: A critical evaluation. *The British Accounting Review, 37*(2), 205–229.

Ogden, S., & Watson, R. (1999). Corporate performance and stakeholder management: Balancing shareholder and customer interests in the UK privatized water industry. *Academy of Management Journal, 42*(5), 526–538.

Owen, D. L., Swift, T., & Hunt, K. (2001). Questioning the role of stakeholder engagement in social and ethical accounting, auditing and reporting. Paper presented at the Accounting Forum. http://lists.exeter.ac.uk/items/BDDBDFDB-0CBB-F6C5-00CC-60A158A4435A.html

Park, H., & Reber, B. H. (2008). Relationship building and the use of web sites: How Fortune 500 corporations use their web sites to build relationships. *Public Relations Review, 34*(4), 409–411.

Passetti, E., Bianchi, L., Battaglia, M., & Frey, M. (2017). When democratic principles are not enough: Tensions and temporalities of dialogic stakeholder engagement. *Journal of Business Ethics*. https://link.springer.com/article/10.1007%2Fs10551-017-3500-z

Perrin, A. (2015). *Social media usage*. Washington: Pew Research Center.

Pfeffer, J., & Salancik, G. R. (1978). The external control of organizations: A resource dependence perspective. New York: Harper and Row.

Phillips, R. A. (1997). Stakeholder theory and a principle of fairness. *Business Ethics Quarterly, 7*(1), 51–66.

Phillips, R. A., & Reichart, J. (2000). The environment as a stakeholder? A fairness-based approach. *Journal of Business Ethics, 23*(2), 185–197.

Polonsky, M. J., Giraud Voss, Z., Voss, G. B., & Moorman, C. (2005). An empirical examination of the complex relationships between entrepreneurial orientation and stakeholder support. *European Journal of Marketing, 39*(9/10), 1132–1150.

Ramanadhan, S., Mendez, S. R., Rao, M., & Viswanath, K. (2013). Social media use by community-based organizations conducting health promotion: A content analysis. *BMC Public Health, 13*(1), 1–10.

Rawls, J. (1971). *A theory of justice*. Harvard: Harvard university press.

Roberts, R. W. (1992). Determinants of corporate social responsibility disclosure: An application of stakeholder theory. *Accounting, Organizations and Society, 17*(6), 595–612.

Rowley, T. J. (1997). Moving beyond dyadic ties: A network theory of stakeholder influences. *Academy of Management Review, 22*(4), 887–910.

Rybalko, S., & Seltzer, T. (2010). Dialogic communication in 140 characters or less: How Fortune 500 companies engage stakeholders using Twitter. *Public Relations Review, 36*(4), 336–341.

Salancik, G. R., & Pfeffer, J. (1974). The bases and use of power in organizational decision making: The case of a university. *Administrative Science Quarterly, 19*(4), 453–473.

Scherer, A. G., Palazzo, G., & Baumann, D. (2006). Global rules and private actors: Toward a new role of the transnational corporation in global governance. *Business Ethics Quarterly, 16*(04), 505–532.

Sharma, S., & Henriques, I. (2005). Stakeholder influences on sustainability practices in the Canadian forest products industry. *Strategic Management Journal, 26*(2), 159–180.

Starik, M. (1995). Should trees have managerial standing? Toward stakeholder status for non-human nature. *Journal of Business Ethics, 14*(3), 207–217.

Sternberg, E. (1997). The defects of stakeholder theory. *Corporate Governance: An International Review, 5*(1), 3–10.

Sternberg, E. (2000). *Just business: Business ethics in action.* Oxford: Oxford University Press.

Steurer, R., Langer, M. E., Konrad, A., & Martinuzzi, A. (2005). Corporations, stake-holders and sustainable development I: A theoretical exploration of business–society relations. *Journal of Business Ethics, 61*(3), 263–281.

Stieb, J. A. (2009). Assessing Freeman's stakeholder theory. *Journal of Business Ethics, 87*(3), 401–414.

Strong, K. C., Ringer, R. C., & Taylor, S. A. (2001). THE* rules of stakeholder satisfaction (* timeliness, honesty, empathy). *Journal of Business Ethics, 32*(3), 219–230.

Suchman, M. C. (1995). Managing legitimacy: Strategic and institutional approaches. *Academy of Management Review, 20*(3), 571–610.

Sundaram, A. K., & Inkpen, A. C. (2004). The corporate objective revisited. *Organization science, 15*(3), 350–363.

Svendsen, A. (1998). The stakeholder strategy: Profiting from collaborative business rela-tionships. Oakland: Berrett-Koehler Publishers.

Swift, T. (2001). Trust, reputation and corporate accountability to stakeholders. *Business Ethics: A European Review, 10*(1), 16–26.

Thomson, I., & Bebbington, J. (2005). Social and environmental reporting in the UK: A pedagogic evaluation. *Critical Perspectives on Accounting, 16*(5), 507–533.

Thorne, L., Mahoney, L. S., & Manetti, G. (2014). Motivations for issuing standalone CSR reports: A survey of Canadian firms. *Accounting, Auditing & Accountability Journal, 27*(4), 686–714.

Tuchman, B. W. (2009). *The march of folly.* Ashland: Blackstone Audio, Incorporated.

UNEP. (1998). *The non-reporting report.* London: UNEP.

Unerman, J., & Bennett, M. (2004). Increased stakeholder dialogue and the inter-net: Towards greater corporate accountability or reinforcing capitalist hegemony? *Accounting, Organizations and Society, 29*(7), 685–707.

Villa, D. R. (1992). Postmodernism and the public sphere. *American Political Science Review, 86*(03), 712–721.

Vinnari, E., & Dillard, J. (2016). (ANT) agonistics: Pluralistic politicization of, and by, accounting and its technologies. *Critical Perspectives on Accounting, 39*, 25–44.

Waddock, S. (2008). Building a new institutional infrastructure for corporate responsibil-ity. *The Academy of Management Perspectives, 22*(3), 87–108.

Wang, J., & Dewhirst, H. D. (1992). Boards of directors and stakeholder orientation. *Journal of Business Ethics, 11*(2), 115–123.

Waters, R. D., & Jamal, J. Y. (2011). Tweet, tweet, tweet: A content analysis of nonprofit organizations' Twitter updates. *Public Relations Review, 37*(3), 321–324.

Weick, K. E. (1999). That's moving: Theories that matter. *Journal of Management Inquiry, 8*(2), 134.

Weiss, J. W. (2014). *Business ethics: A stakeholder and issues management approach.* Oakland: Berrett-Koehler Publishers.

Wood, D. J. (1991a). Corporate social performance revisited. *Academy of Management Review, 16*(4), 691–718.

Wood, D. J. (1991b). Social issues in management: Theory and research in corporate social performance. *Journal of Management, 17*(2), 383–406.

Xifra, J., & Grau, F. (2010). Nanoblogging PR: The discourse on public relations in Twitter. *Public Relations Review, 36*(2), 171–174.

Zadek, S., & Raynard, P. (2002). Stakeholder engagement: Measuring and communicating quality. *Accountability Quarterly, 19*(2), 8–17.

Zöller, K. (1999). Growing credibility through dialogue: Experiences in Germany and the USA. In Zöller, K., *Greener Marketing: A Global Perspective on Greening Marketing Practice* (Vol. *196*, pp. 196–206). Greenleaf Publishing in association with GSE Research.

5 An empirical overview of stakeholder engagement in sustainability reports

5.1 Research context and objectives

Although stakeholder engagement (SE) is recognized as a key process by which to align firm and stakeholder interests and to identify material content for sustainability reporting, research on SE quality in the sustainability reporting context remains sparse (Moratis & Brandt, 2017). In the stakeholder theory literature, little attention has been paid to the properties of information regarding stakeholder engagement policies and practices stated in sustainability reports (Abdifatah & Mutalib, 2016; Brown & Dillard, 2015; Cooper & Owen, 2007; Crane & Matten, 2016; Dobele, Westberg, Steel, & Flowers, 2014; Manetti, 2011; Owen, Swift, & Hunt, 2001). Moreover, non-financial information materiality is a relatively understudied research theme (Fasan & Mio, 2017; Moratis & Brandt, 2017). The present chapter aims to provide a deep, empirical focus on how sustainability reports address the topic of stakeholder engagement, the distinctive features of this process of involvement and the reported role of SE in assessing materiality and defining the content of such disclosure.

As stated by Peck and Sinding (2003), a major concern of companies deals with the increasing need to legitimate their existence and document their performance through the disclosure of social and environmental information. This behavior can be explained in light of legitimacy theory and socio-economic theory (see Chapter 3 of this volume). Given these perspectives, some authors claim that organizations issue social reports to reduce their external costs or to diminish pressures imposed by external stakeholders or regulators (Castello & Lozano, 2011; Deegan, 2002; Gray, Kouhy, & Lavers, 1995; Gray & Milne, 2002; Guthrie & Parker, 1989; Tate, Ellram, & Kirchoff, 2010). In other words, sustainability reports can be voluntarily disclosed for strategic reasons rather than for the company's responsibility toward the community and can be used to influence (or manipulate) stakeholder perceptions of the company's image. Socio-economic theory can complement legitimacy theory to further explain why organizations issue sustainability reports for strategic reasons. Advocates of socio-economic theory state that an organization and its voluntary disclosure practices must be analyzed within a social and political context since the institutional framework helps in understanding their behavior (Clarkson, Li, Richardson, & Vasvari, 2011; Clarkson, Overell, & Chapple, 2011; Deegan, 2002; Deegan, Rankin, & Tobin, 2002; Dowling & Pfeffer, 1975; Laufer, 2003; Patten, 1992). Problems can emerge when there is a disparity between community values and the organization's values and impacts. By using external accountability mechanisms, voluntary disclosure on sustainability issues can strengthen an organization's social legitimacy, which improves its image and perception among external stakeholders and the local community. The manipulation of an organization's image (greenwashing and bluewashing, see Section 3.1.2) is perceived as being easier to accomplish than improving the organization's levels of sustainability performance, its supply chain structure or its value system.

Against this background, industries concerned with particular legitimacy issues represent an appropriate context to study the role of stakeholder engagement in defining the materiality of information for the purpose of preparing a sustainability report. In order to pursue these research objectives, we analyzed a sample of sustainability reports prepared in compliance with the Global Reporting Initiative (GRI) guidelines. As of January 2018, the GRI sustainability disclosure database encompassed 11,744 organizations, 46,637 reports and 29,532 GRI reports published between 1999 and 2017. We aimed for our sample to be up-to-date and to include reports prepared in accordance with the most recent version of the GRI guidelines (G4) in order to study the most current reporting practices employed by organizations (our sample is described in detail in the second section of this chapter).

Beginning with the classification of sectors provided in the GRI sustainability disclosure database, our study focuses on the industries that generally present the most prominent legitimacy concerns: Chemicals, Energy, Food and Beverage Products, Forest and Paper Products, Mining, Textiles and Apparels, Tobacco and Waste Management. More than other organizations, those operating in these sectors must deal with social and environmental issues on a daily basis and must demonstrate that they are sensitive to the interests of several stakeholder groups.

Companies operating in sectors dealing with the extraction and processing of resources – Mining, Energy, Forest and Paper Products and Chemicals – are included because their activities are regarded as among the most environmentally and socially disruptive activities undertaken by businesses (Bini, Bellucci, & Giunta, 2018; Jenkins & Yakovleva, 2006; Peck & Sinding, 2003). Tobacco companies and organizations dealing with alcoholic products (those in the Food and Beverage sector) need to deal with the consequences of the exploitation of natural resources for local communities on one hand and, on the other hand, with an increasing diffidence linked to health and lifestyle changes. The growing demands for worker safety, corporate responsibility and respect for human rights have led international buyers, ready-made garment factory owners, government and many non-governmental organizations (NGOs) to play a pivotal role in improving overall factory working conditions and worker rights in the Textile and Apparel industry in developing countries. Finally, Waste Management represents a crucial segment in terms of environmental sustainability and commitment to corporate social responsibility.

Furthermore, many of the environmental disasters (e.g., the Deepwater Horizon oil spill in the Gulf of Mexico) and human rights incidents (e.g., the Rana Plaza collapse in Bangladesh) that have contributed to the growing public concern about sustainability have occurred in these industries (Cowell, Wehrmeyer, Argust, & Robertson, 1999; Warhurst, 2001).

As a consequence, many studies and reports have been conducted on these activities, contributing to the acknowledgment of the key sustainability issues mentioned by major stakeholders. The same studies document that, in recent years, companies involved in these sectors have begun to pay serious attention to their environmental and social impacts (Dobele et al., 2014; Jenkins & Yakovleva, 2006; Mouan, 2010; Peck & Sinding, 2003). Therefore, organizations operating in these sectors must deal with social and environmental concerns on a daily basis, and their license to operate is very sensitive to the perceptions of their stakeholders. However, practically involving stakeholders is not always a straightforward process in industries that often feature large companies located in different countries around the world (Brummer, Badenhorst, & Neuland, 2006). Disclosing the largest amount of information on this process through sustainability reports becomes imperative in order to fully understand a company's strategies and orientations in light of stakeholders' expectations. Nonetheless, there remains a lack of literature on the characteristics of information on SE processes stated in sustainability reports.

The next section introduces our research design, including descriptive statistics of our sample, while Section 5.3 discusses and comments on our main results.

5.2 Research design

5.2.1 Sample

The empirical study presented in this section is based on a content analysis of 211 annual sustainability reports prepared in compliance with "in accordance – core" or "in accordance – comprehensive" levels of adherence with the GRI G4 standards. We analyzed all G4 reports with external assurance provided by the GRI database that were published in 2016 by companies in the following sectors: Chemicals, Energy, Food and Beverage Products, Forest and Paper Products, Mining, Textiles and Apparel, Tobacco and Waste Management. Of a total of 333 entries complying with these characteristics, we included in the final analysis 211 reports in English, Spanish, Portuguese and Italian; the remaining entries were excluded because the relative reports were in fact unavailable at the time of the content analysis, because they were written in a language that we could not properly read or understand,[1] or because of both factors. Table 5.1 shows the number of organizations in each sector.

Overall, our sample is based on the annual reports of 211 organizations operating in sectors concerned with social and environmental issues that are particularly relevant to the interests of several stakeholder groups. This sample includes 180

Table 5.1 Organizations per sector

Sector	Number of organizations
Energy	56
Mining	51
Chemicals	35
Food and Beverage Products	28
Forest and Paper Products	20
Textiles and Apparel	15
Waste Management	4
Tobacco	2
TOTAL	211

private companies (defined as business organizations owned either by an NGO or by a number of stakeholders), 17 state-owned companies (legal entities created by a government in order to undertake commercial activities on behalf of the owner government) and 14 subsidiaries (companies controlled by another company through the ownership of 50 percent or more of the voting stock). Table 5.2 provides an overview of the types of organizations in our sample and indicates whether these organizations are listed (166) on a stock exchange or not (45).[2]

Table 5.3 indicates the region in which each organization's headquarters are located (in the case of subsidiaries, the country indicates the location of the reporting entity). Europe is the most represented region (82 organizations), followed by

Table 5.2 Organization types and stock exchange listing

Organization type	Stock exchange		TOTAL
	Listed	Non-listed	
Private company	149	31	180
State-owned company	11	6	17
Subsidiary	6	8	14
TOTAL	166	45	211

Table 5.3 Region and size

Region	Size			TOTAL
	MNE	Large	SME	
Europe	26	53	3	82
Asia	15	41	0	56
North America	12	15	0	27
Latin America and the Caribbean	2	17	0	19
Oceania	9	5	0	14
Africa	1	12	0	13
TOTAL	65	143	3	211

Asia (56), North America (27), Latin America and the Caribbean (19), Oceania (14) and Africa (13). Our sample includes 65 multinationals (MNE), 143 large enterprises (Large) and 3 small or medium enterprises (SME).[3]

As previously stated, this study analyzes reports prepared in compliance with the GRI G4 guidelines, which represent the most recent version of the standard. Table 5.4 shows the adherence level of the included reports, which reflects the extent to which the GRI Sustainability Reporting Framework has been applied to a report. In order to avoid introducing biases, we included in the final analyses only reports that officially declared[4] an adherence level in accordance with GRI G4: the vast majority of reports demonstrated a "core" adherence level (177), while 34 reports demonstrated a "comprehensive" level. Thirty-eight organizations issued an integrated report in 2016, including both non-financial and financial disclosures.

English is by far the most common language used in our sample reports. As previously stated, we included in our sample only externally assured reports: Figure 5.1 shows that 60 percent of reports are externally assured by accountants. Regarding the format of the reports, 27 organizations did not provide stand-alone PDF versions of their reports, instead posting them on their websites.

Table 5.4 Adherence level and integrated reports

Adherence level	Integrated		TOTAL
	No	*Yes*	
In accordance - Core	148	29	177
In accordance - Comprehensive	25	9	34
TOTAL	173	38	211

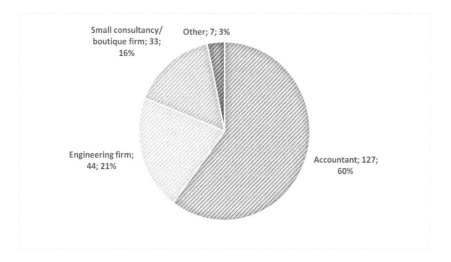

Figure 5.1 Providers of external assurance

5.2.2 Methodology

Our main research objective in this chapter is to study how sustainability reports address the role of stakeholder engagement. In order to answer our exploratory research question, we opted for a mixed methodology built on content analysis: a research technique based on the objective, systematic and quantitative description of the manifest content of communication (Berelson, 1952). This method is conceived as a technique for making inferences by objectively and systematically identifying specific characteristics of certain types of messages (Holsti, 1969). Content analysis is a flexible approach to the examination of various media, documents and texts that seeks to quantify content in terms of predetermined categories and in a systemic and replicable manner (Bryman & Bell, 2015). As reported by Hsieh and Shannon (2005):

> content analysis has a long history in research, dating back to the 18th century in Scandinavia (Rosengren, 1981). In the United States, content analysis was first used as an analytic technique at the beginning of the 20th century (Barcus, 1959). Initially, researchers used content analysis as either a qualitative or quantitative method in their studies (Berelson, 1952). Later, content analysis was used primarily as a quantitative research method, with text data coded into explicit categories and then described using statistics. This approach is sometimes referred to as quantitative analysis of qualitative data (Morgan, 1988).

Currently, content analysis has a long tradition of being used in business, communication, sociology and psychology studies; in the last few decades, its use has shown steady growth (Elo & Kyngäs, 2008; Neuendorf, 2002).

As reported by Bryman and Bell (2015), content analysis has been used mainly to examine media items, as well as texts and documents that are either produced by organizations, such as annual reports, or written about them, such as articles in the business press. In this regard, content analysis is among several approaches to examining texts that have been developed over the years (Bryman & Bell, 2015). It is a research technique widely adopted in corporate disclosure studies (Guthrie, Petty, Yongvanich, & Ricceri, 2004) because it allows repeatability and valid inferences from data according to their context (Krippendorff, 2004; Manetti, 2011). Elo and Kyngäs (2008) provide a review of the main features of content analysis:

> content analysis as a research method is a systematic and objective means of describing and quantifying phenomena (Downe-Wamboldt, 1992; Krippendorff, 2004; Sandelowski, 1993). It is also known as a method of analysing documents. Content analysis allows the researcher to test theoretical issues to enhance understanding of the data. Through content analysis, it is possible to distil words into fewer content-related categories. It is assumed that when classified into the same categories, words, phrases and the like share the same meaning (Cavanagh, 1997). Content analysis is a research

method for making replicable and valid inferences from data to their context, with the purpose of providing knowledge, new insights, a representation of facts and a practical guide to action (Krippendorff, 2004).

Therefore, content analysis aim to attain a condensed and broad description of the phenomenon, and the outcome of the analysis is concepts (or categories) describing the phenomenon; the purpose of those concepts (or categories)[5] is usually to construct a model or a conceptual map (Elo & Kyngäs, 2008).

Consequently, researchers regard content analysis as a flexible method for analyzing text data (Cavanagh, 1997; Hsieh & Shannon, 2005). Particularly when researchers – as in our case – want to code text in terms of certain subjects and themes, content analysis allows a categorization of the phenomena of interest (Bryman & Bell, 2015). Accordingly, as stated by Elo and Kyngäs (2008), content analysis is much more than an unsophisticated technique that results in a simplistic description of data (Cavanagh, 1997) or a counting game (Downe-Wamboldt, 1992). Rather, it is a research technique that can be used to develop an understanding of the meaning of communication (Cavanagh, 1997) and to identify critical processes (Lederman, 1991). Content analysis is concerned with meanings, intentions, consequences and context (Downe-Wamboldt, 1992; Elo & Kyngäs, 2008).

Although content analysis is generally regarded as a quantitative method because it deals with the quantification of recurrent information, it also represents a powerful tool for collecting qualitative data (Hsieh & Shannon, 2005). In other words, it allows us to study the content of sustainability reports from both a quantitative and a qualitative perspective. Qualitative content analysis is defined as a research method for the subjective interpretation of the content of text data through the systematic classification process of coding and identifying themes or patterns (Hsieh & Shannon, 2005). The aim of the approach is to become immersed in the data, which is why the written material is usually read several times (Burnard, 1991). After making sense of the data, analysis is conducted using an inductive or deductive approach (Elo & Kyngäs, 2008; Kyngas & Vanhanen, 1999). As stated by Elo and Kyngäs (2008):

> content analysis is a method that may be used with either qualitative or quantitative data; furthermore, it may be used in an inductive or deductive way. Which of these is used is determined by the purpose of the study. If there is not enough former knowledge about the phenomenon or if this knowledge is fragmented, the inductive approach is recommended . . . The categories are derived from the data in inductive content analysis. Deductive content analysis is used when the structure of analysis is operationalized on the basis of previous knowledge and the purpose of the study is theory testing (Kyngas & Vanhanen, 1999).

An approach based on inductive analysis moves from the specific to the general so that particular instances are observed and then combined into a larger whole or general observation (Chinn & Kramer, 1983; Elo & Kyngäs, 2008). The deductive approach is based on an earlier theory or model, and therefore, it moves from the general to the specific (Elo & Kyngäs, 2008; Grove & Burns, 2005).

If the researcher chooses to use inductive content analysis, the next step is to organize the qualitative data. This process includes open coding, category creation and abstraction (Elo & Kyngäs, 2008). In this approach, categories for coding are derived directly from the text data (Hsieh & Shannon, 2005).

When using a deductive approach, as in the case of this study, analysis begins with a theory or relevant research findings as guidance for initial coding (Elo & Kyngäs, 2008). This step may also involve testing theories, previous literature, concepts, models or hypotheses (Marshall & Rossman, 2014). If a deductive content analysis is chosen, the next step is, as reported by Elo and Kyngäs (2008):

> to develop a categorization matrix . . . and to code the data according to the categories . . . In deductive content analysis, either a structured or unconstrained matrix of analysis can be used, depending on the aim of the study (Kyngas & Vanhanen, 1999). It is generally based on earlier work such as theories, models, mind maps and literature reviews (Hsieh & Shannon, 2005; Sandelowski, 1993).

Of course, researchers must tailor their approach to the requirements of their research by selecting specific techniques and integrating them with other methods, substantive considerations and theories (Weber, 1990). For the purposes of our study, we performed a content analysis on our sample of 211 sustainability reports, with particular reference to the SE sections, in order to build a database capable of complementing information gathered from the GRI sustainability database. In analyzing SE disclosure, attention must be paid to the presence of an SE section, to the intrinsic characteristics of this process (if in place) and to what information has been disclosed and how (Manetti, 2011).

All 211 reports were downloaded from the GRI website (or in the case of web-only reports, linked to them) and identified with a unique ID, and their content was manually analyzed. A specific data entry grid was developed using spreadsheet software (Microsoft Excel) in order to support the data collection phase, the coding scheme and categorization of concepts. Specific coding rules for each cell were defined to avoid the insertion of incorrect values during data entry and to minimize coding errors. To maintain homogeneity, external appendices and secondary reports were not included in the analysis.

Tables 5.5 and 5.6 report the data we collected from the GRI sustainability database and that we manually collected through our content analysis, respectively.

In particular, data listed in Table 5.6 originated from a deep study of each report, with particular reference to our content analyses in the stakeholder engagement section. We collected data on the general characteristics of the reports, the stated methodologies used for SE, the reported categories of stakeholders engaged and the features of reported interactions with stakeholders. These qualitative and quantitative data were collected for all 211 reports included in our final sample.

Table 5.5 List and description of data collected from the GRI sustainability database

Variable label	Description
Organization	
Name	Name of the organization
Size	Size of the organization (SME, Large, MNE)
Organization Type	Type of organization (private, state-owned, subsidiary)
Listed/Non-listed	Whether the organization is listed or not on a stock exchange
Sector	Sector in which the organization operates
Country	Country in which the organization's headquarters are located
Country Status	Whether the country is member of the Organization for Economic Co-operation and Development (OECD), receives funding from the Development Assistance Committee (DAC), or neither
Region	Continent in which the organization operates
Report	
Date Added	Date that the report was added to the database
Title	Official title of the report
Publication Year	Year the report was published
Integrated	Whether or not the report includes both non-financial and financial disclosures, beyond basic economic information
Adherence Level	The extent to which the GRI Sustainability Reporting Framework has been applied to a report
GRI Service	Whether the report has received one of the GRI services: materiality disclosures service, Sustainable Development Goals mapping service, content index service, application level service
External Assurance	Whether or not the report is externally assured
Type of Assurance Provider	The type of assurance provider: accountant, engineering firm or small consultancy/boutique firm
Assurance Provider	The specific name of the firm that provided the external assurance
Stakeholder Panel/ Expert Opinions	Whether or not formalized input or feedback on the report was provided by a panel of stakeholders or expert(s)
Assurance Scope	The scope of assurance (to the entire report or to specific sections)
Level of Assurance	The level of assurance: limited/moderate, reasonable/high, or a combination of both
Assurance Standard: AA1000AS	The application of the AccountAbility AA1000 Assurance Standard (AA1000AS) as disclosed in the external assurance statement
Assurance Standard: ISAE3000	The application of the International Standard on Assurance Engagements (ISAE) 3000 as disclosed in the external assurance statement
Assurance Standard: National (General)	The application of a general national assurance standard (e.g., general accounting principles developed at the national level or by an organization within the specific national context) as disclosed in the external assurance statement

(continued)

Table 5.5 (continued)

Variable label	Description
Assurance Standard: National (Sustainability)	The application of a sustainability-specific (non-financial) national assurance standard (e.g., developed at the national level or by an organization within the specific national context) as disclosed in the external assurance statement
Sector Supplements (Final)	Whether one of the final versions of the GRI Sector Supplements was used in the report
OECD	Explicit reference to/use of the OECD Guidelines for Multinational Enterprises in the report
UNGC	Explicit reference to/use of the United Nations Global Compact (UNGC) and its principles in the report
CDP	Explicit reference to the organization responding to one of the annual Carbon Disclosure Project (CDP) questionnaires or participating in an associated CDP project
IFC	Explicit reference to/use of the International Finance Corporation (IFC) Performance Standards in the report
ISO	Explicit reference to/use of the ISO 26000 clauses in the report

Table 5.6 List and description of data collected from the content analysis

Variable label	Description
General information	
Type	Report format (PDF or web-based)
Language	Language of the report
SE section	Whether there is a specific section devoted to SE
SE role	The role of SE claimed in the report
Stated methodologies used for SE	
Standard procedures	Whether SE is performed through standard procedures such as formal channels, presentation of annual reports, etc.
Focus groups	Whether SE is performed through focus groups and workshops
Interviews	Whether SE is performed through interviews and other one-to-one techniques
Surveys	Whether SE is performed through surveys and polls
Meetings	Whether SE is performed through group meetings, site visits, official meetings, etc.
Social media	Whether SE is performed through social media
Other web app	Whether SE is performed through technological applications other than social media
Others	Whether different SE methodologies are used
Reported stakeholders engaged	
Shareholders	Whether the report presents shareholders and investors as an engaged group of stakeholders

Employees	Whether the report presents employees and their representatives (e.g., unions) as an engaged group of stakeholders
Customers	Whether the report presents customers as an engaged group of stakeholders
Suppliers	Whether the report presents suppliers, contractors and subcontractors as an engaged group of stakeholders
Government	Whether the report presents the government, authorities and regulators as an engaged group of stakeholders
NGOs	Whether the report presents NGOs, members of civil society and non-profit organizations as an engaged group of stakeholders
Local communities	Whether the report presents communities, community members, traditional councils and community trusts as an engaged group of stakeholders
Others	Whether there are other groups of stakeholders reported as engaged

Interaction

SE degree	General evaluation of the degree of stakeholder involvement
Stakeholder perceptions	Whether stakeholder perceptions and feedback on previous reports are reported
Stakeholder issues	Whether stakeholder issues are reported in the SE section or only in the materiality matrix
Quotations	Whether direct quotations from at least one stakeholder are reported
Dialogic accounting	Whether there are forms of dialogic accounting among stakeholders *(see our theoretical framework in Chapter 4 of this volume for details and a literature review)*
SE for materiality	Whether it is clearly stated that SE is used for materiality checks
SE guidelines	Whether and what specific guidelines are followed for SE
Assurance reported	Whether it is reported that an external assurance specifically devoted to SE is in use
Difficulties	Whether the report describes the main difficulties encountered in the SE process
Level of coverage	The general level of coverage of the SE process in the report
Photos	Whether the report makes use of photos
Visual arts	Whether the report makes use of other visual arts
Visual message	The general message of photos and other visual arts contained in the report

5.2.3 Validity and trustworthiness

Content analysts must demonstrate the reliability of their instruments and the reliability of the data collected using them in order to permit replicable and valid inferences to be drawn from data derived from the content analysis (Milne & Adler, 1999).

The reliability of content analysis involves two separate but related issues. First, in terms of trustworthiness, the analysis process and the results should be described in sufficient detail so that readers have a clear understanding of how the analysis was carried out and its strengths and limitations (General Accounting Office, 1996). This step includes the dissection of the analysis process and the validity of the results (Elo & Kyngäs, 2008). This is one of the reasons that motivated us to describe every step and detail of our empirical study in this section.

Creating categories is both an empirical and a conceptual challenge, as these categories must be conceptually and empirically grounded (Dey, 2003). Consequently, successful content analysis requires the researcher to analyze and simplify the data and form categories that reflect the subject of study in a reliable manner (Elo & Kyngäs, 2008; Kyngas & Vanhanen, 1999). Moreover, the credibility of research findings also deals with how well the categories cover the data (Graneheim & Lundman, 2004). It is important to make defensible inferences based on the collection of valid and reliable data (Weber, 1990). As reported by Elo and Kyngäs (2008):

> to increase the reliability of the study, it is necessary to demonstrate a link between the results and the data . . . This is why the researcher must aim at describing the analysing process in as much detail as possible when reporting the results. Appendices and tables may be used to demonstrate links between the data and results. To facilitate transferability, the researcher should give a clear description of the context, selection and characteristics of participants, data collection and process of analysis (Graneheim & Lundman, 2004). Demonstration is needed of the reliability of the findings and interpretations to enable someone else to follow the process and procedures of the inquiry.

Second, content analysts can seek to attest that the coded data or dataset produced from their analysis are reliable; the most common ways in which this is achieved is by demonstrating the use of multiple coders and either reporting that the discrepancies between the coders are few or that the discrepancies have been re-analyzed and the differences resolved (Milne & Adler, 1999). In this case, as reported by Elo and Kyngäs (2008):

> the internal validity of content analysis can be assessed . . . by using agreement coefficients (Weber, 1990). However, there are various opinions about seeking agreement (Graneheim & Lundman, 2004), because each researcher interpret the data according to their subjective perspective and co-researchers could come up with an alternative interpretation (Sandelowski, 1993). Content validation requires the use of a panel of experts to support concept production or coding issues. Graneheim & Lundman (2004) defend the value of dialogue among co-researchers to agree the way in which the data are labelled.

Alternatively, researchers can demonstrate that a single coder has received sufficient training: researchers could require that the reliability of coding decisions made for a pilot sample reach an acceptable level before the coder is permitted to code the main dataset (Milne & Adler, 1999). As reported by Weber (1990):

the central problems of content analysis originate mainly in the data-reduction process by which the many words of texts are classified into much fewer content categories. One set of problems concerns the consistency or reliability of text classification. In content analysis, reliability problems usually grow out of the ambiguity of word meanings, category definitions, or other coding rules. Classification by multiple human coders permits the quantitative assessment of achieved reliability.

By establishing the reliability of particular tools across a wide range of datasets and coders, content analysts can reduce the need for the costly use of multiple coders; well-specified decision categories, with well-specified decision rules, may produce few discrepancies when used by relatively inexperienced coders (Milne & Adler, 1999).

In the case of our study, four content analysts operated under the supervision of two experienced senior researchers. Building on the main existing literature described in this chapter, we defined a strategy to increase the reliability of our analysis (Bryman & Bell, 2015). This strategy followed four steps:

1   Sample definition: we defined the full set of reports to be analyzed (see Section 5.2.1);
2   Draft of the coding categories: we created a first draft of the specific research questions and relative coding categories (cf. Table 5.6);
3   Coding test: we tested the coding rules through a preliminary content analysis on a sample of 81 reports published in 2015 for the mining sector;[6]
4   Revision of the coding rules and final version: after the pilot test, we fine-tuned tools and coding procedures, deleting non-useful categories and adding new, more insightful ones;
5   Inter-rate reliability: we split the sample of 211 reports into two groups, and each group was assigned to two analysts. Both analysts in each pairing analyzed all the reports in their subgroup. This step enabled us to assess a reliability score between analysts in each couple regarding several key categories and to discuss and resolve discrepancies until this inter-rater reliability score (Kohen's kappa) – which can vary between 0 and 1 – surpassed 0.75 and was deemed satisfactory.

After these preliminary procedures, we ran our content analysis on the whole sample described in Section 5.2.1.

For each of the sustainability reports, our analysis created quantitative measures of the attention devoted to various content categories (Weber, 1990). The final deliverable of our data collection phase was a complete database that was the source of the analysis and results discussed in the following section. An analysis of these quantitative data can deliver original insights on the role of stakeholder engagement in sustainability reporting and on the features of this engagement. Moreover, this comprehensive and up-to-date database can easily be a reference for further studies on sustainability reporting, stakeholder engagement and dialogic accounting.

5.3 Discussion of results

Our content analysis, together with the data we gathered from the GRI sustainability database, provided a great deal of quantitative and qualitative information that enabled us to assess the reported role of stakeholder engagement in sustainability reporting. Moreover, we also aimed to understand the distinctive features of the reported SE processes. Most content analysis is likely to entail several research questions that originate from the main one (Bryman & Bell, 2015). Table 5.7 presents these specific research questions and the results from our content analysis (for descriptive statistics for our sample, see Section 5.2.1).

These results will be interpreted in light of the theoretical framework presented in Chapter 4 of this volume. Additionally, we included throughout this section a set of relevant quotations from our sample of reports.

Table 5.7 Research questions, categories and results of the content analysis

Question and categories	N.	%
What is the format of the report?		
• Stand-alone PDF	184	87.20
• Web-based	27	12.80
Has a specific section been devoted to SE in the report?		
• Yes	168	79.62
• No	43	20.38
What is the claimed role (aims and objectives) of SE for this organization?		
• Setting or reviewing strategic objectives	95	45.02
• Setting the content of the report (defining the materiality and relevance of information)	28	13.27
• Both previous elements	68	32.23
• No reference to the previous elements	20	9.48
Does the organization use one or more of the following methodologies for SE? *(Given that this was a multiple-choice question, the percentages indicate the ratio of organizations that make use of that specific methodology)*		
• Standard procedures	170	80.57
• Focus groups	47	22.27
• Interviews	69	32.70
• Surveys	135	63.98
• Meetings	148	70.14
• Social media interaction	127	60.19
• Other web applications	68	32.23

Which stakeholder groups have been engaged?
(This categorization is based on Chapter 3's review of the
definitions of stakeholders. Given that this was a multiple-choice
question, the percentages indicate the ratio of organizations that
declared regularly engaging that group of stakeholders)

- Shareholders   160   75.83
- Employees   194   91.94
- Customers   167   79.15
- Suppliers   162   76.78
- Government   159   75.36
- NGOs   108   51.18
- Local communities   184   87.20
- Media   86   40.76

What is the reported degree of stakeholder involvement?
(Our three-category elaboration is based on Arnstein, 1969
and Friedman & Miles, 2006: see theoretical framework in
Chapter 3 for details)

- Empowered: Proactive role of stakeholders and the   7   3.32
  appointment of representatives in the governing bodies *(7th-*
  12th rungs in Friedman and Miles's model)
- Consulted: Consultation, monitoring and information   136   64.46
  gathering *(5th-6th rungs)*
- Informed: Simple information, one-way dialogue and no   62   29.38
  opportunity for SE to influence decisions *(1st-4th rungs)*
- Absent: No reference to SE   6   2.84

Are stakeholders' perceptions and feedback regarding the
  previous edition of the sustainability report included?

- Yes, only positive   9   4.27
- Yes, only negative   2   0.95
- Yes, both positive and negative   13   6.15
- No   187   88.63

Are stakeholder issues reported in the SE section or only in the
  materiality matrix?

- Yes   98   46.45
- No   113   53.55

Are quotations from stakeholders included in the report?

- Yes, only positive (collaborative/accordant)   17   8.05
- Yes, only negative (agonistic/adversarial)   0   0.00
- Yes, both positive and negative   2   0.95
- No   192   91.00

(continued)

Table 5.7 (continued)

Question and categories	N.	%
Are there forms of dialogic accounting among stakeholders?		
• Yes, collaborative/accordant	7	3.32
• Yes, agonistic/adversarial	1	0.47
• Yes, both collaborative and agonistic	3	1.42
• No	200	94.79
Does the report explicitly claim that stakeholders have been directly involved in providing materiality checks for the reporting process?		
• Yes	159	75.36
• No	52	24.64
Are specific guidelines (e.g., AA1000SES) used for SE?		
• Yes	63	29.86
• No	148	70.14%
Are the difficulties encountered in the SE process stated?		
• Yes	32	15.17
• No	179	84.83
In general, how does the report cover the topic of SE?		
• Deeply	28	13.27
• Intermediate	83	39.34
• Superficially	94	44.55
• Not at all	6	2.84
Do the report make use of photos and other visual arts?		
• Yes	179	84.84
• Yes, with a specific section	1	0.47
• Not particularly	31	14.69
What type of message is the organization trying to articulate with these photos and other visual arts?		
• Positive	187	88.63
• Negative	0	0.00
• Mixed	14	6.63
• Absent	10	4.74

Of the entire sample, 168 enterprises (79.62 percent of the organizations) decided to provide a specific section in their reports to illustrate the SE process. This step is recommended by the GRI guidelines. Our content analysis confirmed that this section usually comprises the following standard disclosures (Global Reporting Initiative, 2013):

- G4-24 provides a list of stakeholder groups engaged by the organization;
- G4-25 reports the basis for identification and selection of stakeholders with whom to engage;
- G4-26 reports the organization's approach to stakeholder engagement, including the frequency of engagement by type and by stakeholder group and indicates whether any of the engagement was undertaken specifically as part of the report preparation process;
- G4-27 reports key topics and concerns that have been raised through stakeholder engagement and how the organization has responded to those key topics and concerns, including in its reporting. It also reports the stakeholder groups that raised each of the key topics and concerns.

These standard disclosures provide an overview of the organization's stakeholder engagement during the reporting period and do not have to be limited to engagement conducted for the purposes of preparing the report (Global Reporting Initiative, 2013). Compliance with the GRI G4 usually allows organizations to comply with the list of principles developed by the Clarkson Centre for Business Ethics (1999), which summarize the ideal features of stakeholder engagement (see Section 4.2.3 of this volume) and define stakeholder engagement as the process of effectively eliciting stakeholder views on their relationship with the organization. Forty-three organizations (20.38 percent) opted not to prepare a specific section of their reports dedicated the SE process and instead disseminated SE information throughout the whole report (referencing the abovementioned standard disclosures through the GRI index at the end of the report) or failed to discuss this information. From the perspective of the report's users, we believe that a dedicating a specific section to SE better serves the purpose of addressing the call for transparency and accountability in the reporting of stakeholder involvement.

SE is reported to be used primarily to define strategies and goals. The large majority of organizations (163 out of 211, 77.25 percent) in our sample claimed in their reports that stakeholders were engaged in order to review strategic objectives. In particular, 95 organizations of 211 (45.02 percent) declared in their reports that they use SE primarily when setting or reviewing strategic objectives; this declaration affects the search for materiality of information, and we must include 68 more organizations (32.23 percent) that use SE both in defining strategic objectives and in setting the content of reports. Twenty-eight companies (13.27 percent) use SE primarily to determine how to implement sustainability reports, defining the materiality and relevance of included information. Only 20 organizations did not openly state the main objective of their SE procedures.

> Waste Management actively seeks out dialogue with all stakeholders who have an interest in our business and hold us accountable to our principles. We engage broadly, and at every level, with industry peers and multistakeholder

groups to discuss the issues affecting our business and the ways in which our operations may affect others. Insights from these engagements help shape our strategic plans and business targets and are especially important for guiding our work within our communities.[7]

Therefore, the role of SE appears to be imperative for organizations, especially those operating in sectors that deal with legitimacy on a daily basis. Dialogue with stakeholders appears to be relevant both for defining strategies and practices and for conducting a materiality check of voluntary disclosures. Particularly, in 159 of 211 reports (75.36 percent), the organization claimed that stakeholders were directly involved in providing materiality checks for the reporting process. Materiality disclosure does not refer to the truthful identification of material issues by companies; rather, it refers to the extent to which companies disclose the materiality determination process and the issues they consider to be material (Fasan & Mio, 2017).

> Material matters are defined as those risks, opportunities and other fac-tors most likely to have an impact on our ability to create long-term sus-tainable value. These matters are continually monitored and evaluated to ensure that our strategy and day-to-day actions address each of them to achieve our strategic goals. We identify our most material matters through our risk management processes, continuous review of internal performance and the external environment, and our formal and informal engagements with stakeholders . . . We analyse and prioritise our most material matters according to the significance of their potential impact on the Company and our key stakeholders . . . The significance of each matter determines the information we report to stakeholders in our Integrated Annual Report, this Sustainability Report and through other channels.[8]

In 98 reports (46.45 percent), the list of issues mentioned by stakeholders is also reported in the SE section, while in the remaining reports, it is included only in the materiality matrix.

> In order to meet the new GRI directives, in version 4, Corticeira Amorim built a materiality matrix based on the results of the stakeholder consulta-tion (. . .) and on the importance of the different sustainability topics for the company. This matrix illustrates the materiality of the different topics of the social, environmental and economic pillars, and served as a base for selecting information to be considered in this publication.[9]

To interact with their stakeholders, companies can use several mechanisms. Which tools and methodologies support this very important process? As shown previously in this volume, organizations often rely on a mix of different tools (for a review of these tools, see Section 4). For example, 70.14 percent of the organizations reported using group meetings, site visits, official meetings and other collective approaches to perform SE; 80.57 percent of the organizations declared using formal procedures such as standardized, general channels of communication (e.g., newsletters, bulletins, etc.) and presentations of annual reports; 32.23 percent of the enterprises rely on their website and other non-social media technological applications (e.g., mobile apps). Other frequently used tools include survey and polls (63.98 percent) and interviews and other one-on-one techniques (32.70 percent). Social media have proven to be a tool capable of supporting a two-way conversation with stakeholders (see Section 4.2 of this volume), and 127 companies (60.19 percent) in our sample claimed to actively use Facebook, Twitter or other social media platforms to engage their stakeholders. Although one-way communication remains the most common strategy adopted by organizations on social media (Waters & Jamal, 2011; Xifra & Grau, 2010), attempts to develop interactions among corporations and users are becoming increasingly popular (Bellucci & Manetti, 2017; Manetti & Bellucci, 2016; Manetti, Bellucci, & Bagnoli, 2016) (see Section 4.4.5 of this volume for more details on the use of social media for SE). While traditional forms of interaction with stakeholders remain the most common, we can imagine how complementary, innovative tools to engage stakeholders will begin to be employed more often in the near future.

We also aimed to assess the stakeholder groups with which organizations claim to have engaged. The categorization we used for this content analysis is based on Chapter 4's review of the definitions of stakeholders. We analyzed each sustainability report to determine if the organization claimed to engage shareholders and investors (75.83 percent of the organization indicated it engaged this group of stakeholders), employees and their representatives (91.94 percent), customers (79.15 percent), suppliers, contractors and subcontractors (76.78 percent), NGOs, members of civil society and non-profit organizations (51.18 percent), communities, community members, traditional councils and community trusts (87.20 percent). In general, more than two-thirds of the organizations claimed to engage employees, local communities, government, shareholders, suppliers and customers. "Make a positive difference in the lives of employees, and the local community".[10]

Our empirical analysis confirms that employees and local communities represent the most important stakeholders for industries with heavy social and environmental impacts (Azapagic, 2004). For example, contrasts between the thoughts of employees and management in terms of working conditions, opportunities for training and career development and respect for human rights have been the cause of major clashes between trade unions and mining companies. Our analysis confirms these trends and suggests that organizations operating in sectors concerned with legitimacy issues are particularly willing to report on the inclusion of the most relevant stakeholders. In particular, organizations in our sample are particularly interested in including employees in their SE strategies because they represent a key group of stakeholders. In this respect, local authorities and governments play a very influential role in supporting sustainability issues, as they define the legislative framework and its enforcement. Several companies offer detailed information about opinion polls and surveys among their employees and communities; employees' and community members' perceptions on a variety of issues – including safety, health and the environment, ethics, accountability, diversity, personal respect and open two-way communications – are often presented (Kolk, 2004).

> Our approach to stakeholder engagement at an operational level is guided by the Anglo American Socio-Economic Assessment Toolbox (SEAT). SEAT provides managers with international best-practice guidance and tools to develop strategies for enhancing the positive contribution of their operations, while also mitigating any negative impacts. Some of the core objectives of SEAT are to improve each operation's understanding of its full range of local stakeholders as well as their views and interests; provide guidance in developing and updating annual stakeholder engagement plans; and increase trust and goodwill among host communities.[11]

Other engaged stakeholders cited in the reports include academia, the media (40.76 percent), other industrial peers, banks, analysts and other representatives of civil society.

Various methodologies can be used to engage different stakeholder groups to different extents. In order to determine the reported degree of stakeholder involvement, we build on Arnstein (1969) and Friedman and Miles (2006) and develop our own four-level categorization:

0   Absence: no reference to SE.
1   Information: one-way communication and no opportunity for stakeholders to influence decisions (1st–4th rungs in Friedman and Miles's ladder; see Chapter 4);
2   Consultation: monitoring and information gathering (5th–6th rungs);
3   Empowerment: proactive role of stakeholders and the appointment of representatives to the governing bodies (7th–12th rungs).

This categorization is based on our theoretical framework (see Chapter 4) and enables us to classify organizations according to their reported degree of stakeholder engagement. On the lower rungs of non-participation lie manipulation; the middle section of the ladder includes degrees of consultation and placation; and the higher rungs demonstrate the degrees of delegated power and full partnership (Arnstein, 1969; Friedman & Miles, 2006). In our sample, 136 enterprises (64.46 percent) carry out a form of level 2 SE, where stakeholders are consulted more than informed through two-way dialogue but are not empowered to contribute to managerial functions or appointed to decisional bodies. This form of consultation corresponds to rungs 5 and 6 in Friedman and Miles's ladder. Of all the organizations, 29.38 percent reported that they inform stakeholders without referencing in their reports any form of active consultation; in other words, their reports communicate that stakeholders are informed of the organization's decisions but are not involved in any decision making at any phase. This finding appears to be a focal point to us, and in the conclusions we will question if this very basic form of interaction with stakeholders, which corresponds to rungs 1 to 4 in Friedman and Miles's ladder, can be considered an effective form of SE or if it is only a way to manage stakeholders' perception. While 6 reports make no specific reference to the SE process, 7 organizations declared that they empower some of their stakeholders by appointing stakeholder representatives to a council with governmental power.

Building on our theoretical framework, we also aimed to assess if practices capable of supporting forms of dialogic accounting (see Section 4.3.3 of our theoretical framework) were implemented. We found that forms of dialogic accounting, such as stakeholders that answer other stakeholders' questions on critical topics or multi-stakeholder initiatives, remain very rare. Only 11 organizations declared having these kinds of practices in place. Seven of these organizations reported a collaborative/accordant form of dialogic accounting (where stakeholders work together to produce a deliberative consensus), while the remaining contemplated a mixed or agonistic/adversarial form (where conflicts among stakeholders emerge).

> Since 2011, we have sponsored the multistakeholder dialogues of the Sustainable Materials Management Coalition. We believe there is enormous value in bringing together diverse viewpoints in a sustained effort to find common ground and mutual understanding of difficult environmental challenges.[12]

Only a few companies provided information about the circulation of reports and the feedback they received on their public communication efforts; in some cases, stakeholders were invited to give their views on the current report (Kolk, 2004). As Table 5.7 shows, 24 organizations included stakeholders' perceptions of or feedback on the previous edition of the sustainability report. The willingness (or not) to report on these perceptions is important in light of legitimacy theory. This value is low, given that GRI guidelines recommend reviewing every version of a sustainability report with stakeholders in order to check its rigor and completeness and to identify opportunities for improvement. It is noteworthy that some of these organizations reported both positive and negative perceptions because it is generally uncommon to find reports of negative or agonistic expressions in sustainability reports: in contrast, we believe it is considerable as a form of commitment and willingness to disclose areas where it is possible to improve in the future. Moreover, 36 organizations of 211 (17.06 percent) declared to the GRI that they took advantage of formalized input or feedback on the present version of the report provided by a panel of stakeholders or experts.

Furthermore, to reflect different stakeholder views, it has become rather common to include stakeholder statements in reports (Kolk, 2004). Quotations from stakeholders – not only on the previous edition of the report but also on the organization's general activities – are more often included: 17 organizations (8.05 percent) included positive (collaborative or accordant) quotations, while 2 organizations (1.23 percent) included both positive and negative (agonistic or adversarial) quotations. These statements included in the reports originated from both internal and external stakeholders (Kolk, 2004).

Sixty-three organizations (29.86 percent) claimed using specific guidelines other than GRI to define the SE processes. In many of these cases, organizations declared following AA1000SES (see Section 3.3.2 of this volume for details).

> "=The CSR team has identified the eight main stakeholders of FPCC by ranking the stakeholders according to international tendency, industrial characteristics, business conditions, and the five principles of the AA1000 Stakeholder Engagement Standard (dependency, responsibility, influence, diverse perspectives, and tension).[13]

Thirty-two organizations (15.17 percent) reported on difficulties encountered in the SE process. Engaging stakeholders is a very complex process that, even for companies adopting best practices, can naturally present logistical, cultural and technical difficulties. We believe that reporting on these difficulties should be interpreted positively, as it signals to the report's users the complexity that concretely lies behind SE and the willingness of the organization to improve year after year in how it involves its stakeholders and in the outcomes of this process.

We also studied the utilization of photos and other forms of visual arts. As Table 5.7 shows, only 31 reports (14.69 percent) did not exhibit a particular use of photos or other visual arts. Photos and other kinds of visual arts are often used to articulate a positive message, to highlight positive features or to encourage a sense of legitimization. In a few cases, photos were used to illustrate that there are unresolved issues or ongoing emergencies, presenting a mixed message (6.63 percent). This kind of behavior is not restricted to photos, as it is commonly found in relation to the entire content of these reports.

The sampled organizations generally provide their sustainability reports in PDF format; a small minority (12.80 percent) present their reports on a dedicated section of their websites. The PDF format is a logical choice because it enables organizations to produce eye-catching, compatible and easily shared reports, making use of paginated texts, figures and photos. PDFs are compatible with a vast set of operating systems and platforms. Moreover, pagination is useful in referencing the GRI Content Index, which is usually located at the end of the report. In contrast, web-based reports can allow organizations to quickly fix errors and typos and even update outdated information during the operating period.

> Openness, dialogue and engagement are essential for developing long-term, constructive and transparent relations with stakeholders. For the past 20 years or so, changes in the regulatory framework have promoted information, consultation and dialogue prior to high-impact decisions being made. In addition to complying with regulations, TOTAL encourages dialogue at every level of its organization. The foremost requirement of the societal directive is that "each asset must consult its stakeholders regularly to gain a clearer understanding of their expectations and concerns, measure their level of satisfaction regarding the Group and identify avenues of improvement for its societal strategy.[14]

After analyzing the content of every report, we gave a general score to the coverage level of the SE section. Not every report disclosed sufficient information on how and why the organization engaged stakeholders, on who were the most relevant stakeholders and, above all, how the organization aimed to involve it community in its decision-making processes. On one hand, 83 (39.34 percent) and 94 (44.55 percent) enterprises provided an intermediate or superficial level of coverage, respectively. On the other hand, 28 organizations fully disclosed every detail of their SE process, with accurate figures and sensitive information: this commitment is significant because it signals that an organization effectively considers SE to be a core process in its definition of its strategy. Six companies (2.84 percent) did not cover the topic of SE at all, even though they declared following the GRI G4 guidelines, which are particularly focused on materiality through SE.

We build on Bellucci (2017) and Manetti (2011) to further comment on our results and the state of the art of SE in sustainability reporting. In particular, we focused on the following levels of comparison:

1) The reported role of stakeholder engagement. Our results confirm that SE is used primarily for reviewing strategic objectives (77.25 percent) and that this use affects the implementation of sustainability reports. Organizations also rely on SE to define the content and materiality of reports (45.5 percent), which is a highly interconnected topic. The abovementioned research by Manetti (2011) on the quality of SE finds that only 10.34 percent of the organizations used SE to define the relevance of the information for the report. We may conclude that our analysis is specific to sectors concerned with legitimacy issues, but these data suggest that SE is increasingly used as a management practice to support both strategy definition and material reporting. Moreover, the recent G4 version of the GRI guidelines stresses the importance of SE as the best way to address the issue of materiality of non-financial information (Global Reporting Initiative, 2013). Consequently, the introduction of G4 facilitated a shift in how organizations approach SE and the involvement of stakeholders in preparing sustainability reports.
2) The reported degree of stakeholder engagement. Our results suggest the mild involvement of stakeholders, who are usually consulted (64.46 percent) more than actively empowered (3.32 percent) or just informed (29.38 percent). These results are consistent with Bellucci (2017) and, in particular, with Manetti (2011), who find that stakeholder involvement concerned a "simple consultation, monitoring, and information gathering" in 3 cases out of 4 (73.56 percent) and that a "proactive role and appointment of representatives in the governing bodies" was reported in only 15.52 percent of the cases.

We can reach several conclusions on the role of SE and the characteristics of this engagement. Building on our theoretical framework presented in Section 4, we used content analysis to study 211 sustainability reports from eight industries that have heavy social and environmental impacts (Chemicals, Energy, Food and Beverage Products, Forest and Paper Products, Mining, Textiles and Apparel,

Tobacco and Waste Management) prepared in accordance with the GRI-G4 guidelines. Further research could build on several key results that emerged from our empirical analysis, particularly the following:

- Organizations reported that SE is used primarily to define their strategies. This use affects sustainability reporting and appears to confirm that stakeholder theory is truly capable of describing organizations' need to define and report on their policies by taking into account stakeholders' viewpoints.
- The majority of organizations affirmed that stakeholders were directly involved in providing materiality checks for the reporting process, appearing to confirm our thesis on the centrality of stakeholders and SE in the materiality assessment process. Using the materiality principle in the context of SR helps organizations select items that inform investors and other stakeholders about a business's ability to create value in a sustainable manner.
- Meetings, surveys, social media, interviews and standard procedures are among the most frequently used methodologies to support SE.
- Employees, local communities, shareholders, consumers and governments are among the most frequently engaged stakeholder groups, although all the other categories are commonly included. If, on the one hand, it is legitimate for organizations to be willing to engage their most relevant stakeholders, on the other hand, the prioritization of the most powerful groups appears to be in line with an instrumental approach to stakeholder theory, highlighting potential connections between stakeholder management and the achievement of the organization's goals. An unbalanced approach risks disregarding important stakeholders for the sake of opportunistic behaviors.
- The concept of consultation aptly describes the overall reported level of engagement, and only a minority of organizations directly empowered stakeholders by appointing them to governing bodies, casting a shadow on the degree to which stakeholders can effectively influence business management. Further studies can examine the background of what is written in public reports and involve stakeholders themselves in research about their genuine degree of participation.
- The adoption of specific standards covering the SE process, particularly AA1000SES, is increasingly popular.
- Forms of dialogic accounting remain very rare or unreported.

In addition to answering our research question on the reported role of SE in sustainability reporting, our empirical study provided a comprehensive database that may be useful for further research on the abovementioned topics. Our data could indicate that companies operating in the most critical industries from a social and environmental sustainability standpoint are more willing to manage their relations with stakeholders and to use sustainability reports as a form of demonstrating the company's legitimacy to them. Further case-by-case research, however, is necessary to complement our data with case studies providing a deep look at how organizations on one hand and stakeholders themselves on the other hand perceive the significance of SE in the frame of sustainability reporting and sustainable development.

In order to better understand the stakeholder-organization relationship, much more research should explore stakeholder perceptions and the factors that stakeholders consider to be necessary and sufficient conditions for stakeholder recognition (Miles, 2017). This research would benefit management by reducing the gap in expectations between management and stakeholders with respect to important business ethics issues, such as accountability and transparency (Miles, 2017). Since it is difficult to ascertain motivations through content analysis (Bryman & Bell, 2015), we should call for further research and case studies to investigate the main reasons behind authentic stakeholder engagement. These in-depth studies could go behind the veil of reports and attempt to understand the degree of genuineness and effectiveness of the processes of stakeholder engagement, their impact on strategies and performance and what stakeholders offer and learn as a result of their involvement.

Notes

1 These languages include, in order of frequency, Chinese, Japanese, Swedish, Polish, German, Greek, Czech and Dutch.
2 For state-owned companies, "Non-listed" means it is fully state-owned and "Listed" means that part of the company is listed on a stock exchange for public trading (partial government ownership).
3 GRI (and this volume) adopts the following European Union definitions of organization size:

Enterprise category	Head count	Turnover	or Balance sheet total
SME	< 250	≤ €50 million	≤ €43 million
Large	≥ 250	> €50 million	> €43 million
MNE	≥ 250 and multinational	> €50 million	> €43 million

4 While our preliminary analysis showed that an undeclared level of adherence does not necessarily indicate a low-quality reporting process, we opted to focus on reports that followed a specific level of adherence in order to have a more homogenous, unbiased sample.
5 Researchers must decide between the terms "concept" and "category" and use one or the other (Kyngas & Vanhanen, 1999); for example, if the purpose of the study is to develop a theory, the term "concept" should be used as a proxy for "category", with this latter term being the most frequently used term in the literature (Elo & Kyngäs, 2008). In this volume, when describing the analysis process, we opted to use the term "category".
6 The preliminary results of this pilot test are discussed in Bellucci (2017).
7 Waste Management Sustainability Report 2016, p. 90.
8 African Rainbow Minerals Integrated Report 2015, p. 32.
9 Corticeira Amorim Sustainability Report 2015, p. 6.
10 Desso Sustainability Report 2015, p. 46.
11 Anglo American Sustainability Report 2015, p. 18.
12 Waste Management Sustainability Report 2016, p. 90.
13 Formosa Petrochemical Corporation Corporate Social Responsibility Report 2015, p. 16.
14 TOTAL Registration Document 2015, p. 147.

References

Abdifatah, A. H., & Mutalib, A. (2016). The trend of integrated reporting practice in South Africa: Ceremonial or substantive? *Sustainability Accounting, Management and Policy Journal, 7*(2), 190–224.

Arnstein, S. R. (1969). A ladder of citizen participation. *Journal of the American Institute of planners, 35*(4), 216–224.

Azapagic, A. (2004). Developing a framework for sustainable development indicators for the mining and minerals industry. *Journal of Cleaner Production, 12*(6), 639–662.

Barcus, F. E. (1959). *Communications content: Analysis of the research, 1900–1958 (a content analysis of content analysis).* University of Illinois, Univ. Microfilms [reprod.].

Bellucci, M. (2017). The role of stakeholder engagement in sustainability reporting. (PhD), University of Pisa.

Bellucci, M., & Manetti, G. (2017). Facebook as a tool for supporting dialogic accounting? Evidence from large philanthropic foundations in the United States. *Accounting, Auditing & Accountability Journal, 30*(4), 874–905. doi:10.1108/AAAJ-07-2015-2122

Berelson, B. (1952). *Content Analysis in Communication Research.* New York: Free Press.

Bini, L., Bellucci, M., & Giunta, F. (2018). Integrating sustainability in business model disclosure: Evidence from the UK mining industry. *Journal of Cleaner Production, 171*(Supplement C), 1161–1170. doi:https://doi.org/10.1016/j.jclepro.2017.09.282

Brown, J., & Dillard, J. (2015). Dialogic accountings for stakeholders: On opening up and closing down participatory governance. *Journal of Management Studies, 52*(7), 961–985. doi:10.1111/joms.12153

Brummer, H., Badenhorst, J., & Neuland, E. (2006). Competitive analysis and strategic decision-making in global mining firms. *Journal of Global Business and Technology, 2*(2), 26.

Bryman, A., & Bell, E. (2015). *Business research methods.* Oxford: Oxford University Press.

Burnard, P. (1991). A method of analysing interview transcripts in qualitative research. *Nurse Education Today, 11*(6), 461–466.

Castello, I., & Lozano, J. M. (2011). Searching for new forms of legitimacy through corporate responsibility rhetoric. *Journal of Business Ethics, 100*(1), 11–29. doi:10.1007/s10551-011-0770-8

Cavanagh, S. (1997). Content analysis: Concepts, methods and applications. *Nurse Researcher, 4*(3), 5–13.

Chinn, P. L., & Kramer, M. K. (1983). *Theory and nursing: A systematic approach.*Please complete ref. ST Louis: Mosby.

Clarkson Centre for Business Ethics. (1999). *Principles of stakeholder management.* Clarkson Centre for Business Ethics, Joseph L. Rotman School of Management, University of Toronto.

Clarkson, P. M., Li, Y., Richardson, G. D., & Vasvari, F. P. (2011). Does it really pay to be green? Determinants and consequences of proactive environmental strategies. *Journal of Accounting and Public Policy, 30*(2), 122–144.

Clarkson, P. M., Overell, M. B., & Chapple, L. (2011). Environmental reporting and its relation to corporate environmental performance. *Abacus, 47*(1), 27–60.

Cooper, S. M., & Owen, D. L. (2007). Corporate social reporting and stakeholder accountability: The missing link. *Accounting, Organizations and Society, 32*(7), 649–667.

Cowell, S. J., Wehrmeyer, W., Argust, P. W., & Robertson, J. G. S. (1999). Sustainability and the primary extraction industries: Theories and practice. *Resources Policy, 25*(4), 277–286.

Crane, A., & Matten, D. (2016). Engagement required: The changing role of the corporation in society. In D. Barton, D. Horvath, & M. Kipping (Eds), *Re-imagining capitalism: Building a responsible, long-term model*. Oxford: Oxford University Press.

Deegan, C. (2002). Introduction: The legitimising effect of social and environmental disclosures-a theoretical foundation. *Accounting, Auditing & Accountability Journal*, *15*(3), 282–311.

Deegan, C., Rankin, M., & Tobin, J. (2002). An examination of the corporate social and environmental disclosures of BHP from 1983–1997: A test of legitimacy theory. *Accounting, Auditing & Accountability Journal*, *15*(3), 312–343.

Dey, I. (2003). Qualitative data analysis: A user friendly guide for social scientists. London: Routledge.

Dobele, A. R., Westberg, K., Steel, M., & Flowers, K. (2014). An examination of corporate social responsibility implementation and stakeholder engagement: A case study in the Australian mining industry. *Business Strategy and the Environment*, *23*(3), 145–159.

Dowling, J., & Pfeffer, J. (1975). Organizational legitimacy: Social values and organizational behavior. *Pacific Sociological Review*, *18*(1), 122–136.

Downe-Wamboldt, B. (1992). Content analysis: Method, applications, and issues. *Health Care for Women International*, *13*(3), 313–321.

Elo, S., & Kyngäs, H. (2008). The qualitative content analysis process. *Journal of Advanced Nursing*, *62*(1), 107–115.

Fasan, M., & Mio, C. (2017). Fostering stakeholder engagement: The role of materiality disclosure in integrated reporting. *Business Strategy and the Environment*, *26*(3), 288–305.

Friedman, A. L., & Miles, S. (2006). *Stakeholders: Theory and practice*. Oxford: Oxford University Press on Demand.

General Accounting Office. (1996). *Content analysis: A methodology for structuring and analyzing written material*. Washington: US General Accounting Office.Please give city.

Global Reporting Initiative. (2013). *Reporting principles and standard disclosure*. Amsterdam: Global Reporting Initiative.

Graneheim, U. H., & Lundman, B. (2004). Qualitative content analysis in nursing research: Concepts, procedures and measures to achieve trustworthiness. *Nurse Education Today*, *24*(2), 105–112.

Gray, R., Kouhy, R., & Lavers, S. (1995). Corporate social and environmental reporting: A review of the literature and a longitudinal study of UK disclosure. *Accounting, Auditing & Accountability Journal*, *8*(2), 47–77.

Gray, R., & Milne, M. (2002). Sustainability reporting: Who's kidding whom? *Chartered Accountants Journal of New Zealand*, *81*(6), 66–70.

Grove, S., & Burns, N. (2005). *The practice of nursing research: Conduct, critique, & utilization*. St. Louis: Elsevier Saunders.

Guthrie, J., & Parker, L. D. (1989). Corporate social reporting: A rebuttal of legitimacy theory. *Accounting and Business Research*, *19*(76), 343–352.

Guthrie, J., Petty, R., Yongvanich, K., & Ricceri, F. (2004). Using content analysis as a research method to inquire into intellectual capital reporting. *Journal of Intellectual Capital*, *5*(2), 282–293.

Holsti, O. R. (1969). *Content analysis for the social sciences and humanities*. Addison-Wesley.

Hsieh, H.-F., & Shannon, S. E. (2005). Three approaches to qualitative content analysis. *Qualitative Health Research*, *15*(9), 1277–1288.

Jenkins, H., & Yakovleva, N. (2006). Corporate social responsibility in the mining industry: Exploring trends in social and environmental disclosure. *Journal of Cleaner Production, 14*(3), 271–284.

Kolk, A. (2004). A decade of sustainability reporting: Developments and significance. *International Journal of Environment and Sustainable Development, 3*(1), 51–64. doi:10.1504/IJESD.2004.004688

Krippendorff, K. (2004). *Content analysis: An introduction to its methodology.* London: Sage.

Kyngas, H., & Vanhanen, L. (1999). Content analysis. *Hoitotiede, 11*(3–12).

Laufer, W. S. (2003). Social accountability and corporate greenwashing. *Journal of Business Ethics, 43*(3), 253–261.

Lederman, R. P. (1991). Content analysis of word texts. *MCN: The American Journal of Maternal/Child Nursing, 16*(3), 169.

Manetti, G. (2011). The quality of stakeholder engagement in sustainability reporting: empirical evidence and critical points. *Corporate Social Responsibility and Environmental Management, 18*(2), 110–122.

Manetti, G., & Bellucci, M. (2016). The use of social media for engaging stakeholders in sustainability reporting. *Accounting, Auditing & Accountability Journal, 29*(6), 985–1011. doi:10.1108/AAAJ-08-2014-1797

Manetti, G., Bellucci, M., & Bagnoli, L. (2016). Stakeholder engagement and public information through social media: A study of Canadian and American public transportation agencies. *The American Review of Public Administration, 47*(8). doi:10.1177/0275074016649260

Marshall, C., & Rossman, G. B. (2014). *Designing qualitative research.* London: Sage publications.

Miles, S. (2017). Stakeholder theory classification: A theoretical and empirical evaluation of definitions. *Journal of Business Ethics, 142*(3), 437–459.

Milne, M. J., & Adler, R. W. (1999). Exploring the reliability of social and environmental disclosures content analysis. *Accounting, Auditing & Accountability Journal, 12*(2), 237–256.

Moratis, L., & Brandt, S. (2017). Corporate stakeholder responsiveness? Exploring the state and quality of GRI-based stakeholder engagement disclosures of European firms. *Corporate Social Responsibility and Environmental Management*, online.

Morgan, G. (1988). Accounting as reality construction: Towards a new epistemology for accounting practice. *Accounting, Organizations and Society, 13*(5), 477–485.

Mouan, L. C. (2010). Exploring the potential benefits of Asian participation in the extractive industries transparency initiative: The case of China. *Business Strategy and the Environment, 19*(6), 367–376.

Neuendorf, K. A. (2002). *The content analysis guidebook.* London: Sage.

Owen, D. L., Swift, T., & Hunt, K. (2001). Questioning the role of stakeholder engagement in social and ethical accounting, auditing and reporting. Paper presented at the Accounting Forum. London.

Patten, D. M. (1992). Intra-industry environmental disclosures in response to the Alaskan oil spill: A note on legitimacy theory. *Accounting, Organizations and Society, 17*(5), 471–475.

Peck, P., & Sinding, K. (2003). Environmental and social disclosure and data richness in the mining industry. *Business Strategy and the Environment, 12*(3), 131–146.

Rosengren, K. E. (1981). *Advances in content analysis.* Beverly Hills: Sage

Sandelowski, M. (1993). Theory unmasked: The uses and guises of theory in qualitative research. *Research in Nursing & Health, 16*(3), 213–218.

Tate, W. L., Ellram, L. M., & Kirchoff, J. F. (2010). Corporate social responsibility reports: A thematic analysis related to supply chain management. *Journal of Supply Chain Management, 46*(1), 19–44.

Warhurst, A. (2001). Corporate citizenship and corporate social investment. *Journal of Corporate Citizenship, 1*(1), 57–73.

Waters, R. D., & Jamal, J. Y. (2011). Tweet, tweet, tweet: A content analysis of nonprofit organizations' Twitter updates. *Public Relations Review, 37*(3), 321–324.

Weber, R. P. (1990). *Basic content analysis*. London: Sage.

Xifra, J., & Grau, F. (2010). Nanoblogging PR: The discourse on public relations in Twitter. *Public Relations Review, 36*(2), 171–174.

6   Conclusions

This volume has aimed to provide an original contribution to the literature on social and environmental accounting, stakeholder theory and the role of enterprises in sustainability by studying the role and features of stakeholder engagement in sustainability reporting and empirically analyzing the properties of information stated in sustainability reports in stakeholder engagement policies and practices. In a global context of growing social and environmental concerns and evolving consumer expectations in terms of responsible consumption, large companies are increasingly expected to provide more than simply a financial report. Even the academic community is reaching a consensus on the responsibilities of large enterprises to report not only on their financial performance but also on their social and environmental outcomes (Deegan, 2002). In deciding what to report on, enterprises must choose from a wide set of aspects related to the triple bottom line. The most relevant sustainability reporting guidelines (AccountAbility, 2008, 2015; Global Reporting Initiative, 2013b) state that this selection is oriented by the principle of materiality, according to which material aspects are those that reflect the organization's significant economic, environmental and social impacts or that substantively influence stakeholders' assessments and decisions. Using the materiality principle in the context of sustainability reporting helps determine those items that inform investors and other stakeholders about a business's ability to create and sustain value. Since it is often impossible or very difficult to set thresholds for non-financial or non-market aspects to assess their materiality, we highlight the centrality of the stakeholder engagement process. An analysis of the stakeholders' interests, in fact, can help define the spectrum of financial, social and environmental aspects for which the organization must be accountable.

Since large corporations are extending their role in our society and the willingness to integrally report on financial, social and environmental outcomes is derived from organizations' new responsibilities, our thesis is that stakeholder engagement can be among the most effective tools for the materiality assessment of information in sustainability reporting and for supporting the orientation of strategies and decision making in light of stakeholders' expectations.

We believe that our research on these topics, which is hereby presented in this volume, led to at least three main deliverables. First, we produced a systematic literature review on topics that are essential to understanding the state of the art of the study of the role of stakeholder engagement in sustainability reporting. In particular, we integrated the main contributions on the extended role of large enterprises in contemporary societies, their responsibilities for sustainability issues and the path to integrated reporting. Naturally, we analyzed the contents of the black box of social and environmental sustainability reporting, which include the motivations underlying sustainability reporting and the critical perspective on this form of reporting. For the purposes of our study, it was very important to frame the materiality principle from the perspective of sustainability reporting guidelines and a materiality assessment of the information to be reported. This literature review of the most influential academic contribution was crucial to establish the context of our research.

Second, we defined a theoretical framework based on stakeholder theory and stakeholder engagement. Starting from the opposition between stakeholders and shareholder theory, we then proceeded to review the different definitions of stakeholders and the positive, instrumental and normative approaches to stakeholder theory. We also provided an original theoretical three-phase segmentation of the process of stakeholder engagement: 1) stakeholder identification and analysis; 2) interaction with stakeholders; and 3) evaluation and reporting. All these steps are needed to implement the principle of stakeholder inclusiveness in sustainability reporting. In both the Global Reporting Initiative (GRI) (2013a, 2013b) and AccountAbility (2008, 2015) guidelines, the aspects that the organization deems to be material in response to its stakeholders' expectations and interests drive sustainability reporting and its content. In other words, stakeholder engagement represents a pivotal component of the process of identifying material topics and material impacts. Our conclusion is that committed, genuine and quality stakeholder engagement represents a fundamental step for organizations willing to disclose truly relevant sustainability reports and drive their strategies to meet the interests of their community of stakeholders.

Third, since in the stakeholder theory literature, little attention has been paid to the properties of information stated in sustainability reports regarding stakeholder engagement policies and practices (Abdifatah & Mutalib, 2016; Aras & Crowther, 2016; Brown & Dillard, 2015; Cooper & Owen, 2007; Crane & Matten, 2016; Dobele, Westberg, Steel, & Flowers, 2014; Fasan & Mio, 2017; Manetti, 2011; Owen, Swift, & Hunt, 2001), we aimed to contribute by providing an empirical analysis of how sustainability reports address stakeholder engagement, of the distinctive features of this process of involvement and of the role of stakeholder engagement in assessing materiality and defining the contents of this disclosure. Building on our theoretical framework, we used content analysis to study 211 sustainability reports published in 2016 and found in the GRI sustainability disclosure database; these reports came from sectors with high social or environmental impacts (Chemicals, Energy, Food and Beverage Products, Forest and Paper Products, Mining, Textiles and Apparel, Tobacco, and Waste Management) and were prepared in accordance with GRI G4 guidelines. Many of the recent environmental disasters or human rights incidents that have contributed to the growing public concern about sustainability have occurred in these industries (Cowell, Wehrmeyer, Argust, & Robertson, 1999; Warhurst, 2001). Organizations operating in these sectors must deal with social and environmental issues on a daily basis and must demonstrate that they are sensitive to the interests of several groups of stakeholders.

Our empirical analysis provides the following key results: a) most of the organizations reported that stakeholder engagement is used to help define both their strategies and the content of sustainability reports, while prioritizing strategy definition; b) the majority of organizations claimed that stakeholders were directly involved in providing materiality checks in the reporting process; c) meetings, surveys, social media and interviews were the most commonly used methods for supporting stakeholder engagement; d) employees, communities, shareholders, consumers and governments were the most frequently engaged groups of stakeholders; e) the most common level of engagement was the "consultation" of stakeholders, which lies between the vary basic "information" of stakeholders and the very rare "empowerment"; and f) forms of dialogic accounting remain very sporadic or unreported.

In conclusion, we can argue that underneath stakeholder engagement lie processes that can truly affect how organizations conceive of decision making, the orientation of strategies and the assessment of the materiality of information for sustainability reporting. This potential, however, has yet to be completely unleashed. We believe the potential of stakeholder engagement for decision making regarding sustainability issues and materiality assessment in sustainability reporting is hampered by at least two factors and has as many practical implications.

First, organizations should take the risk of increasing their exposure. If an organization truly wants to create value for every stakeholder and to seriously take stakeholders' perceptions into account, it must at least be ready to cope with agonistic or adversarial feedback if it is not willing to transfer a part of its decisional power. In light of dialogic accounting, the interactions between organizations and stakeholders and among stakeholders themselves represent a powerful tool for including stakeholders' expectations into new managerial strategies and for supporting a materiality assessment of sustainability reports. At the same time, however, the owner of the stakeholder engagement process must be open and ready to receive both positive and negative feedback; in other words, criticisms, protests, divergent opinions and agonistic behaviors are part of the game. Stakeholder engagement provides opportunities for change precisely through the combination of different, and sometimes opposing, points of view. This reason is also why the basic level of "informing" stakeholders cannot suffice to achieve stakeholder engagement. Considering and reporting on only concordant opinions or "easy" issues will definitely limit the scope of stakeholder engagement for social and environmental accounting. As argued by Neu, Cooper, and Everett (2001), accounting academics have a responsibility to influence social change. Practitioners of social and environmental accounting, in particular, must provide an opportunity for rethinking, take into account critical issues and be willing to expose inconvenient situations (Gray, 2016). The same argument applies to the need to transparently include in sustainability reports the most critical and less "shiny" issues. This step would have practical implications for conceiving of reports as legitimization devices, as these reports would include more negative or mixed feedback and could illuminate areas where companies can improve their responsibility. We also believe that consumers would reward this choice. We are now living in an increasingly mindful context in which consumers include ethical and environmental factors in the formation of their preferences.

A second element that hampers the potential of stakeholder engagement is the limited use of new technologies. This element is connected to the previous one: generally speaking, organizations are not searching for new ways to interact with their stakeholders in public because they fear the adverse publicity they could receive. This limitation is an issue because there are currently new technologies, particularly web-based technologies that could support organizations in reaching a broader set of stakeholders. For example, we believe that social media can be powerful mechanisms for reaching and keeping in touch with a large number of stakeholders, thus guaranteeing interactive dialogue with them at very low costs. We have already begun to explore the utilization of social media as an instrument for stakeholder engagement in sustainability reporting that is capable of identifying, dialoguing with and engaging the largest possible number of the organization's stakeholders while also taking into account their opinions and expectations, even if they diverge from the organization's point of view (Bellucci & Manetti, 2017; Manetti & Bellucci, 2016; Manetti, Bellucci, & Bagnoli, 2017). Nonetheless, we believe that topic is increasingly relevant and has many practical implications, as social media are becoming one of the main channels through which organizations promote their activities and communicate with customers, users, communities and other primary stakeholders. Companies could create more interactive and fruitful conversations without significantly impacting their budgets.

Further research could build on the limits of the present study by providing additional empirical evidence on the role of stakeholder engagement in sustainability reporting, the real motivations underlying social and environmental reporting and the legitimization processes behind the voluntary disclosure of non-financial information. First, from a qualitative standpoint, further case-by-case research is necessary to complement our data with case studies that provide a deep look at how organizations on one hand and stakeholders themselves on the other perceive the significance of stakeholder engagement in the context of sustainability reporting and sustainable development. Our data suggest that companies operating in the most critical sectors are willing to manage their relations with stakeholders and to use sustainability reports as a way to demonstrate to stakeholders the organization's legitimacy. Further research should make use of case studies to investigate the main reasons behind authentic stakeholder engagement. These in-depth studies could go behind the veil of reports and attempt to understand how truly genuine and effective the processes of stakeholder engagement are, their impact on strategies and performance and what stakeholders offer and learn as a result of their involvement.

Second, from a quantitative standpoint, software-assisted content analysis could be useful to study the manifest content of a broad set of sustainability reports. Quantitative content analysis could help to measure the number of concepts and words related to sustainability and legitimacy in different reports from organizations operating in different fields. In particular, a study based on word counts and quantitative content analysis could identify the sectors in which key words related to sustainability issues or legitimacy issues emerge with greater frequency. Implementing a dynamic setup, this analysis could also take into account the occurrence of scandals or environmental disasters (e.g., the Deepwater Horizon spillage, Volkswagen's "Dieselgate", etc.) and study if these companies changed the information they disclosed after these episodes, which would suggest a proactive attempt to restore eroded legitimacy.

References

Abdifatah, A. H., & Mutalib, A. (2016). The trend of integrated reporting practice in South Africa: Ceremonial or substantive? *Sustainability Accounting, Management and Policy Journal, 7*(2), 190–224.

AccountAbility. (2008). *AA1000 AccountAbility principles standard 2008*. New York: AccountAbility.

AccountAbility. (2015). *AA1000 Stakeholder engagement standard 2015*. New York: AccountAbility.

Aras, G., & Crowther, D. (2016). *The durable corporation: Strategies for sustainable development*. Boca Raton: CRC Press.

Bellucci, M., & Manetti, G. (2017). Facebook as a tool for supporting dialogic accounting? Evidence from large philanthropic foundations in the United States. *Accounting, Auditing & Accountability Journal, 30*(4), 874–905. doi:10.1108/AAAJ-07-2015-2122

Brown, J., & Dillard, J. (2015). Dialogic accountings for stakeholders: On opening up and closing down participatory governance. *Journal of Management Studies, 52*(7), 961–985. doi:10.1111/joms.12153

Cooper, S. M., & Owen, D. L. (2007). Corporate social reporting and stakeholder accountability: The missing link. *Accounting, Organizations and Society, 32*(7), 649–667.

Cowell, S. J., Wehrmeyer, W., Argust, P. W., & Robertson, J. G. S. (1999). Sustainability and the primary extraction industries: Theories and practice. *Resources Policy, 25*(4), 277–286.

Crane, A., & Matten, D. (2016). Engagement required: The changing role of the corporation in society. In D. Barton, D. Horvath, & M. Kipping (Eds), *Re-imagining capitalism: Building a responsible, long-term model*. Oxford: Oxford University Press.

Deegan, C. (2002). Introduction: The legitimising effect of social and environmental disclosures-a theoretical foundation. *Accounting, Auditing & Accountability Journal, 15*(3), 282–311.

Dobele, A. R., Westberg, K., Steel, M., & Flowers, K. (2014). An examination of corporate social responsibility implementation and stakeholder engagement: A case study in the Australian mining industry. *Business Strategy and the Environment, 23*(3), 145–159.

Fasan, M., & Mio, C. (2017). Fostering stakeholder engagement: The role of materiality disclosure in Integrated Reporting. *Business Strategy and the Environment, 26*(3), 288–305.

Global Reporting Initiative. (2013a). *Implementation manual*. Amsterdam: Global Reporting Initiative.

Global Reporting Initiative. (2013b). *Reporting principles and standard disclosure.* Amsterdam: Global Reporting Initiative.

Gray, R. (2016). Reading for displeasure: Why bother with social accounting at all? *Social and Environmental Accountability Journal, 36*(2), 153–161. doi:10.1080/0969 160X.2016.1197625

Manetti, G. (2011). The quality of stakeholder engagement in sustainability reporting: Empirical evidence and critical points. *Corporate Social Responsibility and Environmental Management, 18*(2), 110–122.

Manetti, G., & Bellucci, M. (2016). The use of social media for engaging stakeholders in sustainability reporting. *Accounting, Auditing & Accountability Journal, 29*(6), 985–1011. doi:10.1108/AAAJ-08-2014-1797

Manetti, G., Bellucci, M., & Bagnoli, L. (2017). Stakeholder engagement and public information through social media: A study of Canadian and American public transportation agencies. *The American Review of Public Administration, 47*(8). doi:10.1177/0275074016649260

Neu, D., Cooper, D. J., & Everett, J. (2001). Critical accounting interventions. *Critical Perspectives on Accounting, 12*(6), 735–762.

Owen, D. L., Swift, T., & Hunt, K. (2001). Questioning the role of stakeholder engagement in social and ethical accounting, auditing and reporting. Paper presented at the Accounting Forum, London.

Warhurst, A. (2001). Corporate citizenship and corporate social investment. *Journal of corporate citizenship, 1*(1), 57–73.

Index

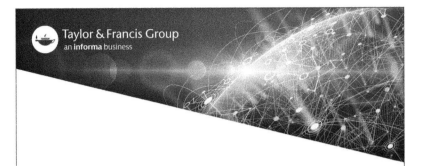

For Product Safety Concerns and Information please contact our EU
representative GPSR@taylorandfrancis.com
Taylor & Francis Verlag GmbH, Kaufingerstraße 24, 80331 München, Germany